The

TOURIST

PHIL TUFNELL

The

TOURIST

What happens on tour stays on tour...
UNTIL NOW!

HarperCollins*Publishers*

HarperCollins*Publishers*
1 London Bridge Street
London SE1 9GF

www.harpercollins.co.uk

HarperCollins*Publishers*
Macken House, 39/40 Mayor Street Upper
Dublin 1, D01 C9W8, Ireland

First published by HarperCollins*Publishers* 2023

1 3 5 7 9 10 8 6 4 2

A catalogue record of this book is
available from the British Library

ISBN 978-0-00-864161-0

Printed and bound in the UK using 100%
renewable electricity at CPI Group (UK) Ltd

MIX
Paper | Supporting
responsible forestry
FSC
www.fsc.org
FSC™ C007454

This book is produced from independently certified FSC™ paper
to ensure responsible forest management.

For more information visit: www.harpercollins.co.uk/green

To Mum and Dad, without whom
I'd never have got anywhere.

CONTENTS

Introduction   1

1 The Fear   9

2 Blond Bombshell   29

3 Independence   41

4 Come Fly with Me   63

5 The High Life   81

6 Ya Pommie Bastard!   105

7 An Innocent Abroad   123

8 Blighty   147

9 A Tour Like No Other   169

10 Which End?   193

11 And Here's Your Room, Sir   211

12 Back in the Jungle   225

13 Misunderstandings   255

14 Food   267

15 'Work'   275

16 The Dawn of Tourism   297

17 You Only Live Once   307

    Acknowledgements   311

INTRODUCTION

I've been on more than a few adventures in my life. As an England cricketer I went on eight of the best holidays anyone could ever have. Not only that, but I did so along-side a whole bucket-load of my heroes. I know people will say, 'They weren't holidays – they were professional cricket tours.' And they're right. Sort of. While I know there was work to be done on those trips, it would be disingenuous to suggest there wasn't a whole lot of fun and excitement to go with it. You only get one life, and if I was lucky enough for the world to be laid out in front of me, I was only going to enjoy it.

Equally, when I retired,* no way was I going to become a shrinking violet and start unfolding a picnic table in a layby on the A45.

* * *

* I knew it was time to jack it in when the Middlesex fast bowlers were slapping on a bit of 'product' in front of the mirror and requesting Gatorade at the end of the day.

Even now, more than 20 years since I last played for England, it's my touring tales that people ask me about more than anything. The reason for that is I had – or, more accurately, was given – a reputation for being a bit of a loose cannon. Some people went further and said I was a bad tourist. In which case, it's pretty remarkable that I should have spent pretty much the entirety of Nineties' winters jetting around the world playing for my country. Maybe there's a conclusion to be drawn there – that actually I was a very good tourist.

OK, there was the occasional bit of tomfoolery. Yes, there was that one time at the signing day before we departed Heathrow when I autographed several bats, T-shirts and team sheets as Mickey Mouse – if you have one of those bats, apologies, although to be fair so many different faces played for England at that time that it wasn't totally inconceivable that Mickey might have got a run-out. But all in all I was a pretty decent person to have along, happy to be in the thick of the action and always on hand to make a complete and utter fool of myself.

There'll always be people who'd prefer a more sedate presence – Judith Chalmers perhaps, or Fiona Bruce – as a travel companion, but if you prefer someone who might decide to zip wire down a suburban Melbourne clothesline at 3 a.m. then I'm your man. Or was. My days of zip wiring down clotheslines are long gone. These days I see a clothesline and wonder if I've got time to air my cardigan before the rain comes on.

INTRODUCTION

Similarly, while I'm still not averse to the occasional blowout, my present-day travelling companions tend to be a little quieter than Allan Lamb and Ian Botham. I like people who are a calming influence; people who aren't going to persuade me that helping a grand piano down a flight of stairs is a good idea, and that putting a shark in the captain's bed will be seen by all concerned as a jolly good jape.

These days, I do the majority of my travelling with my lovely wife Dawn. Not only is she the best company I could ever have, but she constantly reminds me that messing about with grand pianos will definitely put my back out.

Me and Dawn have always enjoyed a getaway. There's a big wide world out there – Europe, Africa, the Isle of Man – and we've been lucky enough to see quite a lot of it.

But recently we've mainly been seeing the interior of Tufnell Towers. Poor old Dawn has had a hip operation and so I've been looking after her. To be honest, I thought it would be the other way round, that I'd be the first one to have my hips pawed at and mauled in an operating theatre. For someone known for his love of sleeping, I've spent far too much time on my feet, most of it on the cricket pitch, a lesser, but still sizeable percentage, stood at the bar afterwards and a small, but nevertheless significant, amount running away from Graham Gooch.

Then there was my run-up. OK, rarely was I mistaken for Dennis Lillee, but doing that little hop, skip and a jump a few hundred times a day is bound to lead to wear and tear. After a long day in the field, next morning I could barely move. I was one of the few players to carry a can of WD40 in his holdall.

Remember as well I did *Strictly*, and pointing your feet one way while going another is never going to be good for your skeleton. Gorka Marquez and Giovanni Pernice might look good now but come their 50s they'll be hobbling down the promenade at Southend like the rest of us. I tell you, the minute I was eliminated I parked up my American Smooth forever.

And yet it's Dawn who's stuck in bed recuperating while I play nursemaid. I've got legs like Chris Hoy I've been up and down the stairs so many times.* That's without the burns up my forearms from ironing and shoving shepherd's pies in the oven. I'm like a tiger – a series of dark stripes where I keep catching myself on the grill.

The way I look at it, your house is where you relax. You go out, do whatever it is you're doing that day, come home, empty the cat tray, do a bit of cooking and have a sit on a nice plump settee for a few hours. Now I've reached the point where if I manage a sit-down with a cup of tea and a biscuit and catch ten minutes of *Bargain Hunt*, I'm happy. I actually look forward to *Bangers and Cash*. I sit there with a bourbon in one hand and a tub of

---

* I've also acquired a real empathy for Carson in *Downton Abbey*. I've had a few injuries in my time but never did I think I'd get housemaid's knee.

cold cream for my litany of wounds in the other. Last week I got three *Countdown* conundrums in a row.

If there was to be a documentary made about these few weeks, it would be called *Hip Operation: The Aftermath*. Tragic scenes would unfold of a bloke wandering round his house with a little bottle of beer in one hand and a feather duster in the other. Like a dog on a chain, I can only get so far. While dogs can't get past the front door to bite the postman without the chain tightening, I can't get beyond the airing cupboard. I have fevered dreams of donning my wife's Lycra and escaping to the village hall for half an hour of keep-fit. More than once I've thought about scrawling 'Help Me!' in the condensation on the front window.

The only time I've been out in the past few weeks is to get some bits from Asda. Once or twice while wandering the aisles I've wondered if the whole thing is an elaborate hoax. Whether Dawn is actually fully recovered and just runs upstairs and jumps into bed when she hears me come back. Maybe I need to install CCTV.

There is some good news, though. In two days I'll have a bit of company. Someone's coming round to help me dismantle a bed. Until then, I've got an emerging friendship with the Amazon driver who delivers here, mainly because he's round so often. He dropped a parcel off the other day. 'Here, Phil,' he said, 'this is a really special one.'

'Oh yeah, why's that?' I asked.

'It's for you.'

You might well ask what's happened to the person once dubbed 'the wild man of English cricket'. Well, here's the answer. He's in a pair of Marigolds removing stubborn hairs from the plughole in the bath.

And yet there has been one positive in all this. Being stuck at home has made me think about my times as a tourist. I am, after all, fairly well travelled. I've been to the majority of the Test-playing nations of course, but more than that I've been all over the place with Dawn, friends, family and all kinds of TV shows. I'm not comparing myself to the great explorers of yesteryear – at no point have I been greeted on the shores of Lake Tanganyika with the words, 'Dr Tufnell, I presume' – but I have seen some pretty remarkable sights. Even more remarkable than Mike Gatting emerging from the shower at Lord's.

As I've polished the pelmets and shoved the hoover round, my mind has drifted to the splendour of Sydney harbour, the immensity of the Kruger National Park and Blackpool Illuminations. Same when I've got a load of washing in. I'll watch it spinning round and be taken off in an almost hypnotic state to a far-flung part of India.*

The more I've thought about it, the more I've blessed my good fortune in being able to travel so fulsomely across the globe. It's not something I ever considered when I started out playing cricket. Back then, a cheese sandwich in the pavilion at half-time was considered exotic. Little

---

* Hopefully not that time I was stuck on a train with a rat.

did I know that my ability to spin a small red ball would result in rather more magnificent feasts being placed before me, like swordfish steaks and, erm, witchetty grubs. Same with some of the most incredible views on Earth.*

I thought it might be nice if I shared a few of these great memories with you. I hope you enjoy accompanying me on this voyage. If at any stage you'd like to stop at the services, please do let me know. Only ten minutes, mind – we've got a lot to get through.

* Again, not Mike Gatting getting out of the shower.

1

THE FEAR

My older brother Greg, who got all the sense when it was being doled out to the Tufnell boys, will tell anyone who'll listen that from a very early age if anyone told me not to put my hands on a hot grill pan I would immediately do exactly the opposite.

'Why don't they want me to touch the hot grill pan? What are they not telling me? Why are they trying to trick me? Oww!'

However, this anecdote is far removed from my own memories of being a kid. The way I remember it I was petrified of everything. And I wasn't alone. Thing is, when I was a child it was dangerous to go anywhere or do anything. How did I know? Because public information films said so. You couldn't turn the telly on without some kid being thrown 50 feet from an electricity pylon while retrieving a kite or falling foul of some terrifying piece of farming equipment. Even breakfast cereals made you glow orange.

The whole world was a minefield. One public information film stated, 'Don't leave a mat on a varnished floor

– you'll slip and kill yourself.' I don't know if statistics were kept for the number of mat-related deaths in 1974 but if they were I'd like to see them. Another had some poor devil frying in a bath after dropping a hairdryer. And in another someone overloaded a plug and their house burnt down. That was three ways to perish before you'd even left the front door.

Venture outside and it only got worse. Even having a picnic was a matter of life and death. There was one public information film which showed a couple, albeit a little bit messy, sat on a rug in a field – 'Ooh, look, there's a farmer down there with a very red face!' He looked like he was going to shoot them. 'FOLLOW THE COUNTRY CODE!' we'd be told at the end. All right. All right. I was only leaning on a gate.

The 'Charlie says ...' adverts were the same. These had an unusually socially aware cat which issued warnings of imminent danger – running into roads, messing about with matches, global thermonuclear war, that kind of stuff. I saw the one about not taking sweets from adults about a hundred times. Someone's dad offered me a fruit pastille at a party and I had to be restrained from punching him in the face.

Even if you did the right thing and went somewhere that was supervised by adults, you couldn't do anything when you got there. Remember that board they used to have up at the swimming pool?

'NO KISSING. NO PETTING. NO SPLASHING. NO BALLS. NO DIVING.' I wouldn't have been surprised if I'd turned up one week and it said, 'NO SWIMMING'.

There's a whole generation of us out there who grew up paranoid, thinking everything held a hidden menace. Fridges – you could get trapped in them. Loose stair-rods – they'd have you tumbling headfirst into a solid oak front door. Paddling pools – watch out for the rip current.

If it wasn't public information films, it was disaster movies. After *The Towering Inferno*, I never went up a skyscraper for about 30 years. Switch the channel and there'd be a bedraggled vicar trying to claw his way through an upside-down iron hull on *The Poseidon Adventure*. After that it would be *The Omen* with plummeting lifts and blokes getting trapped under ice-covered ponds. You needed a tranquiliser just to watch TV on a Saturday night. You'd be scarred for life. To a young kid these films sent out an unavoidable message – in any given situation, no matter how apparently safe and normal, at any minute something could go horribly wrong.

'Do you fancy going to the zoo tomorrow, Phil?'

'The zoo? Are you mad? What happens if there's an earthquake and everything escapes?'

Or you'd have stayed up and watched *King Kong* the night before – 'I'm not going anywhere near that gorilla!'

'Don't worry, Phil, it's toughened glass.'

'That won't stop it. Didn't you see? It plucked a biplane out of mid-air and crushed it like matchwood.'

That's where I get a little bit health and safety. These things do actually happen. A gorilla escaped at London Zoo a few years ago and drank five litres of Ribena before it was tranquilised. As someone who's always liked Ribena I found this very disturbing indeed. What if I happened to be down there one day and it got a whiff of it on my breath. There could be very big trouble indeed.

If we did actually summon up the courage to leave the house, and no horrendous fate befell us, we'd fill this void of terror by immediately taking the opportunity to scare ourselves half to death. We'd sit around in the woods telling ghost stories, desperately trying not to be the first one to start crying.*

And then there'd be that spooky house we'd be scared of and yet were always drawn to for some reason. Over the fields from us, for instance, there was this great big old asylum. We'd all head over there on our bikes, for no reason other than no one dared say it was a really bad idea. When it started going dark, just as you were looking forward to going home, some fool would pipe up, 'Come on! Let's go and have a look around.' The correct response at this point would be, 'No, I'm not going to do it. It'll be beyond terrifying. I'm going to go home for my tea.' But next thing you knew you'd be pulling yourself through a window of this dilapidated, derelict old building, the kind

---

* This would later form an integral part of pre-season bonding sessions when first-class teams spent a week living rough in a forest in preparation for a solid tilt at the Benson & Hedges Cup.

12

of place even the Munsters would find a little chilling. A couple of minutes later you'd hear a bang down some distant corridor and that would be it, you'd be legging it out of there as quick as you could, ripping your coat on a hook or piercing your leg on a railing. Every time it happened – because obviously the week after you'd be back there again – I'd think, 'This is mad – why am I putting myself through this stuff?'

Kids of that era had very vivid imaginations. We had to – we didn't have computer games. We made dens in woods and shot baddies with cap guns. I mean, when you look at it, most computer games are the same. They involve going into dingy places, fighting fantasy enemies and firing guns. Today's kids just do it all sitting down. We were actually out there risking life and limb. We deserve our pensions just for that.

In the end, round about the time I was awarded a benefit year, I worked out that I actually had no intention of climbing electricity pylons and the chances of becoming entangled in a threshing machine in London were relatively low. By then I was also quite big to be offered a sweet by strangers.*

However, I still take any warning sign very seriously. I tell you, I've seen more people slip over on wet floors than I care to mention. When I see that little sign out, 'WARNING SLIPPERY FLOOR!', I'm down on all fours.

* I'll still call the police if you offer me a Polo.

'Don't be silly, Phil,' friends tell me, and then next thing, they're collapsing like a house of cards. Down they go, back of the head – whack! Growing up in the Seventies did have its benefits after all.

My fear of the unknown has naturally extended to travel. If I go on a cruise, I want a cabin with a balcony just in case. After all, boats do end up at the bottom of the sea. And I don't just mean the occasional one. I read a book about Cornish shipping disasters once when I was down that way and there's hundreds of them. You can barely have a paddle round Land's End without tripping over a piece of mast or a cannonball. OK, a lot of those wrecks date from hundreds of years ago, but the principle remains the same. They didn't just sink. They smashed against cliffs or were caught up in some terrific storm. On the plus side, I believe Cornish villagers have stopped luring them on to the rocks.

Even when they started building ships properly they still plunged to the ocean floor. They said *Titanic* was unsinkable and it was three miles down in the North Atlantic in less than two hours. I'm not sure how much help having a balcony would have been in that situation but I'm always trying to shift the survival odds slightly more in my favour.*

*　*　*

* For similar reasons I always ask for a room with a bath – an excellent makeshift lifeboat.

14

Thing is, I'm very aware of my surroundings when I travel. Like a cat down a back alley, I'm on heightened alert. Everywhere I look I can see potential disaster. When I board a train, for instance, I always sit at the back. That way there's always a few carriages in front to take the impact. Same with planes. I know it's an old joke but you really have never heard of a plane reversing into a mountain. Odd really. I've been quite adventurous in my life and yet when it comes to travelling I've always had a lot of trepidation. I think it's because, be it train, plane or boat, you never know who's up front driving the thing. If someone's speeding me through the English countryside at 200mph, it would be nice to think they haven't become engrossed in a Sudoku or the last episode of *The Crown*.

And yet, whatever my fear, I've pretty much always, somehow, worked through it, even if ten minutes later I was wishing I'd let my yellow streak win. Not too long ago, for example, me and Dawn did a bit of parasailing in Mexico. It's great fun, but when you're up in the air you can't help noticing that the only thing keeping you airborne is a tiny little knot on a rope. 'Hang on! Is that it?' If that knot had come loose I'd have been landing ten hours later in Texas. Those weren't Chinese spy balloons they kept spotting high in the skies over the US, they were people like me.

I've got a strange sort of bravery where I'll do something, but after I've done it no way will I do it again. If I was invited to a revolving restaurant at the top of a skyscraper, I'd do it, but chances are afterwards I'd feel really sick.* Hopefully not because of the food but more because I'd start really thinking about how unnatural it is for human beings to sit in spinning buildings. I put that down to the fight or flight instinct. We are, after all, land-dwellers. If we'd been meant to go up high we'd have looked like pigeons (more on Henry Blofeld later).

When I filmed the travelogue *This Could Go Anywhere*, where me and the former Kiwis captain, batting legend and pioneering England coach Brendon 'Baz' McCullum criss-crossed New Zealand doing odd and inadvisable things, I was required to do a bungee jump into a deep gorge. It wasn't just the jump, it was the build-up. In an attempt to settle my nerves, I had a few drinks the night before, went to bed, didn't sleep a wink – gripped by the kind of nausea I'd not experienced since witnessing Angus Fraser cutting his toenails – and then all too soon the birds were singing and it was time to get up and do the deed.

No joke, as me and Baz left the hotel I was visibly shaking. 'Bloody hell, mate,' said Baz, who, heroically, would watch the whole thing from the ground, 'are you all right?'

'No,' I shrieked. 'I really don't know if I can do it.' Sadly for the Louis Vuitton† store next door, I then threw up all over their front step.

---

* Never eat mussels in a revolving restaurant.

† Louis Vuitton – please don't feel the need to send me any freebies for the brand mention in this book.

It was odd. Usually, I'm quite good at blanking out what's to come. It's like sport. Overthink it, let it get to you, and doing it becomes harder and harder. My general approach to any kind of challenge is to go out the night before, have a nice dinner, a couple of glasses of wine and then get up next morning ready to go. I'm quite bullish like that. But with the bungee jump the anticipation was horrific, building up for days to this horrible crescendo.

Brendon, as seemed to be the way in this show, drove me to the scene of my execution, and was, as also seemed to be the way, deeply entertained by my need for him to pull over so I could again be sick at the side of the road.

On arrival, I approached the side of the gorge and the bungee people slid me out to a platform, a sickening height above what I'm sure I would otherwise have viewed as a beautiful example of New Zealand's incredible geography. By now I wasn't far off being in tears, actually retching. Somehow I managed to stand on the edge of the platform, now paranoid that I hadn't been attached properly to the rope – 'Please check! Please! Just do it for me!' In fact, I asked, 'Am I attached?' so many times I'm thinking of patenting it as a catchphrase. I just wanted the misery over and done with, to jump right then, but then these mechanical arms began extending from the platform to take photos.

'No! Just do it! Get me down there and I can go and have a lie-down somewhere.' Like I say, I'm reasonably bold, but doing a bungee jump was a whole different level of scary. I really don't think I'd have managed to do it if they hadn't given me a little shove in the back to send me screaming into the abyss, relying on nothing but an elastic band to stop an imminent argument with the extremely rocky floor of the canyon.

All through this experience, the one thing that had reassured me was the presence of the *This Could Go Anywhere* camera crew. I don't know why, but I always think nothing can go wrong if there's a camera crew there. Daft – all it really means is that there'll be great high-definition footage of my final moments.*

'He said he wasn't attached,' the newsreader will say, 'but no one listened and just minutes later he dropped like a stone to his demise. And now the weather …'

They say never say never. But I can say, with all honesty, never, ever, ever will I do a bungee jump again. At no time while I was dangling on the end of that elastic band did I think, 'You know what? This really is the hobby for me.' In fact, I decided there and then that the next travel show I do will be me going round being asked to do things and saying, 'No! Absolutely not!' I'm available for all programmes of that nature right now.

I wasn't going to do 30 bungee jumps any more than I was going to take up abseiling on a professional basis after being asked to descend 160ft down the side of Guildford Cathedral. The abseil was for the very deserving cause that is The Children's Trust so I didn't need that much persuasion. It was just a coincidence that it was 11 o'clock at

---

* To be fair, I do need a bigger presence on TikTok.

night in a pub when I was asked if I'd do it.* Only when I woke up the next morning did I remember I was afraid of heights.

When the day in question arrived, I was very glad indeed that Dawn had agreed to undergo the abseil too, because when I dragged myself up to that famous spire I wasn't feeling particularly confident about going back down swinging from a rope. When I tell people about abseiling off Guildford Cathedral, they tend to opine that it must be a great view from up there. I will point out by way of reply that while indeed you can see for miles, I was a little more concerned with the distance to the pavement below. I know it's 160 feet, but in reality it felt like I was miles up in the air, sat on the edge of this little wooden platform with the whole of Surrey laid out in front of me. Again, I'm not sure I'd have been able to make the first move if I'd not had a little nudge. I've said it many times – there's only so long you can sit on a church spire trying to build up your courage. The actual abseil was more like a long diagonal zip wire that bit by bit I had to ease myself down. It was a very slow process, during which I will admit to wondering why charity endeavours never seem to involve lying in bed watching telly, or sipping a Pina Colada down the pub.

* * *

* I have since instigated a hard and fast rule of not agreeing to anything past 9 p.m.

I'd have perhaps looked on the above events a little more favourably had I not taken part in Channel 4's truly terrifying winter sports show *The Jump*. Fellow contestants were dropping like flies as every discipline – slalom, luge, etc. – seemed to result in another dislocated shoulder or cracked bone. It wasn't so much The Jump as 24 Hours in A&E – On Ice.

The biggest challenge, as the title might suggest, was the ski jump. We wouldn't be going off the top of the platform – even reality TV hasn't reached those lengths – but they still took us up there to have a look. Again the mere sight of the drop caused me to throw up.* Even going off the little trainer jump was worrying enough, and again once I'd whizzed – well, plopped – down, no way was I going to be queuing up for another go.

Another issue I suffer from is sympathetic travel nervousness. You know you hear about blokes getting sympathetic pregnancies – they can feel the baby kicking inside them and can't stop eating charcoal, that kind of stuff – well, I get the travel version. Take the time Dawn went over to Spain to see her dad for a week. I'd stayed behind, with various instructions to follow to keep things ticking over at home. She's good like that, Dawn. When she's not here she makes me lists – when the bins need to go out, best mop to use in any given situation, where to find the toenail clippers, etc. Anyway, a day or two before she was due to fly back, the ash cloud happened. An eruption of the Eyjafjallajökull

* Sorry if this is an emerging theme.

volcano – try saying that when you've had a few (in fact try saying that when you haven't had a few) – in Iceland pumped great swathes of ash into European airspace. I was watching TV and they were saying how flights were being cancelled everywhere, including Spain, because the ash was a danger to aircraft engines. I didn't like hearing that at all. In fact, I could feel myself starting to panic. It was a real nervousness in the pit of my stomach. And not just because the freezer meals only went up to Wednesday.

On the day Dawn was meant to be flying, I rang her to see what was happening. She reported that they were on the way to the airport. All was looking good. Next time I checked she was on the bus from the airport out to the plane. Then she was saying the bus had stopped and it was turning round. Then it looked like, no, it was going out to the plane after all. Then it had stopped again. By this time my guts were doing somersaults. In my head I had a vision of the aircraft, and more importantly Dawn, heading into an ash cloud never to be seen again. I was in agony just thinking about it. In the meantime, she'd managed to have a word with someone from the airline and it looked like, yes, they were definitely going to give it a try. A try? I didn't want to hear the word 'try'! This was my Dawny not *Those Magnificent Men in Their Flying Machines*. By this time I was phoning every five minutes. 'Crikey! What's happening? What's happening?' It seemed they had actually now got on the plane. But then they sat there for an hour. Dawn told me there was some 'deliberation' about whether to go or not. Again, 'deliberation' – not a word I wanted to hear. There was talk of a 'flight plan' and a 'slot'. But the majority view was that they were going to call it off and everyone was going to have to get off. I was relieved. I had visions of the engines clogging up with dust. I'd seen it happen with the hoover and it didn't look good. And then the next thing I know Dawn's rung me – as they're taking off! The captain, although possibly not in these exact words, had told the passengers, 'Ladies and gentlemen, sod it! We're going!' and that was it. It was the last plane out for a week and a half.

Well, for the next two and a half hours I was an absolute mess. There was no way I could contact Dawn once she was up in the air. It was awful. I did everything – dusting, washing-up, hard skin removal – to distract myself from my worries but nothing worked. I thought about putting the TV on but knew for sure the first thing I'd see was an episode of *Air Crash Investigation*. It was horrible – the longest two and a half hours of my life.

When eventually the call came to say she'd landed safely, the relief was unbelievable. God knows what I'd have done when that last lasagne had gone.

I had a similar thing happen when I was on holiday in Turkey with Dawn and my stepson. They were up for a scuba dive whereas I prefer the bits of the world with air in it. Well, it was more scary being the one left behind than the ones 30 feet down. It was late in the day and the light was going a bit as they disappeared beneath the waves.

While they were down there a bloke came round in a boat and started taking these great big things with antennas out the water. Being a bit nosey, I asked what he was doing.

'Oh,' he said. 'We bring these in at night. They're the things that stop the sharks coming in.'

'WHAT? SHARKS! Hang on! My wife and stepson are down there. Put them back in!'

Then something else occurred to me. 'What sharks?' Nobody had ever mentioned sharks in the first place. Six months down the line, a mako ate someone off a neighbouring beach.

Dawn is very much someone who'll try anything. This means I'm permanently waiting to have to extricate myself from a potholing weekend. If I do have one proper 'phobia', then it would be claustrophobia. I have no wish to crawl through a confined space known as the 'cheese-press' or hold my breath for 90 seconds while navigating a pitch-black sump. I'm just not convinced of the appeal of getting in very small caves with water levels that can very rapidly rise. It's for the same reason I've never been a fan of the Blackwall Tunnel. I'd always hope against hope there wasn't a traffic jam halfway through. If I did get stuck, I couldn't help thinking about how just above that tiled ceiling was a massive great river full of water. I'd be peering up through the windscreen in fear of the first few drops coming through the roof, waiting to be deluged at any moment.*

* For reasons why I avoid the Woolwich Ferry, see earlier mention of *The Poseidon Adventure*.

23

I'm not afraid of water. I can swim, just not like Dawn. She's akin to a fish and beats me hands down if we have a little race in the sea on holiday. Also, I'm very aware of the dangers of deep water. It's not my natural home. In fact these days I'm very much a stand in the shallow end with a lager on a floating table kind of bloke. I'm also a bit fussier about where I want to swim. I'm straight in the Caribbean Sea, for example, because it's so lovely and warm. The North Sea off Gateshead, on the other hand, perhaps not.

The water off the coast of Dubai is incredible, like sitting in a hot bath, although me and Dawn did have a slightly worrying experience there. We'd been out the night before and, as we strolled a little hungover down to the beach the next day, perhaps weren't quite as aware of our surroundings as we might have been. Which is why we missed the board telling people not to swim that day. Anyway, we had a dip and a loll before deciding to go up on a parasail. We were up there wafting about and looked down to see that the exact spot where we'd been swimming was completely surrounded by sea snakes, jellyfish and sting-rays. Two minutes longer in there and we'd have been eaten alive. When they wound us back in, I was shouting to Dawn, 'Keep your feet up! They'll have you! Keep them out the water!'

* * *

There's another travel fear that's plagued me down the years – leaving pets behind at home. Oscar was our beautiful silver-shaded Persian, pedigree as long as your arm – not that it mattered, within two days of his arrival the vet had relieved him of his testes. Oscar was a very expressive cat, always happy to join in a party, and we both loved him to bits. When it came to holidays, we hated leaving him and he hated us going. As soon as the suitcases came out his face used to change. In fact, he'd sit in them to try to prevent their use. He also had a sixth sense for when we were coming back. I'm sure we never left him an itinerary, but be it two in the morning or 11 at night, he'd be there waiting. Whatever night out he'd got going on, he knew he had to be back to greet us at the appointed hour.

When Oscar passed away, we did what any owners would do – cremated him and had him made into keyrings. Well, what I mean is we've got two keyrings with his ashes in them. At least we think they're his. Who amongst us can honestly say they'd know a cat's ashes from a dog's or even a lizard's? I could be walking around with a six-foot python in my keyring. To be fair, they did put a bit of Oscar's fur in there too, and I've never seen a furry boa constrictor.

I digress. Point is Dawn was away with some friends when Oscar took a turn for the worse. At this point we'd gone through a run of holidays which entailed a mildly terrifying and historically unlikely weather event. We'd be in Majorca and there'd be the first recorded cyclone in 45 years, or walking down the promenade in Mauritius when it suddenly start raining fish, these sort of things. Anyway, in Dawn's case she was on a Greek island in the middle of August when a freak weather front dumped a load of snow on her head. Oscar had been showing a few signs of getting a bit poorly at this stage. He'd been into the vet's for various scans, which in itself was a shock to the system. I reckon it costs more to put a cat through a CT scanner than it does a human. It doesn't seem to matter that they're about a tenth the size.

While Dawn was away, Oscar would come and lie next to me. As you do, I was telling him not to worry, that Dawn would be back in a couple of days, and she'd know what to do.* In the meantime, seeing he was feeling a bit sorry for himself, I thought I'd make sure he was at least getting some good grub. I went out to M&S and got him some smoked salmon.† In his later years Oscar developed the ability to read the name on the carrier bag as I came through the door. Waitrose, he was purring. Asda, it would be paws up with full claw extension.

Eventually, I picked Dawn up from the airport. Again, it was like Oscar knew where I was going, possibly because

---

* Some people believe cats can't understand English, but I can think of multiple cats – Top Cat, Garfield, Lenny the Lion – who were fluent in the language.

† Actually, I'm wondering now if that might have finished him off – maybe it was a bit rich. To be honest, though, if I was a cat I'd rather go with the smell of smoked salmon in my nostrils than have Go-Cat for my last meal.

Dawn's imminent return from an excursion tended to be marked by me squirrelling away takeaway boxes and giving the hoover a quick shove around. I swear old Oscar hung on until she came back. When we got in from Gatwick he was lying on the floor with his tongue hanging out. Dawn wrapped him up in her arms and we scooted off to the vet's.

I'll be honest, as we sat in the waiting room I was crying my eyes out. I did think, 'Come on! It's only a cat! And he's just had Loch Fyne salmon!', but anyone who's lost a pet will tell you it is a very emotional time. When my stick insect passed away while I was on tour with Middlesex U-13s I was inconsolable. In his surgery, the vet confirmed that Oscar's time was up. He'd chased his last shrew, flicked his last ball of wool round the carpet, eaten his last wasp.

We've yet to replace Oscar. We've talked about perhaps getting another cat, potentially even a dog, but the worry of us both being away in time of need is overwhelming. Really we need something we can take with us. A tape-worm perhaps.

Tapeworms aside, the point I am trying to make in this chapter is the world is an unpredictable place. Our planet has all sorts of highly dangerous elements to it. Sharks, volcanoes, electricity pylons, slippery mats and overloaded plugs form just a tiny number of them. I haven't even mentioned lions, lightning strikes and a full-flow Jonny Bairstow. In fact, just writing this now has made me think it's a miracle I've been anywhere – that I ever stepped out of my childhood bedroom. Had I thought about the perils of travel too much, chances are I'd have lived like a medieval monk. Oh, how my captains would have loved that vow of silence.

For the fact I did break the shackles and see so much of this great world of ours, I can thank two people – Mum and Dad.

2

BLOND BOMBSHELL

As a kid I had blond hair. My mother used to call me a 'blond bombshell'. It's one of the few things I had in common with Diana Dors.

I was very lucky to be taken abroad for holidays and that non-stop exposure to the sun would bleach my hair almost white. The Tuffers of this infant era is best exhib- ited by a picture of me wearing a yellow short-sleeved button-up shirt, yellow knee-length socks, white shorts and a pair of white plimsolls standing on the steps of, if I recall correctly, the El Cid Hotel,* in Benidorm. It's a lovely picture, quite emotional to look at now, of me, my brother and my mum (Dad would have been taking the picture), probably on our way out to dinner. Even today, that yellow shirt is the brightest thing I've ever seen, brought to life in the most vivid way imaginable by the brilliant light of the Med. Thing was, compared to being

* The Castilian knight was well known for his love of Benidorm, much preferring it to Torremolinos.

at home, where the brightest thing was the sign at Woolworths, everything in Benidorm was bright. It was like being in a completely different world. With the sun came a real sense of freedom. One of those public information films that haunted me showed a kid running on a beach, freeze-framing at the point where his foot was about to be sliced open by a broken bottle submerged in the sand. But I wasn't haunted here. Running on lovely soft warm sand on magnificent beaches felt like the most wonderful, natural, thing ever. Public information films belonged to that other world – the one back in Britain.

Benidorm quickly became our go-to destination. If we weren't on the beach, me and my brother would spend endless glorious days running around and hurling ourselves into the hotel swimming pool. We were both kitted out in the most ridiculous trunks,* while my dad's swimming attire was possibly the most 1970s thing I've ever seen. He had shorts made up of vertical black, blue, orange and brown stripes. They were the only shorts that came with matching wallpaper. For some reason, a lot of swimming gear back then was made of a quite unpleasant synthetic material that never felt comfortable to wear. I keep meaning to check if Michelin ever did swimwear.

Meanwhile, there was little adherence to sun-protection guidance. In fact, completely the opposite. My dad used to cover himself in suntan oil and lie there like a massive

---

* To be fair, there wasn't much else knocking around in those days and I didn't have the figure for a bikini.

chip. He wasn't alone. Everyone did it. People would even have reflectors, essentially Bacofoil, around their necks to make sure no part of them was missed. I was always reminded how much they looked like those frilled lizards you'd get on David Attenborough wildlife programmes. 'And here they are, sunning themselves in their natural habitat, a swimming pool on the Costa Blanca. Any minute now their rest will be disturbed by one of their young, a blond boy in ill-fitting Speedos, asking for his 15th Coca-Cola of the day.'

For some reason I never used to burn in the sun. I think it was because I was moving so fast – the sun could never quite catch up with me. But Mum would always battle to get the sun cream on me anyway. I'd be there with my armbands on, shark inflatables bigger than I was, desperate to get to the pool. Every smear was another vital second lost. I'm sure most of it was washed off the minute I hit the water.

I don't know what everyone else's childhood holidays were like but I remember a lot of near drownings. On one occasion my dad did pretty much actually save my life. It was a red-hot day and I was in my rubber ring (don't laugh, this is serious) in quite a busy swimming pool. Next thing I knew the ring was somehow round my ankles, the effect being to turn me upside down. I couldn't for the life of me right myself. I'm sure it was only seconds, but it felt like I was under the water for about five minutes. I could just see all these legs thrashing around, like an exceptionally poor synchronised swimming team. Finally, I felt someone grabbing my hair. Thankfully, Mum and Dad had been keeping an eye on me and when they saw I was in a spot of bother Dad launched himself into the water like David Hasselhoff in *Baywatch* – only with much worse shorts. In rescuing me, he took out half the other people in, and actually out of, the pool on the way. When I opened my eyes there was a right commotion going on – sunbeds, Spanish waiters and bits of tapas everywhere. The Cat had used up his first life.

Nothing, not even an unexpected drink of three litres of chlorinated water, could spoil a Benidorm holiday. After a couple of days, in contrast to my white hair, I'd have this lovely little tan going on. 'You're a very handsome boy,' my mum used to tell me. 'Naughty, but handsome.' My blondness actually gave me a bit of early notoriety. Hotel staff were endlessly ruffling my hair. Either that or they were using it for a tea towel.

Down at the beach, we'd take a pedalo out. We'd look back at the beach and because a few Brits had arrived there'd be windbreaks everywhere. All this was very new and the average Brit was still in the Skegness mindset – 40-mile-an-hour gusts with a wind-chill factor of minus ten. This was Spain in high season. The air would be totally still and it was 90 degrees. If anything you wanted something that would create a breeze, not stop it.

I loved how the food was different from home too. In Spain you could get Pez sweets, like little bricks, and Orangina. There was lemon Fanta in a little bottle and chocolate milk. All these wonderful things that I'd never encountered. The proper food was also new and exciting, except to my dad – 'Oh, I don't know whether I like all this foreign muck!' At the dinner table, Dad got more joy out of picking up a bit of octopus or lobster and swinging it on our faces. We'd be screaming and laughing, hiding under the table. I don't know why but it always seemed to be the British people messing about. To the inhabitants of no other country does the squid have so much comic potential.

Whatever was put in front of us, however 'foreign', we always ate it, and I actually genuinely enjoyed it. I was quite good like that. I'd look around at other tables and there'd be kids crying, shouting for beans on toast or a bag of Chipsticks, but I would always tuck in. To me, the food was another reminder that we were somewhere out of the ordinary. Aged five or six I'd even be asking for a little taste of the local wine. 'Well, you're a bit young, son,' my dad would say, 'but we're on holiday so you can have a sip of my shandy.' I hadn't started smoking – although it had crossed my mind.

It wasn't just the food that was different, it was the entire act of eating. The hotel would have a dinner-hall kind of affair composed of stiff-backed chairs with a raffia seat. Mum would get her best frock on and dress up while Dad would put on his slacks and a striped towelling short-sleeved shirt. I'm pleased to say this particular fashion recently came back round and I've got one myself. He'd finish it off with a pair of boat shoes. One of his great heroes was the actor Tony Curtis and I think he was trying to encapsulate the look – hair Brylcreemed back and everything. We'd sit down and immediately spy a packet of breadsticks. These were great fun. You could stick them in your ears, up your nose, play the drums with them, throw them at your brother – anything but eat them really. A great way of passing the time before the main course arrived.

At the end of the night the entire family would collapse into bed in the same room, me and my brother on little put-me-ups. We'd be so tired, having swam and run around for 14 hours solid, that we'd just pass out. The minute I woke up, I'd be saying to Mum, 'Come on, let's go down to the beach! I want another chocolate milk!'

Before that would come the continental breakfast, which never quite hit the same heights as the evening repast. If you were lucky there might be the odd croissant or pain au chocolat knocking about, but generally it was dry bread and a bit of cheese.* The alternative would be a somewhat poorly put-together attempt at a full English. My dad would be having none of it, holding up some limp bit of bacon and two-inch sausage. 'Sylv?' he'd ask Mum. 'What's this? This ain't a sausage. Look at it! And where's the toast? Sylv, they ain't got toast here. They just keep giving me these dry bread rolls.' He'd be banging them on the table to emphasise his point.

*　　*　　*

* For me, considering it represents the entirety of Europe, the continental breakfast has always been a little disappointing. They could at least chuck a bit of coq au vin and a pint of Bavarian lager in.

34

Once I was out of the rubber-ring phase,* I had a bit more freedom. By the second day my mum and dad would have inevitably bumped into someone who lived two doors down the road. We'd hook up with their kids and that would be it for the week. 'Clear off down the beach and build some sandcastles – we're going for lunch.' Suddenly you had free rein. In the evening, there'd be some entertainment on – a couple of blokes singing, three women with maracas (#Eurovision) – and again while Mum and Dad had a glass of wine we'd be allowed to go off and explore, which basically meant running feral with a group of seven or eight other kids. Usually, we'd end up under the stage, finding a little cubbyhole next to where the dancers changed into their tinselly dresses.†

As I got a bit older, I'd have what might loosely be termed my first holiday romances. In Spain, the pool was always a good area to bump into the female sex. Generally, the way these things worked was you'd make friends with a boy who had a sister. You'd then tease her relentlessly because you were so embarrassed that you fancied her. I wasn't schooled in the ways of romance – I'd yet to build a library of Mills and Boons – and so generally I'd get a girl's attention by pushing her in the pool. 'That'll endear me to her,' I thought. If that worked out OK, then I'd very

* I'm not far off being back in it.

† This would later form the basis of a brief infatuation with The Nolans.

gallantly offer her a sip of my chocolate milk. Although not too much of course.

The more we holidayed in Benidorm, the more I was struck by how the Spanish people who holidayed in these resorts were exotic in the extreme. They might wear high-waisted bikinis or, very occasionally, even be topless, which was like something from another dimension. You never saw that in Worthing. My older brother would suddenly be very keen to go and build some sandcastles on that particular part of the beach, even if it was half a mile from where my mum and dad had set up. It was like a world free of rules. I imagine it to have been like the Sixties in England when there was this sudden leap from mole-neck jumpers and long skirts to people baring 12 inches above the knee.*

But then again, everything was geared to this free-wheel-ing attitude. It just fitted in with the whole vibe of people feeling happy with themselves and their environment. It was the same with how people spent hours just launching themselves into waves. You adapt to your environment – same as if the Spanish had booked two weeks in Morecambe they'd be clad in 14 jumpers just to have a paddle.

We'd go to Spain every couple of years, interspersed with cruising† on the Norfolk Broads. The Broads were very different from Benidorm – in Norfolk they only go topless for a harvest moon – but still great fun for a young-

* This might not have happened in the Shetland Islands.

† This meant something different back then.

ster. It always amazed me that my dad who, let's face it, had never driven a boat before, was allowed to pick up something the size of a small bungalow and five minutes later be motoring along what could be quite a busy waterway. To drive a car requires a deep knowledge of both *The Highway Code* and the controls. A boat is different. The only instruction Dad had was, 'That's forward. That's back. And by the way there's no brakes.'

It felt like every half hour we were crashing into something or other. People would be shaking their fists shouting that we were on the wrong side. We'd be shouting and swearing back. I don't think the Norfolk Broads knew what had hit it – quite literally.

Parking up was another point of high drama. Even if we did manage to do it without hitting something or someone we'd be in the wrong place. On one occasion we were driving along and it was getting later and later. My dad was panicking a bit, obviously thinking we needed to moor up for the night. Me and my brother were chief moorers on these trips while my mum would be shouting instructions to my dad on the rudder – 'Right hand down, Alan!', that kind of thing. Any other poor sod trying to have a relaxing evening when we turned up would be left wishing they'd saved a few hundred quid and gone and stood by a motorway. On this particular occasion, I leapt from the boat, rope in hand, on to what I thought was dry land only to discover it was actually a reed bed. I was completely underwater before I knew it, coming back up to the sight of our barge chugging just feet from my head, pumping oil and all sorts in my direction. Between shouting for help, crying and hoping not to get my foot hooked in an old mattress,* I was desperately holding on to the rope. This time it was my mum who jumped in and saved me.

Then there were the bridges. I'm not sure quite what vessels Norfolk's bridges were built to accommodate but most of them seemed to have about two inches clearance. There's a famous one at Wroxham where these days you're required to have a pilot jump on board to steer you through. There was none of that back then. Dad – after a pub lunch – was lining up and hoping for the best. I vividly remember looking at this thing getting nearer and thinking and saying out loud, 'We're never getting through that!'

'Don't worry,' Dad declared. 'Your mum says I'm a very good driver.'

'But, Dad, that's in a car! This is a three-berth 45ft pleasure cruiser, not a Ford Cortina.'

Kerr-unch!

On occasions, me and my brother would be allowed to do some night fishing. We'd get some maggots,† borrow a fishing rod and sit there with a torch gaffer-taped to our heads. These were the first times I'd ever been allowed to stay up really late, until about two o'clock, and as a kid it felt incredibly exciting. Next morning we'd feast eagerly on our catch of three Wellington boots and a bedframe.

---

* We're back to those old public information films.

† An experience of which I'd be reminded when a load of the horrible little blighters were tipped on my head in the jungle.

All too soon, these holidays would come to an end. Nowadays most of us think nothing of heading off for ten days or even a fortnight, but back then the majority of people would go for a week because they had to return to work. My dad was no different. He had to get back to run his silversmithing business. Like he always used to say to me, he had a half day off on Christmas Eve and was back at work the day after Boxing Day. Paternity leave, even a day off sick, was a pipedream. The way he saw it, if your feet could hit the floor you went to work.

'If I don't go,' he'd say, 'all those herberts who I employ will do absolutely **** all.' Whenever he went on holiday, he'd leave a list for his deputy. 'Right, you're in charge. There's the work you've got to do. There's 40 pots, 20 pans and 15 dishes. I want them done by the time I get back.' None of it would even have been touched. The minute he left they'd be down the pub.

Across the country it was a different era, a time when entire towns, factories and industries used to go on holiday en masse. The city of Liverpool would move 30 miles down the road to Rhyl, Blackpool would become 95 per cent Glaswegian and on the east side of the country they'd hit Scarborough and Cleethorpes. In going abroad, we were the exception not the rule. People weren't flying around like they do now, and I remember how, as a kid, the drive to Gatwick, usually getting up about three in the morning to get the eight o'clock flight, was a big exciting thing all on its own.

For my mum and dad too, going to Benidorm must have been a big deal, very different from the holidays they'd have had when they were kids. But I think Dad's job opened their eyes to what travel, albeit limited travel, could add to a life. Because of his trade they hobnobbed with the boss of the jewellers Mappin & Webb, who used to head over to France a lot in his boat. Knowing someone like that maybe normalised the idea of going abroad and before they had me and Greg they would drive Mum's white Triumph Vitesse to the south of France, top down, sun in their faces, hair blowing in the wind. I think that's one of the main reasons they had their kids so late in life, because they were having too much of a good time! When they did have kids they realised that foreign travel didn't have to stop, it would just be a bit different. I totally get why they still wanted to see somewhere else, take in a different view, feel the sun on the back of their necks, and I'm so very grateful to them for giving me the bug. Even as that little lad with his white shorts and button-up yellow shirt, I always had that 'going back home' feeling, an unshiftable weight of disappointment in my stomach. I knew that if I could I wanted to see as much of the world as I could. Don't get me wrong, I love my country and there's nothing better than summer in England's green and pleasant land, but there's a big wide world out there and I've always had an urge to throw myself in it.

I suppose maybe once or twice I threw myself just that little bit too hard!

3

INDEPENDENCE

When I was 16, I went back to Benidorm with my mates. A sweet lad in a yellow short-sleeved button-up shirt, yellow knee-length socks, a pair of white plimsolls and little white shorts I was not. Neither for that matter were the rag-tag bunch of misfits and ne'er-do-wells who accompanied me. With the knowledge of what unfolded on that 'holiday', I really do believe that any group of 12 16-year-olds heading to Benidorm should be incarcerated at the airport until the relevant flight has left the tarmac. If not, perhaps a siren could be sounded across the Spanish mainland, a bit like the new emergency test alert the government put out on mobile phones in Britain.

'Absolute carnage' is pretty much the only way to describe that particular break. First night there a fight erupted with a load of northern lads twice our size and age. I'm not entirely sure what started it, although I'm fairly sure the spat wasn't born of an intellectual basis. I don't think one group heard the other contemplating the theory of relativity and, offended by the views espoused, decided to step in and do something about it. I suspect it was more of the 'you northern ****s'/'you soft southern ******s' kind of thing.* There was a giant kerfuffle, in which heroically I wasn't involved, a couple of tables got knocked over, a paella thrown, and then we legged it.

The northerners, big lads, possibly on a mini-break from an abattoir, weren't at all happy with this situation which then meant they were pursuing us for the rest of the holiday. On a night out we'd nervously poke our heads into a bar – 'It's all right, they're not here – come on.' But when you're trying to avoid a bunch of rabid northerners with a score to settle, Benidorm isn't the biggest place. It's not like London where the chances of seeing a detractor are minimal, or New York where if the mob are on your back you can keep your head down on the Upper East Side for a few days. This is a one-time fishing village on the Costa Blanca in which everyone descends on the same few hundred square yards every night. Like a smashed bus stop, a bunch of drunk scrawny southerners will always stick out.

With two days to go they found us. As bad news goes, this was very bad indeed. Over time, only the words 'and from the Pavilion End, Courtney Walsh' would instil the same level of fear. These lads were after blood. Forget straw donkeys, they wanted our livers for souvenirs. After a chase round the back streets, and drawing on lessons learnt from watching *The Great Escape*, we split up and

* Of which more later.

found places to hide. I spent most of that night in a deserted porch in the company of a small lizard.

By this time we'd also been thrown out of our hotel. Not a total surprise. What went off that balcony doesn't bear thinking about. About 4 a.m., after a fairly typical night of letting off fire extinguishers and throwing beds down stairwells, we were awoken by the Guardia Civil. A national police force of a military nature, the Guardia Civil are not the sort of people you particularly want to see at the end of your bed, baton in hand, in the early hours. In fact, given the choice, I'd rather see Godzilla.

There were three rooms, each with four of us, and the officers, batons flying, steamed straight in. They gave us a good going over before ordering us to pack our bags and get the hell out of there. Still the worse for wear from the night out, we were now scrabbling around trying to get our Fila tracksuits and Ellesse shorts together while being beaten on the back of the calves.*

They chucked us out the hotel door with the not very tourist-friendly message, 'And don't come back, you English bastards!' and so we spent the last two days kipping on the beach. Even now I'm still finding grains of sand in unusual places, but it wasn't too big an ordeal as most nights, by the time we got out the clubs, it was daybreak anyway.

*   *   *

* Better hangover cures are available.

43

With Anglo-Spanish relations in ruins, we all came home thinking how exciting the whole thing had been. To have been let off the leash at that age, drinking shots, trying to impress girls, getting horrendously drunk and throwing up every five minutes, was amazing.* Not clever, I know, but we were so young. I looked at the photos recently and we all look about 12, so pale and skinny, like a Rodney Trotter convention. None of us came home with a tan. We were either in bars or asleep under a sunbed on the beach. Thinking back, I'm not sure if any eating happened either. I've an idea a single burger at Heathrow saw me through the entire seven days.

By then, I was travelling around a bit at home as well, having become part of the MCC Young Cricketers, a pathway to the professional game which involved the occasional tour, the first one of which took us up north – a place which, justifiably in my opinion, I now viewed with considerable trepidation – to play some pretty serious club and representational teams. Like most southerners we never went up north† and this was the first time I'd really strayed the other side of Watford Gap services.

We got on the bus looking very smart in our MCC blazers. Benevolently, my dad had given me 50 quid which, like a lot of the lads, I used responsibly by immediately

---

* Anyone expecting me to make a joke about how this was great preparation for my later life as a touring England cricketer can expect to be disappointed – I never drank shots on tour.

† By the Eighties, pies were freely available in the south.

buying a load of cans of beer and cider to tide us over while chugging up the M1 in the coach.

That first night, we stayed in a small Yorkshire town. I can't quite remember where, but it was either Halifax or somewhere Halifax-esque, somewhere a bit *Last of the Summer Wine.** We were staying at whatever the 1980s version was of Premier Inn. I'm thinking Trust House Forte. Dumping our bags, we headed straight into town to try to find a bit of nightlife. As we enjoyed a few pints – I don't think they did Campari and soda in West Yorkshire – it was obvious there was a feeling of negativity towards us from the locals. It was the repeated threats of bodily violence that gave it away. Before we knew it there was a massive scrap going on. Like one of those cartoon fights where all you can see is fists and feet emerging from a cloud of dust. We ended up legging it back to the Trust House Forte.† Inspecting my wounds, and pockets, I realised I had now spent my entire 50 quid. It was a ten-day trip. From then on, I worked out a survival strategy. I formed a plan involving the hotel maid's cleaning trolley. As well as various sheets, pillowcases and cleaning products, the trolley would also be laden with supplies of those

---

* Women in wrinkled tights shouting, 'Get off my step!' – that kind of thing.

† Being pursued by northerners really was a common theme of my youth. I'm happy to report it's something that's improved over the years and I'm now only rarely chased to my vehicle after commentary stints at Headingley, Chester-le-Street and Old Trafford.

little biscuits they put by the kettle. Every time she left it outside the next-door room I'd sneak out and pocket several dozen packets. I lived on those biscuits for more than a week. I don't know what was in them but I played some pretty good cricket. I've thought a couple of times about recommending them to the England nutritionist.

The on-pitch stuff was a real eye-opener for me. We were playing proper old established clubs, some who played in the Lancashire League, which had some incredible players at that point. We were just lads, coming up against players who might well have had a few games for their counties or maybe featured an overseas pro from the West Indies. We weren't a bad outfit ourselves and so had some right old ding-dongs, and there again it all got a little bit lively. This was my first experience of sledging.

'You little southern *******s. Look at you. You come up here in your ****ing blazers thinking you're it.'

We'd be giving it back. 'We'll show you, you silly northern ****s.'

There'd be a call to the big quick bowler looming on the boundary. 'Come on, Nobby, get in there and knock his ****ing head off.'

It was proper full-on stuff. More like boxing than cricket. Afterwards, instead of a drink with the opposition, we'd be herded away to the minibus – 'Look, lads,' the club chairman would say, 'you'll have to go. There's a bit of ill-feeling in the bar.'

It was a steep, occasionally painful, but very valuable learning curve. Faced with that environment you very quickly realise you have to toughen up. There was no one to go running to – 'Miss, he's just had a go at me!' Aged 16 or 17 we had to rely totally on ourselves. In all honesty, I wasn't averse to saying a few words back – 'Come on, then, you old has-been. What have you done? Played for Yorkshire seconds twice?' I wasn't the biggest bloke, left-arm spinner, and all that, and I'm pretty sure the opposition didn't expect that from me. But I was a little trump card. As a player I was able to back those words up with action. A lot of the time we were playing on sticky dog wickets. I'd come on, knowing they'd want to smack me out the park and, with a bit of flight and guile, get them out. I used to clean up and make them look a bit silly. They'd get very upset about that, which, from my point of view, made it even better.

In a good way, those games made you learn who to sledge and who not to sledge. If you had the local blacksmith walking out at number ten with tattoos all over his face, 'H A T E' on the knuckles of his gloves and 'Made in Huddersfield' on the back of his neck, then you knew it was perhaps not a great idea to get him offside.

It was a well-publicised tour so there'd be decent crowds as well. There'd be three or four hundred people dotted around, and a lot of them would join in the banter. At a young age, that tour taught me game and crowd management, because if you got it wrong there was a good chance of someone marching into your little changing hut to give you a slap.

All in all, I got on the coach home with an idea that the north was quite an aggressive place.* When I thought more about it, though, it wasn't aggression that I'd experienced, it was just real grown-up men's cricket – sport where nobody took any prisoners. Put the ball round their earholes and get stuck in. For one or two of the MCC lads it was the moment they found out that maybe adult sport was all a bit too much for them. These were the young players who looked good in the nets and had amazing technique but in the face of a six-foot-five bloke steaming in trying to knock their nut off, screaming and shouting at them in the follow-through, didn't quite fancy it. I never judged them because I totally understood where they were coming from. It took a bit of getting yourself together to deal with something like that.

When not touring, playing for MCC Young Cricketers meant a lot of driving to away games. It never seemed to be straightforward. There were no satnavs in those days and we were always breaking down. We'd be 17, packed into a decades-old Hillman Imp donated by someone's nan, cricket bats hanging out the window, trying to get to some remote part of Devon. More than once a few of us turned up late, causing a delayed start, lots of tuts and even more raised eyebrows. It would have been easier herding cats than getting some of us to away games.

* Although I did like the gravy.

At the same time, it was so much fun – just hysterical. We'd pull off the motorway to ask directions and find ourselves in some odd deserted hamlet, reminiscent of an episode of *The Avengers* – one of those places where the postman is also the policeman, the publican, the doctor and an eminent Russian spy.

'Excuse me, could you please point us in the direction of the road to Ottery St Mary?'

'Ottery St Mary is it? And what might a bunch of laddies like you be wanting there?'

'We've got a game of cricket.'

'Cricket is it? And what might a bunch of laddies like you be doing playing cricket?'

'Well, we play for the MCC.'

'MCC is it? And what might ...'

No wonder we were always late.

My first car was my mum's old Volvo which remained in the family after she passed away. The Tufnells were a Volvo family. Because of his silversmithing business Dad needed an estate. In typically understated style he went down to the dealer's and got a job lot, well, two, one for him and one for mum.

Volvos were actually a bit exotic back then – 'What? Really? Your car's Swedish? Like Abba?' – and were built like tanks. You could drive a Volvo over a Morris Marina and barely feel the bump. OK, the Volvo wasn't exactly a head-turner – you saw very few of them harbourside in Monaco – but that didn't concern me. I had a car, that's all that mattered. I customised it a bit. I liked a bit of music when I was travelling and so stuck some vast speakers in the back, the kind of things you might see beside the main stage at Glastonbury. I'm pretty sure it was the first time a Volvo had been associated with the term 'boy racer'.

There were times when turning out for MCC Young Cricketers felt a bit like being the Harlem Globetrotters, the American exhibition basketball team who used to pop up a lot on TV in the Seventies.* I'm not saying we balanced cricket balls on the ends of our fingers and took wickets by bowling from under our knees. What I mean is it was our first taste of actually being paid to play, train and tour. For what were still pretty young kids, it did make you feel like you were the bee's knees, even though, in the big scheme of things, we were, at best, more a butterfly's armpit. We had some very talented lads, several of whom went on to play county cricket. It was also the first time you got a real feeling of playing for a team – a good team – turning up with your shoulders back, your sponsored kit and, with a fresh bowl cut, perhaps thinking you looked a little bit sharp. Having the MCC name behind you meant you could puff your chest out a little bit and look the opposition in the eye as if to say, 'Come on then – we'll show you!'

I'll be honest, I'm not sure the Harlem Globetrotters drank as much as some of us, although again, in this envi-

---

* On light entertainment shows, not *Emmerdale Farm*.

ronment it was encouraged. A lot of club cricketers will be familiar with the old thing of getting a jug in at the bar if you get five wickets. Here, if I remember rightly, if you got one batsman out you were required to get the beers in. It was a great feeling, as young lads starting out, to go to some place, potentially a little unfriendly, knock the Essex second eleven over and then have a great night out on the beer.

One or two of us had already experienced life on the road to some degree, having been on a trip with Middlesex under-13s to the Midlands. On that occasion it wasn't so much a brush with the locals as a brush with authority that marked it out for me. Before anyone says, 'Bloody hell, even at 12 he was causing chaos on away trips,' and asking how I was possibly getting served in a high street pub in Halesowen, this was friction with a coach rather than an issue of being caught creeping in at 3 a.m. after a night on the rum punch.*

I actually performed very well on the tour, and was probably the best player, but expect I might have been overheard using some, what have been termed, 'industrial language' or been seen mucking about with my Middlesex partner in crime Jamie Sykes, going up and down in a lift at half past ten or something equally terrible, and so was dropped from the team when we got home. In the meantime, as could happen, a lad who was always called something like Ponsonby-Smythe, who'd scored seven

* That happened the year after.

runs in five innings, would be declared the player of the tournament – my first inkling that cricket might not always be about what you do on the field; that people in authority can do you over. That incident actually messed my career up for a while because I became a little disillusioned with cricket and genuinely thought about going off and doing something else. I didn't want to be around something where people weren't treated the same.

For me, the best coaches were the ones who worked with your character rather than against it. Don Bennett, who was at Middlesex for half a century as player and coach, was a case in point. Don was an old school coach and a very tough guy – strict but very good at getting the best out of people. Players respected him and in return he did his best to make them the best they could be. He'd knock off your rough edges without you even realising it. When he talked to you about how you were carrying on, you listened to him. Early on in my first-class career I bowled out Lancashire and was being a bit chirpy in the dressing room, thinking I was the dog's bollocks.* Straight away he was in there – 'Well, that's your job isn't it? What do you want me to do, piss in your pocket?' An unusual turn of phrase – and one I assume rarely answered in the affirmative – but I got what he was saying. It didn't stop me feeling a little hard done by, but it pushed me on, made me work harder.

* A phrase I've never understood – I've walked behind a lot of dogs in my time and their bollocks are always awful.

If you got a compliment from Don you knew you'd done something special. It came my way once, after we beat Glamorgan in a ridiculous game at their place in 1993. Both teams had scored more than 500 in their first innings, with the great Viv Richards knocking a double century, and the game was meandering to a draw on the last day when I popped up with a miracle spell of 8–29, including Viv first ball, to win us the match and the Championship. In the bar Don sidled up to me over a beer. Two words was all he said – 'Well done.' Not much but it meant the world to me. I'm not one for the whole 'in my day ...' thing, but one thing I will say about the modern game is praise can be bandied around a bit too easily. 'That was a great innings! You're world class, you're brilliant. Here's a million quid.' Hang on a minute! He got 30! A great knock is 190. But cricket's forever changing and maybe that effusiveness reflects the era we're now in.

For sure, there was no big fanfare to announce my first Middlesex contract – two and a half grand for the summer. When Mark Ramprakash (Ramps) signed, the *Evening Standard* and *Daily Mail* turned up – 'Middlesex Sign Wonderkid!' – to get the classic pen-to-paper shot. In my case, someone wandered into the dressing room, said, 'Oi, Phil, sign this,' and that was the end of it. Not that I minded. I was allowed to develop a little bit under the radar in those early days by playing a lot of games in the second eleven. I had the most wonderful two or three years going up and down the country with my mates and that second-eleven dressing-room taught me a lot. It was chaos in there. A lot of strong characters, London lads, and a real hierarchy. Thankfully, I was always good at using humour to fit in, the complete opposite to the 16-year-old Ramps who would just sit quietly in a corner. At that point Ramps had never fielded for an entire day and was worried whether he could do it. Against Sussex at Horsham, towards the end of the day he chased a ball to the boundary down the slope and was so exhausted that he fell into the rose bushes in front of the pavilion.* He couldn't pick himself up so we went down to help. As we dusted this little lad down I couldn't help thinking, 'He should be at home doing his prep!'

Next day, he was waiting to go out to bat. He clearly didn't know what to do with himself. When the third wicket fell, someone actually had to say to him, 'Mate, you've got to go in now.' Again, it felt like a child playing with the grown-ups. We all felt he wouldn't be much cop, that perhaps he was better suited to the under-16s. He walked out to face a pretty lively attack and he had a couple of nervy moments. Then one of the Sussex bowlers had a little sledge. The look on Ramps's face changed. Next delivery was a short one and Ramps rocked back and whacked him. 'Ahh,' we thought, 'better look after

---

* Rose bushes are a very poor choice of pavilion plant. Much better is something soft, like moss.

this bloke.' Next season, aged 17, Ramps made his first-team debut, immediately making a fifty.

My debut wasn't quite so memorable. As a bowler, when you start out, even a fairly average county pro is capable of taking you apart. Worcestershire's Phil Neale did just that. No disrespect to Phil, but ten years later I could have bowled at him with my eyes closed. However, faced with a spinner fresh to the county scene, he saw, and took, the chance to dominate. I was 20 when that first-team debut came. I didn't get any wickets and was absolutely annihilated. I'd been performing against some good batsmen in the seconds and now I was being smashed to all corners of the ground. I couldn't understand it at all, but that's the difference in class between first- and second-eleven cricket. When the call comes, suddenly you've got to find your place.

I was in and out of the team for a couple of years before what was to be a landmark game against Essex at Uxbridge.

'Listen mate,' Mike Gatting, our skipper, said to me, 'there's been a lot of chat about whether you can do it or not. We've given you a few chances and you haven't done much. I can't keep protecting you. You can't just be a luxury. I've got people saying you're a bit of a pain in the arse* and questioning whether you're actually worth it. Look at this as a bit of a decider, not necessarily about your attitude but whether you can get people out.'

* Bit harsh.

It was a flat wicket but I bowled well, including knocking a young Nasser Hussain's stumps over. I'd shown I could be a crucial cog in moving us forward in the game. An added bonus was that Gatt didn't particularly like Nasser, dating back to Nasser not walking when playing for Combined Universities against Middlesex in the Benson & Hedges Cup. Gatt always got stuck into Nass. 'Who does this bloke think he is? He thinks he rules the place.' Gatt loved it when I bowled him – 'Yes! Go on, Tuffers! Get rid of that show-off!'

Gatt had spelled out my position to me and I'd responded. That then gave me a confidence boost. I began to see the craft of being a professional cricketer – that there's a bit more to it than just running up and bowling. I became more and more aware of the little tricks and pointers, like how a batsman sets up or opens up his hands. I began building a knowledge bank of batsmen. Did they sweep? Did they slog? What fielding positions forced false shots?

Another major confidence boost was taking 6–60 at Kent in one of legendary left-arm spinner Derek Underwood's last games for the club. Still the 'Deadly Derek' of old, Underwood, then aged 42, took 5–43. After the game, he sat down with me, exactly half his age.

'Listen, boy,' he told me, 'well bowled. Keep that up and you'll go a long way in this game.' He talked about the ins and outs of bowling left-arm spin and by the time we went our separate ways, I really did feel I might actually have a future in the first-class game.

*   *   *

There was something else about reaching the first eleven – I became entitled to a sponsored car. That was it as far as I was concerned. 'I've cracked it. I've arrived as a professional cricketer. I must have because I've been given a Peugeot 205.'

Along the side, it had my name emblazoned – 'Phil Tufnell, sponsored by Dave's Peugeot, Hammersmith', or some such. Collecting the cars was a huge day. The garage would want all the publicity it could muster and so they'd all be lined up, a fleet of low- and mid-range Peugeots, gleaming in the Lord's sun for the photo-op. We'd then turn up in our Middlesex kit and drape ourselves sexily over the vehicles. It really was very Formula 1.

The way it worked was the more senior the player, the better the spec of vehicle. After the photocall, there'd be a mad dash to the office to pick up your keyring with your name and registration on it. It was like having Christmas in spring. At the top end they'd be hoping for a GL, while as captain Gatt would have a 'special edition'.* At the other end, the peripheral lads got all the shitty ones. In all honesty, I didn't care what I got. All that mattered to me, as it did to most of us, was I'd got a brand new car, free.

We must have made for quite a sight, in formation whizzing up and down the motorway in our sponsored fleet. One time, not long after we'd been given the cars, we were heading up to Durham and decided to give them a bit of a

---

* Walnut dash, tape player, heated gear knob.

workout. It was late, this big wide road was literally empty, and everyone was taking turns on the front. It was like a very poor version of the Red Arrows. As we pulled up in Durham we could almost feel these poor cars panting, trying to get their breath back, wheezing, 'Thank **** for that!'

As I progressed through my career, each year the car I was handed would improve, potentially with a leatherette armrest or teak ashtray. After a while, the Peugeots were replaced by a real wowser of a manufacturer – Vauxhall. A rep would come in and ask what range we were interested in. I had a look and plumped for the Frontera, one of the first mass-produced 4×4s. The only problem was it topped out at 70mph and sounded like a taxi. I parked it outside my dad's and walked in one day and his first question was, 'How come you got dropped off in a cab?' Thankfully, I did move on to a very smart top-of-the-range Cavalier estate that went like a bomb.

After England won the ashes in 2005, the team all got sponsored Jaguars. Everyone was delighted, except Kevin Pietersen, who preferred to drive his own car. But, in all honesty, I was extremely grateful for any vehicle. The condition we gave them back in is another matter entirely. Cricket gear slung in and out, tearing up and down motorways – bumps, bangs, scratches and crashes. We drove them like we'd stolen them. I left about three clutches on the M4. We tried our best, but the cricket season is tough for a human let alone a sponsored car. At the end of September, if they could have talked, those vehicles would have said one thing, 'Please! Set me free! Don't make me go back to Middlesex.'

I often wondered whether it ever produced any noticeable benefits for the garages in question.

'Oh, hi – I saw Mike Gatting in one of your Peugeots yesterday. I was umming and ahhing about my next car and seeing the captain of Middlesex poking his nose at the lights in one of yours was the clincher.'

Certainly, having your name emblazoned on the side of your car wasn't always a positive. Normally in a car park if you back into someone you have a quick look round and off you go.* No chance of that when your name is on the side as well your employer. Also, you might have to be a little bit careful where you parked in case an Essex fan wiped a chip wrapper on your windscreen. It could all get a bit surreal, hacking down tree branches in pub car parks and laying them over the bonnet. I really should have carried some First World War camouflage netting around in the boot. Or had a false panel made up with Jamie Sykes's name on.

Having said that, those cars were rarely stationary long enough for any negative attention. The amount of driving we did back then was crazy. There can only have been HGV drivers doing more miles than your average county cricketer. It was so dangerous. You'd be sat in a car with a bloke at the wheel who'd batted for three sessions or bowled 45 overs to try to force a victory. On another

* At least, this is what I've heard.

occasion, that bloke at the wheel would be you. We'd finish at Llandudno at 6 p.m., shovel some food down and face a six-hour drive down to Sussex ready to go again the next morning. If I'd been bowling all day and was fortunate enough not to be driving, I'd be gone, curled up on the backseat for the duration. Amazing to think that on several occasions it would be Wilf Slack at the wheel. Wilf, a lovely bloke and a fantastic batsman, an absolute rock of the dressing room and the team, had lost consciousness three times while batting for Middlesex late in his career. I recall one of those games quite clearly. He was taking guard and then just fell over. Everyone rushed out to help him. Another time, at Leicestershire, Jonathan Agnew was at the end of his mark and Wilf just slumped to the ground. No one could figure out what was going on, least of all him. Eventually, one such collapse would prove fatal. Batting in a friendly match in Gambia, Wilf passed out and never woke up again. A post-mortem showed he had a cardiac issue, but while that went undiagnosed he was like the rest of us, driving all over the country. With medical testing lacking, he was oblivious to his condition.

Eventually, some counties dropped car sponsorships and began travelling by coach. We did try that but with Middlesex being a London club it could take some of the boys an hour and a half just to get to Lord's before we'd even set off. The journey itself would then take forever as we trundled along in the bus. It was much easier to pick up the bloke who lived nearest and make the trip yourselves. That wide dispersal of players meant Middlesex could lack a feeling of community. Occasionally, we'd go round to each other's houses for barbecues, but London is a big place. It was hardly like nipping over to your neighbour down the road. The upside of that was the club never felt too incestuous, a difference from certain other counties where it was rumoured players were, shall we say, a little too close to one another's wives. In those counties, infighting was common, whereas we went to work, played our cricket and then went our separate ways. I quite liked that. It didn't feel like we were in each other's pockets. I could compartmentalise my life. I had Middlesex and outside of that I still had my mates who couldn't care less what I did.

Looking back on my early experiences of travel, as a young man and as a cricketer, it's clear I was never going to be content just to be a passenger. I always wanted more. On the pitch I wanted to perform; off the pitch I wanted to enjoy the life that had come my way, one free of the confinement of the office or factory walls.

I wanted to live life to the full – an attitude I've maintained. My playing career might now be sinking into ancient history, and the old knees might be a bit stiff, but I'm as keen as ever to get out and have new and fascinating experiences. It's just, as anyone who travels regularly will know, it isn't always that easy …

4

COME FLY WITH ME

I've spent an awful lot of time in airports down the years and I have to say they're places where nothing ever seems to go well. Departures get delayed, tempers get frayed and entire families disintegrate before they've even got on the plane.*

Some people think that if you've been on the telly it delivers you into a wholly different airport experience. They've seen fly-on-the-wall documentaries where A-listers such as Keith Richards, Angelina Jolie and Maureen from *Driving School* are ushered past awestruck passengers and fast-tracked straight on to the plane. This is a world where queues don't exist and a giant Toblerone isn't considered an offensive weapon. Essentially these people emerge from a limousine and are whisked on a magic carpet ride to their place of opulence in first class, or, more likely, a private jet. All everyone else can do is look up from the hard metal

---

* To be fair, this can be an interesting diversion once you've finished your word search.

chair they've slept on for two days and nudge the person next to them in awe, wonder and deep, deep resentment.

I can confirm that an appearance on series 47, episode nine of *Blankety Blank* confers on you none of the above privileges. In fact, I've concluded that at airports even the tiniest bit of notoriety can seriously work against you. Take the speedy boarding queue. I will generally pay my eight quid for speedy boarding. It's not exactly a bank-breaker and if it means not standing in a line at the gate for 45 minutes then I'm more than happy to shell out.* Even so, when the speedy boarders call has been issued and I've stepped forward I have occasionally felt someone give me a bit of an, 'Oh, here he is – Charlie Big Bollocks!' look. A couple of times I've actually felt a little embarrassed, and then I've thought, 'Well, hang on, all I've done is pay eight quid for speedy boarding. I'm not being carried on to the plane in a sedan chair while people feed me grapes and wave fans above my head – and it's not just me, there are quite a few of us.'

The situation is never helped by the lack of clearly marked lines for speedy and non-speedy boarders, leading to vicious accusations of queue-jumping and mutters about being 'like Phil and Holly'.

'Oi! Just because you've been on the telly, don't mean you can push in.'

---

* I've spent a lot of time standing. Aside from when Merv Hughes puts you on your backside, cricket is a standing game. If you want to do sport sat down, become a rower or a racing driver.

'No, no. It's OK. I've paid my eight quid for speedy boarding.'

'Come off it, pal, I know your game. You've been on *The Jump* and now you think you can do what you want.'

'No, look, honestly. All I've done is pay eight quid. My wife's had a hip operation and she can't stand for long. That's it.'

Next thing you know you're all over social media – #pushingin #whodoeshethinkheis? #questionofqueuing #bringbackthestocks

All because of a lack of direction to the speedy boarding queue.

If you do get on board without being strangled, there's then the question of whether your luggage has actually travelled with you. I've lost my luggage a few times down the years. On my very first England overseas tour, to Australia, my entire cricket kit didn't turn up – lucky pants, lucky socks, the lot. This was very bad news indeed. As a cricketer, you become very familiar with your kit. Socks become nicely moulded to feet, shirts soften and become less itchy, undercrackers become nicely moulded to … well, you get my meaning. Boots are especially important. I'd hear about David Beckham sporting a new pair of boots every time he walked out on to the pitch and find it unimaginable. I enjoyed the sensation of something being worn out in all the right places – like an old pair of slippers if you've got them right.

I'd worked this out the hard way. Early in my career, while all the other boys were there in lovely Reeboks with lots of padding and inner soles, I, on the other hand, had accepted a small sum to don the output of a rival footwear manufacturer. Being a young chap I was very amenable to being paid to wear shoes.* Who wouldn't be? But it only took me a couple of minutes in the nets to realise these were the most uncomfortable boots imaginable. It was like playing cricket with two ice-cream tubs strapped to your feet. At the end of each day as I hobbled off, like a little old lady on her way home from the shops, someone, a player, or a member perhaps, would stop me and ask, 'Phil, are you all right?'

'I'm fine,' I'd say, smiling through gritted teeth as I thought about the money.

In the end, I had to bin the boots. I phoned the company up and explained my predicament. 'I can't wear these anymore,' I told them. 'I can hardly walk in them let alone bowl. I've got bow legs and there's blood in my socks' – the screws that held the spikes in place had actually worn through the soles. As part of the deal I was required to say the boots were like walking on air. Correct – if the air happened to be full of drawing pins. In a matter of months they'd turned me into John Wayne. A tip for any young sportsperson – go for comfort, not cash.

I wasn't so worried about my batting gear. If anything, I was hoping that would get lost. But with no sign of the

* I'd have worn stilettoes for the right price.

rest of my kit I had to go down to a local sports shop in Brisbane. Nothing was how it should be. The shorts were rough, the socks were all horrible and thin rather than those lovely thick ones you get in England, and the trousers didn't fit right, tight round the crotch and disappearing up my arse. I looked at this paltry offering and thought, 'How am I going to do 30 overs in 40-degree heat in this stuff?' I walked out the first day of the Test match in what felt like hessian. I must have looked a right idiot. Thankfully, a couple of days later my luggage did turn up and I got all my stuff back. I hugged those socks in the manner of a kid reunited with a lost teddy bear.

Losing luggage was an occupational hazard of being a touring cricketer. In Antigua at the start of a West Indies trip a few of the boys' cases didn't turn up for a few days. The rest of us dumped our bags and headed straight down to Millers beach bar, sat there sipping cocktails in T-shirts and flip-flops while everyone else was sweating their backside off in the same clothes – shirt, trousers and brogues – they'd boarded the plane in back in England.

Of course you don't have to be a cricketer to feel that will-it-won't-it luggage dread. That awful wait at the carousel has happened to everyone. In fact, so convinced am I that we'll be one of the unlucky few, even before we get to the baggage reclaim I'll have said to Dawn, 'Forget it, it won't be there.' You can feel the tension as the bags start coming round. Everyone gets a bit nervy. People are pushing to the front to get the best view, congregating by the prime spot where the bags emerge, elbows sticking out. If your bag isn't among the first two to come out, that's it, you won't be told otherwise – it's lost. I had my car stolen once and was walking up and down the street looking for it for about 45 minutes before I had this crushing realisation – 'It's been nicked!' It's exactly the same with an airport carousel.

'It's not here, Dawn!'

'Give it a chance, Phil, it'll turn up.'

'No, no. It's disappeared. We might as well just go now.'

Eventually, there'll be just you and one other bloke. A last case will plop on to the carousel and he'll take it and go. At that point, there's just you standing there disconsolately for a quarter of an hour, staring at an empty conveyor belt, before finally you give up.*

This is why as well you have to be ultra-alert when the cases do come out. Let's face it half of them look exactly the same. It's not beyond the realms of imagination that someone else might mistakenly clear off with yours. That exact thing has happened to Dawn, and ever since I've swathed the Tufnell bags in all sorts of rags, ribbons and bandages to make sure they stand out on the carousel.†
Sounds extreme but it's either that or unzip your suitcase

---

* Some people try to minimise the consequences of lost luggage by wearing multiple layers on board. However, this can compromise the ability to fit through the exit doors in an emergency.

† A pair of Y-fronts wrapped round the handle generally ensures a bag is left well alone.

at the hotel to find Katie Price's autobiography and ten sets of ladies' underwear. I mean, look, I'm no fashionista, but I draw the line at wearing stockings and suspenders to the beach.

I've now mastered the art of the small carry-on bag. Going somewhere for a week, I'll pack seven T-shirts and seven pairs of shorts. I'll also have two pairs of flip-flops, a pair of posh shoes, two pairs of going-out trousers and five decent shirts. Potentially, I have to compromise on my velvet smoking jacket but that's the price you pay for easy luggage. Indeed, I'd recommend this method to any travelling gentleman.

Whatever my luggage preference, it's generally only a matter of time before a customs officer is rooting through it. I don't know if I've got the face of an international drugs mule, but I'm seemingly always pulled over for a baggage check, so much so that me and Dawn will have a bet on it beforehand – two to one on that it'll be me given the third degree. It's as if someone has rung ahead. 'Yep, he's on the flight. Could staff on the ground please get the rubber gloves ready for when he disembarks.'

It's reached the stage now where I'm expecting to experience a cavity search at every travel hub. 'But this is Euston Station! I'm only going to Watford! I'm not sure a train conductor is allowed to do that.'

We were coming back from somewhere a bit ago, it was about three in the morning, and as we trooped through arrivals I turned to Dawn – 'I bet I get called over again.' No sooner had the words left my mouth than I heard the customs bloke – 'Right, OK, over you come!' I didn't even bother looking round. I knew it was me he was speaking to. For once – and the early hour certainly didn't help – I actually lost it a little bit.

'Well, what a surprise. Me again. Who'd have thought it? Come on then, Dawn, get the keys to the case out. Let him have a look.'

The bloke looked at me, a little bit taken aback. 'Oh sorry, Phil. Go on, mate. On your way.'

I couldn't believe it. Don't get me wrong, I was very grateful to him for being so kind and feeling sorry for me enough to let me continue unhindered, but if anything I felt a little bit let down. I mean, surely that's against the rules, isn't it? That can't be how it works, can it?

'Come on, Mr Escobar, let's be seeing your case.'

'Oh what? Again? It's every bleeding time!'

'Oh, OK – sorry, mate. We'll leave it. Go on, I can see your armoured Hummer's waiting. Have a nice day.'

Occasionally, though, something unexpectedly pleasant will happen at an airport – and I'll give you a very good example. Not too long ago, me and my *A Question of Sport* pals Matt Dawson and Sue Barker were doing a speaking event on a cruise liner. I've done them before, on a sporting theme. For that one, me and Dawn flew out and joined the boat in La Rochelle and then three days later flew back from La Coruna. I enjoyed the cruising experience immensely. Anywhere you can get a

hamburger at four in the morning has to be good fun.*
On our boat there were endless restaurants, theatres, a
casino and a swimming pool. I found that last one a bit
hard to get used to. You're at sea and everyone's sat
round a pool? That is odd when you think about it. I
preferred it when we entered a port and could go and
have a wander round, have a bit of lunch, then get back
on board for dinner and a nice bottle of wine. From that
point of view, I can see why Captain Pugwash liked the
ocean life so much.

On the way home, I thought I'd be romantic and so I
bought Dawn a ring. I'd given it to her at dinner on the
last night only for her to wake up the next morning unable
to get it off her finger. We tried everything – hand cream,
lard, the lot – but there was no shifting it. By the time we
got to the airport the digit was swelling alarmingly. We
started worrying about the pressure in the cabin on the
plane. Surely that would only make it worse. By now we
were really panicking, sat in the bar at the airport desperately googling potential solutions to the situation. By now
people around us were beginning to take an interest in
what was happening, a bit like when someone starts playing a piano in a public area, only in our case the only noise
was gentle weeping.† Someone suggested looping a thread
of cotton round the ring and easing it off that way. I set off

---

* Cruises essentially revolve around food and booze. They only
stick a gym on board to rub it in.

† From me – Dawn was OK.

around the airport shops in search of a thread but could only find a box of chocolates with a bow and so we had to use that.* Anyway, that didn't work either. A few other people suggested stuff, with no joy, and so in the end I went off to some sort of maintenance department to see if they had anything in there. Ten minutes later I came back with two massive pairs of pliers and some bolt cutters.

Dawn was having none of it. 'No, no. Keep them away from me! You'll end up hacking my finger off.'

By now the flight was nearly ready for boarding and she was beginning to feel woozy with the anxiety. We had no choice but to try with my scavenged instruments. We were just trying to wrestle the pliers between the ring and the finger, with accompanying shrieks and caterwauling, when this little bloke in a beige safari suit† appeared among us. He was grey-bearded and had a quiet, almost spiritual, demeanour.‡ He knelt down to inspect Dawn's hand which by now was resting on a cushion turning a garish shade of purple. Whereas before the panic had been spreading amongst us, now suddenly we were all becalmed. The man laid his hand on Dawn's, and within a minute, almost imperceptibly, had removed the ring. He then picked up his bag and disappeared back into the bowels of the airport. During the entire time, neither he nor any of us had spoken a word.

* The bow, not the chocolates – they only make your fingers bigger.

† Not Don Estelle.

‡ See Chapter 16 – Stonehenge.

Funnily enough, it turned out this man of mystery was actually on our flight. A friend sat next to him and asked him what he did for work. In a very quiet voice, he replied, 'I'm an engineer.' My guess was he'd removed a few tight washers in his time. From that point on, in mine and Dawn's minds, this chap has always been 'the engineer ghost of La Coruna', a little apparition who, whenever you're in trouble round that way, will arrive, rescue you from your plight, and then wordlessly disappear. If ever you're in strife at the airport in La Coruna, look skyward and ask quietly for '*el pequeño ingeniero*', and with you very shortly will be 'the little engineer', a small man in a safari suit who has powers beyond this world. Some say, many years ago, the engineer died at the airport, possibly sucked into an engine, and now returns to help people before they get on the plane. You'll neither see him nor hear him – but he'll find you.*

Whether approached by a miniature man with mystical powers or not, the modern airport is far from the worst place to spend a few hours. They're essentially a vast indoor shopping mall with large numbers of mildly stressed people wandering around.† My issue with flying is more to do with the bit where you're up in the air. I

---

* I've since suggested La Coruna Airport as a great location for a future episode of *Most Haunted*.

† Like Bluewater.

don't care what you say, but flying just isn't normal. It is
for birds, but if you notice we haven't got wings. Like it or
not, we're ground-dwellers. The problem being that walking to Barbados takes a very long time.

While I can think of a few people who won't fly – Dennis
Bergkamp, the old Arsenal forward, being one of the best
known – I've always made myself get on the plane. I must
have flown two thousand times in my life – it was an
unavoidable part of my job.* But that little bit of fear never
leaves me. I'll always take on board my old St Christopher
which my mum gave me, and I'll back its powers up with a
bit of a snifter. Three bloody Marys is my go-to medicine,
which has the added bonus of being three of my five a day.
I did that all the way through my cricket career and,
impressed by its stress-soothing properties, continued afterwards as well. That might sound a bit OTT but I've had a
few dodgy old times on planes and they've always stayed
with me. I have a recurring dream where I'm on a jet heading at speed towards the ground. In it, I'm shouting, 'I told
you! I told you this would happen! And would you listen?
You all said I was overreacting and now look at us. I told
you!' Just before impact, I wake up in a cold sweat.†

Again, it didn't help that back when I was growing up
there were endless films about things going wrong on

* In the old days, the England cricket team would sail to away
fixtures. An Ashes trip Down Under meant three weeks on an
ocean-going liner. If you didn't like deck quoits, you'd had it.

† For really bad nightmares I keep a Qantas sick bag by my bed.

planes. Engine failures, lightning strikes, hijackings. Every year there was a new one of the *Airport* films. The pilot would have a seizure and an alcoholic nun would have to guide a 747 down to the ground. Is it any wonder everyone was so scared of flying? Luckily, early on, I taught myself the art of kipping on a plane. I've got it down to a T.* I get on board and put myself into a trance. I know the safety display is important but for me it's a hypnosis tool. I'm surprised a flight attendant has never noticed my altered state and taken the opportunity to get me to bark like a dog or do an impression of Elvis. So quick is this slip into unconsciousness that Dawn will get her seatbelt on, take her book out her bag, look round and I'm gone. If ever I'm on a plane that plunges into the Atlantic, I can tell you now what my last words will have been. 'Whatever you do, Dawn, don't wake me up.' It's like I've got an off switch. I only turn back on just as we're about to land. It's a self-imposed coma. The drooling isn't attractive but there you go.

Sadly, self-imposed hypnosis isn't an option in a hot-air balloon. Not unless you want to fall over the side. I don't know what possessed me, but I did once go up in one of these things. I mean, what could possibly go wrong with something with no brakes, no steering wheel, a massive gas cooker and an outsized laundry basket? No wonder it never caught on as a mode of transport.†

* Preferably iced, with a drop of brandy.

† There's a reason the president of the USA has 'Air Force One' emblazoned on a 747 and not a hot-air balloon.

Me and Dawn went up in one in South Africa. As we rose from the ground, I couldn't help thinking how much at the mercy we were of such basic elements as fire and wind.* The higher we went, the more I clung, dry-mouthed, to the side. It's hot in South Africa and my mind turned to Icarus, that bloke who flew too close to the sun.† We had a good view up in that balloon, but I'd have given anything to be one of the wildebeest below. Unlike us, the wildebeest isn't constantly trying to push the boundaries. If it's got a bit of grass, it's happy. As a species, we could learn a lot from wildebeest.‡ Cowering away from the side, I couldn't help thinking how much easier it would have been just to have gone up a really tall building. That way you're not cheek by jowl with gas bottles, breathing in cooker fumes and worrying that the bottom of the basket might fall out. Even what should be the joy of landing is messed up by being dragged along for half a mile.

Ballooning is very much more Dawn's thing than mine. She's mooted a romantic ride above the English countryside once or twice. I get where she's coming from but, the way I see it, the romance soon ends if you career into an electricity pylon or drift over a nuclear power station. For me, it was watching a programme about the *Hindenburg* that really put the kybosh on travelling around in big

* Also water – let's face it there's no toilet.

† Icarus perished that day, but he taught us all an important lesson – don't use beeswax in aircraft construction.

‡ How to cross crocodile-infested rivers not included.

gas-filled containers. There's something about the broad-caster Herbert Morrison shouting 'Oh the humanity!' as the airship bursts into flames on landing at Lakehurst, New Jersey, that really does concentrate the mind. To be fair, safety restrictions are much tighter now.*

I spent most of my short dalliance with ballooning pondering a long-held thought – people have forgotten that most things look quite good from the ground. You don't necessarily need to see everything from above. Is looking down on the Empire State Building from a heli-copter any better than looking up at it from the pavement? When you think about it, it's the same view just the other way round.

One of the very few times I've ever felt lucky to be up in the air was when I was filming the TV show *My Family at War*, looking into my grandad William's involvement in the First World War. When I signed up for the programme I never imagined it would lead to me going up in a Sopwith Camel. But as a coppersmith, grandad was good with his hands. Joining the Royal Flying Corps in 1916, he went out to France as a mechanic with 46 Squadron and worked on the planes on the front. He never really used to talk about it, but I got the gist of his experience from my dad.

* Did you know you could actually have a fag on the *Hindenburg*? Even I'd have drawn a line at that. The burner on a hot-air balloon, on the other hand, would make a fantastic lighter so long as you weren't too attached to your eyebrows.

Sopwith Camels were used for reconnaissance and really were sitting ducks. They'd only just been invented and so were very basic, without guns or anything. Forget a bullet, someone chucking a tomato could have brought one down. The biplane, re-created using original blueprints, I went up in was based at a lovely little flying club in Yorkshire. With a hut and a few benches, it actually reminded me a bit of a village cricket club. The difference was the hangar. After a few pleasantries, the enthusiasts who looked after the aircraft opened the doors and pushed it out. Talk about atmospheric, it really did hit a note, like being taken back in time a hundred years.

The driver was a retired fighter jet pilot, and really looked the part – moustache, silk scarf and leather hat. I was reassured by his presence. As a nervous flyer, there's definitely something about a highly qualified fighter pilot that puts your mind at rest. Even when he said, 'Don't be alarmed if the engine stops,' I wasn't too worried, whereas on a normal flight such a pronouncement would spark a desperate search for a parachute.*

That's not to say there weren't concerns. I did fret slightly, for instance, when I discovered that not only would I be sitting above the fuel tank, but I'd be doing so on a wicker seat. Like something from a garden centre. I definitely wouldn't be lighting a fag, that's for sure. Anyway, despite my issues with the flammability of the chairs, I climbed in. The driver got the old girl fired up

---

* And new underpants.

and, rather marvellously, did actually say, 'Chocks away!' before we wobbled off on what looked a little bit too much like bicycle wheels.

It felt like we'd reached about 20 miles an hour when the Sopwith Camel fluttered gently up into the air. There was none of the old Red Baron business, swooping around and loop the looping. It was just this fluttering the whole time. There's no roof of course. You're just sat there with your elbows on the side, leather jacket and gloves, and the wind rushing through your hair. The plane's fragility and lack of speed again made me think again how totally vulnerable such aircraft must have been over the trenches. Made of the flimsiest of woods, they would burst into flames when hit, and indeed the lads who flew these things had a life expectancy of two weeks. The people in charge didn't even give them a parachute, the thinking being it would be too easy for them to abort the mission. Instead, pilots had a pistol with which to shoot themselves in the head – because that was considered by their superiors the best way out. Eventually, those in authority began to realise that the pilots were actually more important than the planes – it's easier to build another plane than it is to train another pilot – and so gave them a parachute after all.

It really was quite emotional flying around with all those thoughts in my head – what those blokes had to put themselves through. They were very brave boys. They'd have been courageous to get in this odd new machine and go up in the air over a village fete in Surrey let alone over the battlefields of the First World War. Incredible people.

After a few minutes, feather-like, we fluttered down. I was very lucky to experience that flight. Very few people have got to do so. It's something I'll never forget – and it may be the one airborne experience I wouldn't mind doing twice.

5

THE HIGH LIFE

I might not have been a natural when it comes to flying, but I wasn't averse to a bit of the high life.* The main problem was finding where the high life existed. As a newcomer to the England set-up, it was all a bit mysterious. My first experience of the national team was on a tour Down Under and I soon began to notice that on days off a few senior players – Allan Lamb, Ian Botham and David Gower in particular – would disappear. The rest of us newbies would be sat round the pool, or having a round of golf, only to see their helicopter vanish into the distance. Later that night they'd return, a little the worse for wear, clearly having had a fantastic time.

Having watched a few episodes of *Columbo* I vowed to get to the bottom of the situation. Enquiries revealed that nine times out of ten they were visiting a winery, of which there's no shortage in Australia. But what actually

* Before anyone mentions the story about weed smoking in a New Zealand bar toilet, that was shown to be a hoax.

happened when they got there? I found out the answer in typically unorthodox manner.

Early on in that trip, the team – players, management, the works – went out to a very busy and highfalutin fish restaurant in Melbourne. There was a big, long table, with the more experienced blokes at one end and the likes of me down the other. We were all talking, having a few glasses of wine while we were eating, and possibly I didn't realise quite how tipsy I'd become. That wasn't really an issue until '(I Can't Get No) Satisfaction' by the Rolling Stones started up over the speakers, at which point I was gripped by a strange urge. By the restaurant bar was a mannequin. For the next three minutes it would be my partner in possibly the most excruciating dance interpretation of 'Satisfaction' ever seen. Around all these tables packed with Victoria's most eminent individuals, me and my smileless (understandably) companion went, me gyrating and giving it the Mick Jagger* lips, even at some points rolling around on the floor. To this day it's the only time I've seen a mannequin look embarrassed. As the song finished, I regained my senses. Looking round, I realised

---

* I did actually happen across Mick Jagger, a big cricket fan, during a later tour in the Caribbean. He was in the same bar as me and a couple of the other boys. I resisted the temptation to grab the nearest statue and repeat my Melbourne spectacular, but I was introduced to ol' rubber lips – 'This is Phil – did you know he does a really good impression of you? Go on, Phil, show him!' I declared a sudden need for the toilet and departed at speed. Whether he tells the same anecdote from the opposite perspective – 'I was waiting for him for three hours – he never came back!' – I don't know.

the entire place had come to a stop, conversations halted, forks halfway to mouths. Waiting staff had frozen mid-ladle. The maitre d' was as white as a sheet from Brentford Nylons. Each and every one of them was staring directly at me.

If ever you find yourself in this situation – maybe you've battled a life-sized cut-out of Arnold Schwarzenegger in a cinema foyer, or perhaps done something unspeakable with a giant pepper pot in an Italian restaurant – there's only one way to deal with that awful moment of realisation that you've just made a complete arse of yourself. Style it out. I returned to my table and sat down as if what had just happened was the most normal thing in the world, something I did every Thursday and twice at weekends. I looked at the halibut on my plate and carried on eating.

Looking back, I'm convinced it was this display of unadulterated ridiculousness that meant the next time the senior boys were having a day out, they gave me the nod. Back then, most players favoured the traditional way of becoming part of the senior set-up. They would put in solid performances on the pitch and pipe up with suggestions regards fielding positions at team meetings. They could have bypassed all of that by drinking too much Chardonnay and making a grotesque fool of themselves in front of a city elite. It's an approach that forms a key tenet of the *Phil Tufnell Coaching Guide*.

Anyway, like I say, the call soon came – 'Tuffers, we're off to a winery tomorrow. Want to come?'

Well, what are you going to say to that? 'Er, no thanks, I'm going to read the latest copy of *Titbits* while getting third-degree sunburn by the pool'? I don't think so. The only time I've moved quicker was when Linda Lusardi's 1981 calendar hit WH Smith's. I couldn't believe it. Finally, I was not only going to see what happened, but actually experience, one of these legendary winery days out. I was beyond excited. It was like someone with a Cold War fascination being shown the nuclear button.

Next day, I rushed down to the hotel lobby like a kid waiting for the coach on a school trip. Soon enough, the trio appeared. The smooth nonchalance of Gower. The sheer presence of Beefy. The confidence of Lamb. And into that mix stepped me, in two minds whether to ask for a packed lunch from reception.

We were, it transpired, heading to a winery owned by Geoff Merrill, who'd been inviting England cricketers to visit since befriending Bob Willis in an Adelaide hotel on a previous Ashes tour. Back then, England players might head to the nearby Barossa Valley to sample a bit of grape juice. Merrill is said to have asked Bob, 'Why don't you come and try some decent wine rather than drinking that Barossa stuff?' To which Bob replied, 'Well, why don't you come and drink some of this weasel's piss you call beer?' It's easy to see why Bob's laconic wit and acerbic eye made him such a hit when he later became such a key and now much-missed figure on Sky. Anyway, on such beautiful exchanges lifelong friendships are made. Geoff Merrill was a fantastic host and for years England players enjoyed his incredible hospitality.

After a couple of minutes, a limousine arrived and took us off to a waiting helicopter, at which point we whizzed down to the winery and landed, in a manner usually reserved for royalty, on an immaculately manicured front lawn. I stepped out of that helicopter into another world.* I had never seen anything like it. I tell you, if tables could groan then these would have sounded like an early morning commuter stuck on the M25. There were lobsters, crabs, pigs on spits, bunches of grapes. It was like the set of *Caligula*.

I was salivating wildly when Gower produced a sabre and promptly sliced the neck off a bottle of Grand Cru Champagne. Whether Geoffrey Boycott could do the same with a bottle of milk stout I'm unsure. Years later I learnt this was an old trick of the officer class in Napoleon's light cavalry. Napoleon himself was a big fan of a glass of bubbly – 'I drink Champagne when I win, to celebrate, and I drink Champagne when I lose, to console myself.' I can see where he was coming from.

From there, the jollities began. It wouldn't just be us there, there'd be all sorts of really quite notable people – business types, artists, Madge and Harold Bishop from *Neighbours*. Before you knew it, you'd be messing about

---

* I've never read *The Lion, the Witch, and the Wardrobe*, but I imagine it was a bit like the feeling those kids had when they nipped through the back of that cupboard. Or Norse warriors have when they reach Valhalla.

having a little game of cricket on the lawn, or being taken on a tour of the vineyards. It was a level of being looked after I'd never experienced in my life, and that's coming from someone who'd played at Derby.

The winery itself was beautiful, and of course something we rarely see in Britain.* It was an education for me. Like most British people, I'd always thought of Australia as being a dry and arid place – more dust than a hoover bag. But here I was seeing open green Australian countryside, lush and full of life, and made so, so beautiful by the most incredible light. I was absolutely blown away.

The wine was also lovely, although, I'll be honest, at that time I didn't know one end of a bottle of Shiraz from another. While other people sipped and swilled, my approach was more 'mouth under water fountain'. I'd glugged a few glasses down when someone mentioned they were now getting the 'good stuff' out. I hadn't an earthly what they were on about. What was the stuff we'd just been drinking then? Dishwater?

'Would you like a drop of the '75?' someone enquired. It's not a question you tend to be asked when you predominantly drink lager. I'll be honest, to my untrained palate, the '75 didn't taste much different to the '88 or whatever we'd had previously. Clearly, though, from the appreciative noises being made by everyone else this was a very wholesome drop indeed. I got the idea they didn't sell it at Kwik Save.

* I've yet to hear of one opening in Stoke.

A bit later, a never-ending supply of quality brandies came out, again something entirely new to me, and then a bloke in a bowtie and black gloves showed up with an array of cheeses and bottles of port. It just never stopped all day – food, wine, food, wine. For someone like me, still a little new at this business, lasting the course would mean the occasional employment of the tactical chunder. 'Won't be a minute, everyone. Just going to take another look at the vineyard.' Blooaarrr! I mean, if being sick throughout a feast was good enough for the Romans, why not me? No way was I going to miss out on what else was to come.

For someone like me, barely into my 20s, the whole day was an amazing eye-opener. I came to realise that Lamb, Beefy and Gower had opened up this world by being talented on the pitch and getting to know some remarkable people off it. But, like pretty much every-one else, until I saw it for myself, I had no idea this side of touring existed. Me and my England colleague Phil de Freitas had been going down the KFC. I just felt so lucky, like I'd been invited into the best club ever. These senior players had worked out the recipe for enjoying the good things while not compromising their place in the side. As more of these days out unfolded, they'd say to me, 'This is the life, Phil, so don't get too stupid.' I got what they meant. Four months Down Under, four or five star all the way, it doesn't get any better than that. All the time I was in their company I was picking up lots of little things, hoovering up the crumbs, of just how the big boys operated in this world. That trip, in so many ways, was my apprenticeship.

The New Zealand tour the year after would be the same. Again, with the older boys, one time I travelled right out into the hills. Like that incredibly verdant Australia, it was unlike anything I'd ever seen, the most luscious country-side, but as if it was on steroids. Phenomenal. After a jaw-dropping 90-minute drive we ended up at what looked little more than a wood shack with a few hay bales chucked around. There were a couple of blokes there cooking lamb on a barbecue. Unbelievably good – the best I'd ever had. Afterwards, we went white-water rafting down a crystal-clear river.* We then pulled over for a bit of fishing. A couple of rainbow trout were soon caught and a bloke filleted and cooked them on a makeshift stove. We were lying on the riverbank with these amazing summer white wines and it was just idyllic. Even now I can summon up exactly how it felt to be lying back on that grass with the loveliest mellow feeling. Just as in Australia, those sort of trips would pop up all the time. If it wasn't fishing, it was clay-pigeon shooting, or, again, wineries. Other players would go off and have a game of golf, but I couldn't be bothered. Why would I play golf when there were these memories-for-life alternatives just waiting to be sampled?

* Nobody mention *Deliverance*.

88

I appreciated the fact these senior players had shown me what touring could mean before they disappeared from the scene. They were sporting heroes coming to the end of their journeys while I was just starting out. On your first senior tour there will always be an element of finding your way. In all honesty, I hadn't really met many of the older pros on that first trip. Maybe they'd have been away on England duty when Middlesex played their county, or I'd not run into them other than a brief hello in the bar. When it came to really big names like Gower and Botham, the fact I'd worshipped them as a kid did actually make me feel a bit self-conscious. All you can really do is try to forget that a few years ago you were sat in short trousers watching them on TV and try to be yourself. That was what worked for me. It didn't take them and a couple of others long to see that maybe there was a little twinkle of mischief in my eye. I was always the one saying or doing something daft. Basically, I was like a performing seal. 'Oi, Phil, wander round with a lobster on your head for half an hour will you, mate?' And off I'd go.

Inevitably, on any tour, there's a few days of trying to work out what people are like as characters, but I soon got to understand that most cricketers, of whatever genera-tion, have more in common than separates them. Myself and Graham Gooch, my captain in my early England days, famously were poles apart when it came to matters like exercise and early nights. He lost most of his hair because of me. But then I was told that in his youth he would turn up at Essex on a scooter dressed as a Mod. The man I saw as being a little over-keen in the discipline stakes wouldn't have looked out of place as an extra in *Quadrophenia.*

Of course, when it came to bonding with established players, it helped as well if quite early on in your Test career you did something on the pitch. I was fortunate that in my second Test, at Sydney, I took 5–61 in the second innings and nearly conjured up an unlikely victory. Until other players see what you can do, you'll always have a bit of self-doubt about whether they think you belong and can perform when the chips are down. You do look for that appreciation from your teammates. I'd had it from my county colleagues but, like I say, some of these England guys were my heroes. In the back of my mind, I knew they were asking, 'What can he do?' Everyone in a cricket team is ultimately dependent on one another, and, no matter what they've done in county cricket, a new face will always raise questions. It's the cricketing version of, 'Yes, he's a decent footballer, but can he do it at Middlesbrough on a wet Wednesday night in January?' After Sydney, I was welcomed with open arms – 'Oh, right, this boy can actually bowl.'

That pressure to gain recognition from teammates can hold some players back. They become over-desperate, and it affects their game. I get why. You just want to prove to your peers, and yourself, that you belong in the same dressing room. Especially when they're icons and you're just some little kid. The same thing happened in New Zealand a year later when I bowled England to victory with 11 wickets in the first Test at Christchurch. As a youngster, if you don't have a good start to your Test career it must play on your mind a hell of a lot. Then again, maybe that was just the bad old days. I think nowadays everyone is given proper support and a decent chance.

Players deal with pressure, on and off the pitch, in different ways. Jack Russell was a case in point. I'd never actually batted with Jack until the 1994 Test match in Barbados. It was red-hot, he had about seven jumpers on, his eyes were like beach balls and there was snot all over his moustache. I don't know whether the sun had got to him but he was practically drooling.

'Come on, Tuffers!' he greeted me. 'Are they watching? Are they all watching?'

I didn't have a clue what he was on about. 'Is who watching? Are they all watching what? Jack, what's happening? What's happening to you?' It was like a possession – not so much going out to bat in a Test match as entering a scene from *The Exorcist*.

Over time, I came to see that this was just how Jack batted; how he got the best out of himself. On one occasion, I defended a delivery, went to pick the ball up, and from 22-yards way he bellowed, 'Don't ****ing touch it!'

Jack was never anything but up for it, something I'd noted the first time I'd seen him bat on the county circuit with all his gear battered and taped up, like he'd made it himself, which actually he probably had. Gloucestershire were a long way behind in the game, basically in an irretrievable position. He reached the middle and shouted to his mate, 'Come on! Come on! We can do this!' I was thinking, 'Hold on a minute. Calm down. It's only Gloucestershire versus Middlesex on a Thursday.'

'We'll have these bastards!' Jack snarled through his grille.

'Well,' I thought, 'I admire your tenacity and determination, old boy, but you've got a long way to go to "have us". Have you had a look at the scoreboard?'

As a spinner, I was also spared some of the physical pressure of the fast blokes. At Adelaide on that first Ashes tour, I was with my Middlesex colleague Angus Fraser at the hotel when he declared he was going upstairs to the gym. 'Do you want to come?' A foolish question really. The gym was never a room I had a great relationship with. More than anything, it lacked a bed. I said I'd see him up there in half an hour. I finished my fag, had a club sandwich, flicked through a couple of magazines and headed on up. Gus was flogging himself on what looked like a piece of medieval torture equipment. I wasn't sure if it was meant to get people fit or extract a confession.

'Why are you doing that?' I asked.

'You wouldn't understand,' he replied, 'but I'm a six-foot-seven fast bowler who's got to run in from halfway to the boundary and then wind myself up into a position where I can bowl the ball as fast as I can.' He'd bowled for about two hours in the nets that day.

As I went outside and slipped into the rooftop Jacuzzi I compared Gus's day to my own. Twenty minutes of practice, a few high catches, a little jog round the Adelaide Oval.

The weary paceman joined me. We'd had very different days but we both agreed we wanted this life to last a very long time. For me, part of that was learning how to enjoy all the fruits of touring without, like those senior boys had warned me, pushing things too far and so jeopardising my position in the team. 'All right, have a good time and enjoy yourself. But then, when the nitty gritty comes, don't be too much of a dickhead because you can throw this life away.' No way did I ever want to do that, but at the same time I appreciated what had come my way and was going to enjoy every minute of it. The way I saw it, I'd have been mad not to. That's why, without fail, on every tour I went on I went out every night. Even if it was just to meet at the bar, have a drink and a pizza, I did it. I was living the dream of being on tour with the England cricket team. I wasn't going to stay in my room, watch the telly, and order a cheese and pickle sandwich on room service.* For all I knew it could all end tomorrow. I could have got injured or not performed or fallen out of favour with the selectors.† As a sportsperson, so much is out of your hands that you really do have to make the most of it while it lasts. That's why I always wanted to be doing something, anything – and why I'd always get pissed off when certain people said I wasn't a good tourist. I was a great tourist. I

* I've endorsed many products down the years but never cocoa.

† As if.

was always trying to get something going – go there, do this. I'm so glad the likes of Nasser Hussain and a few of the other boys have stood up for me on that point. Each to their own obviously, but if everybody sat in their room every night, a tour would be terrible.

There's another thing. Considering I was consistently branded as being a nightmare on tour, England gave me a plane ticket an awful lot of times. Although that might have been because the England team at that time was under-performing and no one else wanted to go!

Sounds mad, but I always had in the back of my mind how club cricketers went about a tour. You know, if, say, Mansfield second XI had a couple of weeks in Cornwall, what would they do? They'd go on trips, have a few drinks, enjoy a few curries, do this, do that, have a bit of training, play the fixtures.* This was England, so of course we were professional when it came to the matches, but in the time in between I and a lot of the others were going to have some fun. I worked out that it was what worked best for me. Three or four months is a long time to be away and you've got to keep yourself bubbling along. Was that wrong? The evidence would tell you not. Look at some of the players who came after me. Jonathan Trott became

* I've plucked the name of Mansfield out merely as a hypothetical example – apologies to Mansfield if it's a club of teetotal hyper-fit librarians.

totally focussed on his cricket, his performance, to the point of obsession, practising and re-practising the same shot in his hotel room. Marcus Trescothick also had terrible anxiety about touring. I totally understand their issues. On a tour there will always be times when you feel down, where negative thoughts get into your head, where you can actually feel quite overwhelmed. It's very easy to shut off. Believe me, there were many occasions when I sat in my room and had a bit of a wobble, the most infamous being on the Ashes trip of 1994/95, where I completely lost it, smashed up my room and was dragged off to a mental health unit in Perth. Me being me, that big outburst of emotion was kind of what I needed, and next day I went down to breakfast at the hotel (I'd legged it from the mental health place after an hour) and carried on the tour like nothing had happened. But everyone's different. Players need to address and balance their mental health in whatever way suits them, but being aware that it's important is the first step on the road.

Incredible to think how cricketers were isolated during Covid – periods of prolonged isolation unlike any other sport in the world. I think in particular of the West Indies team who toured here at the peak of the lockdown in summer 2020, and also the England boys who went to Australia in extreme circumstances the winter after, confined to a tight bubble and thousands of miles away from their families. I did fear a little bit for cricketers at that time. The amount of time they were spending in bubbles was quite astonishing and a recipe for mental health issues if people weren't careful. I'm so grateful to those people for giving the rest of us some entertainment in a difficult time, but I hope that psychologically they were looked after. Players who performed in lockdown had that decision to make – career versus state of mind.

Working on the West Indies series for *Test Match Special* (*TMS*), we operated in 'bubble' conditions ourselves, the modern trend of ground redevelopments including hotels making the situation considerably easier. Our bubble felt relatively sociable as we were able to mix and eat together. In strict conditions, proper isolation, I'm sure I would have struggled. It wouldn't have done for me at all. I like seeing other people too much, getting out and about. Also, as a player, the one thing I always wanted to do at the end of a day's play was get away from the ground, be in a different environment, different bar, different restaurant, whatever. It's not like anyone was slumming it, but those players had to face the realisation that they couldn't just nip out, get a paper from the corner shop, go for a bit of a wander, reignite the spark.

All through that West Indies series, I was amazed at two things – how good the cricket was and how well the broadcasting went, because the potential was there for either to be a load of old rubbish. Playing in a completely silent stadium? What must that be like? I couldn't help thinking that if I was bowling and some bloke hit me for a couple of sixes, I'd probably just wander off for five minutes and have a cup of tea. I know also that when you cross that white line you click into gear. Empty ground or not there's always professional pride. You want to win for you and your teammates, which is why the standard of the cricket was first class. My suspicion also is that, for most teams, playing during a pandemic brought everyone very close together. In any side, you are friends with some people more than you are with others. But here everyone was sharing a difficult experience and so that has to build unity.

I'm so glad to have played in a time when touring meant a huge amount of freedom, much of it a natural and essential accompaniment of a very lengthy tour. While now the England team lands somewhere, plays three Tests and clears off, for us the cricket was only part of the experience. That meant you saw the whole culture of a country, not just the inside of hotel rooms and cricket grounds. To be honest, if you'd said to Lamb, Gower and Botham that they were going somewhere to play a couple of Test matches and then coming home, they'd probably have said they weren't available – 'Play cricket and then come home? What's the point of that?'

Obviously, those long tours could be a double-edged sword. They meant long periods away from family, and there were always times when you felt a bit lonely or down, but in between there were many, many brilliant days. I always appreciated the life that had come my way so much. I knew all too well that in another existence I would be bashing pans in my dad's workshop. He knew that too, which is why he and Mum backed me all the way with my cricket. As Dad pointed out, 'With cricket you've got a great opportunity. You don't work when it rains. You go to all these lovely hot places. Make the most of it.' Which I did.

And look at me now. I've travelled from not knowing what on earth I was chucking down my neck on these winery trips with Beefy and the rest of the boys – 'Oh? The 1965? Righto!' Glug! – to having my own label, Tuffers' Tipple. It's been a fascinating process, the tasting especially of course, but also the idea of being able to blend the kind of wines which I, and hopefully a lot of other people, would appreciate, and wines also which would fit in with the kind of occasions I enjoy, be it a sunny afternoon in the back garden or a meal with friends.* There's a Tempranillo from Spain, a Sauvignon Blanc and GSM (a blend of Grenache, Syrah and Mourvèdre grapes) from France, a Shiraz and Sauvignon Blanc from the Margaret River region of Western Australia, and an English Bacchus hailing from New Hall Vineyard in Chelmsford. They're lovely wines, even if I say so myself, although I am told that I do look a bit Christopher Lee on the label of the Tempranillo.

In the absence of helicopter flights with Beefy, Lamb and Gower, I have also headed down to the Barossa Valley,

---

* Just to head this particular question off at the pass, there isn't one that goes with dancing round a southern hemisphere fish restaurant with a bemused bust.

northeast of Adelaide, with Dawn and had a wonderful time, even tasting a wine from the year of my birth, 1966. Pleased to report it had a tang of sticky toffee pudding, although a tang of jam roly-poly would have been more befitting my early years. I was also lucky enough to go to New Zealand's Craggy Range winery with Brendon McCullum while filming our amazing journey around the islands. Set beneath the Mata Hills in the Hawke's Bay region it has to be one of the most spectacular wineries on Earth. Don't think twice about going if ever you're in that area.

Perhaps the most luxurious place I've been is the yacht belonging to the late Sir Paul Getty, the cricket-loving philanthropist who, amongst many other things, served as president of Surrey, funded a new stand at Lord's and built a sumptuous ground in his 2,500-acre estate in Buckinghamshire, complete with thatched pavilion. Of course, when I say yacht, I'm not talking about one of those you see bobbing around in the waves off Weymouth. This particular vessel was 82 metres long, had two funnels and was valued at $50 million.

Sir Paul had moored up in Jolly Harbour, Antigua, and with the England boys in town for a Test invited us on board. With Andrew Flintoff's pedalo service not yet up and running, a fleet of motor launches carried us across. The boat was parked up, handbrake on, amongst a whole host of other superyachts – basically a floating country house. Stepping on deck I was immediately reminded of a recent viewing of *Death on the Nile*. If I'd looked around hard enough I'm sure I'd have happened across Hercule Poirot.

We were escorted to this beautiful bar and lounge area on the deck with lovely low-level sofas, coffee tables and rugs, like a very posh hotel or high-class spa. It really did look like we were in for a very good night. You never know who's who at these kind of dos – even the waiters were better turned-out than most of us – but I asked a bloke wandering around if there was any Dom Perignon Champagne. 'Listen,' I said, 'the boys have got a couple of days off here and they might fancy a drop of the good stuff.'

He looked me up and down, possibly wondering if I was a pirate jumped aboard from a nearby vessel, and then uttered the words I was so hoping to hear – 'Would you like to follow me, sir?'

For the next five minutes I followed this bloke down endless corridors, him showing me a few bits and pieces of the boat – en suite bedrooms, dining rooms, bilge pumps – along the way, before we plunged down into the very bowels of the ship. Either there was something of great interest down there or he was going to feed me into the boiler.

'This, my friend,' he explained (I was reassured by his use of the word 'friend'), 'is the stores.'

He proceeded to pull open these huge double doors. Inside was an Aladdin's cave of top-notch booze. Looking at the treasure, mildly drooling, I was surprised he hadn't cried, 'Open Sesame!' At a conservative estimate there must have been two thousand bottles of Dom Perignon. That's without the countless bottles of Scotch, gin and every other alcoholic beverage you could think of. It was as big as most luxury yachts in itself.

My guide turned round. 'I don't even think you could finish this lot,' he remarked.

'Well,' I replied, 'I'll have a good try.'

I can't be sure if I met Sir Paul himself. At occasions like this, you get talking to people without ever really understanding who they are. It's a hazard of any official do, mainly because quite often the really well-off and powerful people aren't the ones in the big flashy dresses and suits. You're standing there having a drink with a little old fella in an old linen shirt, fading corduroys and a dodgy old pair of brogues, and only afterwards do you find out he owns half the world's oil reserves. You do have to be careful not to put your foot in it sometimes. You'll see someone wandering around in red moleskin trousers and a weird tie, ask if they'd mind refilling the tea urn, turn a corner and spot an oil painting of them up on the wall.

In Barbados, meanwhile we were invited to the residence of the late horse-racing mogul Robert Sangster. He lived in the bricks and mortar version of Sir Paul's yacht, with equally good ocean views. It was a charity do with fellow guests invited to pay $100 to meet such luminaries as myself and Robert Croft, although the star was actually Sangster's black Labrador Archie which had a habit of hunting down golf balls chucked by Beefy, back in the

Caribbean as a commentator, into the illuminated swimming pool. If nothing else, it made a change from his more usual habit of hurling fellow humans into water features.

Sometimes on these occasions I'd try to sneak home a little souvenir. I've had some fantastic ashtrays down the years. Sadly, those on Sir Paul's yacht were large, heavy and unwieldly, possibly fashioned from a precious metal – definitely not seven for a quid from Home Bargains – and I abandoned the plan. Fall overboard with one of those down the front of my trousers and I was a goner.

The thing about going out on any boat for a few hours is that when you get back on dry land you tend to have a bit of a sway on. It would happen quite a lot in the Caribbean. Again in Antigua, me and a few of the boys went out on a boat for a few drinks the day before a Test match. As ever, we then lost the toss and had to bowl. There were a few of us stood on the outfield literally rocking about. I was standing at fine leg and it felt like I was on a canoe. It did nothing for your accuracy when you came on to bowl. Better that than batting though – half the team would have been out first ball.

I will admit – and turn the page now if you're eating – on one sorry occasion it was me making a fellow passenger feel queasy. Me and Dawn had been to Sharm El Sheikh in Egypt for Christmas. We'd had a wonderful time – actually perhaps too much of a wonderful time on Christmas Eve because on the big day itself I awoke a very unpleasant shade of green. I managed to get up and about, trying not to look at the people shovelling mince pies down at 9 a.m., but was still feeling rough in the extreme. Dawn then suggested a parasail. I couldn't have been less enthusiastic if she'd suggested a raw egg eating competition. I didn't want to be a total killjoy so said I'd go along for the boat ride. Naturally, the sea was a bit rough and so the boat was bouncing up and down, up and down, over and over. I'm not sure if I've ever felt worse, like all my bodily organs had been put in a cement mixer. In my befuddled state I'd forgotten to pack some of my things and so Dawn had bought me some very strange swimming shorts from a nearby bazaar; a cheap throw-on pair to make do, almost like boxer shorts.

Anyway, by now I was stood at the bow of the boat, legs wide open for support, groaning and throwing up over the side. The boat then picked up a couple of women who were also parasailing. One of them twigged who I was. 'Merry Christmas, Phil,' she said, as I retched over the side. I managed to chat with her for a while. She was telling me how much she loved A *Question of Sport* but for some reason her eyes kept flitting from my face to my midriff. After about five minutes of this I thought I'd better have a quick look to see what the issue was. Turns out that so tight were these shorts that my testicles were hanging out of one side.

'Oh my God!' I spluttered, going from green to bright red in an instant. 'I'm so sorry.'

'Oh no,' she said. 'I've had a great time. I've spent Christmas Day talking to Phil Tufnell and his bollocks for

15 minutes.' I dread to think how many people she told when she got back home. I just hope she didn't manage a crafty photo.*

* Although it could make an interesting cover for my next book.

6

YA POMMIE BASTARD!

There's two things going on as a tourist in a foreign land. Your attitude to it, and its attitude to you.

'I hope you like hospital food,' was the lovely greeting I had once in Australia. That particular bon mot came from the ever-large mouth of Aussie fast bowler Craig McDermott, a big gingery bloke who in his heyday looked like he wouldn't be averse to barbecuing your kidneys between overs.

To be fair to Craig, being horrible to Englishmen was in his job description. If being an Aussie quick entailed a job interview, then 'How many ways do you know to call a Pom a ****?' would be the first question on the panel's lips. What was more shocking was the abuse that came away from cricket, emanating from the most unexpected places, like airport security officers. We'd turn up off the plane from England, full of wide smiles and expectation,* and the first thing we'd hear would be, 'Come this way, ya Pommie bastard.'

* And gin.

I'd be thinking, 'Did I just hear that right? Did the customs officer just call me a Pommie bastard?'

'This way, Mr Tufnell.' Oh, I must have misheard. After all, it's been a long flight and I am a little tired. 'By the way, you Pommie bastard, you're going to get your ****ing head knocked off.' No, I was right first time.

Over I'd go with my bag.

'Warney's gonna getcha!'

'I beg your pardon?'

'And Merv. He eats number elevens like you for breakfast.'

'Right, well, thanks very much. If I could just have my bag, I'll be on my way.'

Even when you got to the hotel, face to face with people whose actual job it was to be nice to you, to be as polite as polite can be, it wasn't any different. The concierge out front would open the door for you. 'Ah, good morning, Mr Tufnell – ya little bastard.'

Even the maids – *the maids!* – would do it. I'd get back from breakfast and there one would be cleaning my room.

'Ah, cricketer are you, mate? One of the Poms?'

'The England cricket team, yes, that's right.'

'I thought you were. I could see your bat.' Pause. 'You won't be needing that.'

This was someone whose role was to make my bed. That's all. Make my bed.

'Well,' I replied, somewhat dumbfounded, 'I thought I'd better bring it just in case.'

'No, mate. Forget it. Have you seen the look in Merv's eyes – he's gonna kill ya.'

And then off she tootled towards the door, hand out expecting a tip!

It was like no one could resist having a pop. I had visions of the Aussie prime minister shaking my hand before the Test Match in Sydney – 'Lovely to meet you, Mr Tufnell. Still got both bollocks, have we? Can't be having that!'

I mean, this kind of stuff didn't happen when the Aussies came to England. The doorman at the Ritz never greeted Ricky Ponting with a brisk, 'Afternoon tea is it, sir? I hope you bloody choke on it you Aussie t***.' You can't imagine the MCC members at Lord's lobbing stones at the Aussies and calling them a bunch of w*****s.

To be fair, it wasn't much better in the Caribbean. In Antigua it would be the bus driver taking us to the ground. He'd be turning round at the wheel. 'Curtly gonna get ya! Curtly gonna get ya today, boys!'

'Right, OK, pal. Thanks.'

'And Lara – he's coming for ya.'

'For God's sake, man – keep your eyes on the road!'

About four days before a Test in Antigua I twisted my wrist getting out of a swimming pool. The physio arranged for me to have an X-ray the next day. A very early appointment as I remember, which was a shock to the system after a few rum punches the previous evening. My nausea wasn't hugely helped by being transported in a Mini Moke, not the smoothest ride, to this small Caribbean hospital. It was all very laid back, and everyone was very nice, but nevertheless it still had that hospital disinfectant smell of which I've never been a fan. I could feel myself getting faint. I had the flashing lights in front of my eyes.

A bloke came in. 'Right, Mr Tufnell. Take your top off. We're going to do an X-ray of your shoulder before we do the operation.' A shoulder operation was news to me since I was there for a check-up on my wrist.

The bloke disappeared behind a screen, at which point I slumped on the floor. He reappeared. 'Bloody hell. You haven't even had the injection yet. This is just the X-ray!' As the nurses picked me up, he whispered in my ear – 'And you're England's secret weapon are you?' Even when I was passed out in a hospital people couldn't resist having a dig.

Another time in Antigua, I'd settled down to a nice dinner in a restaurant, delighted to see the waiter heading my way with a lovely plate of the most amazing looking seafood, only for him to lean in as he placed it in front of me. 'There you are, Mr Tufnell. You do know you're going home in a body bag?' I wasn't sure if he was trying to tell me that the chef had put arsenic on the prawns or that Curtly Ambrose was going to knock my block off.

It wouldn't have been so bad but for the fact that when you reached the playing area, the abuse continued – this time broadcast via the PA system. One announcer in particular was something else, feeling compelled to give his opinion of each new batsman as he walked to the middle.

'And coming to the crease now is Andrew Caddick. Now let's have a look.' There'd be a pause at this point while the relevant statistics were uncovered. Then would come the critique. 'Average 7.5. That's with the bat. Not very good against fast bowlers. Or any bowlers really.'

This stuff would be delivered to the crowd as you were walking to the middle. You'd hear it as clearly as everyone else. A batsman might stroll out feeling pretty happy with life and then halfway to the middle they'd hear. 'Not a bad average ... Oh, hang on! What's this? Only one hundred. Wow, that conversion rate is terrible.'

Over time his analysis became something of beauty. We actually began looking forward to hearing what he said about us. If I recall correctly, he accompanied my trip to the middle with, 'I've seen him bat before – he better be a bowler.'

If you were a spectator, PA announcers would be worth the entrance fee alone. We were playing Jamaica one time when the bloke piped up and asked if the owner of a vehicle could move it as it was blocking an entrance. Five minutes later he was back on – 'As already requested, will the owner of the white car blocking Gate B please move their vehicle urgently?' Another five minutes passed – same request, a bit more irritable. Five more and the PA crackled into life again. 'The owner of the white car don't need to worry about moving it no more – it's on fire.'

You're trying to play cricket and at the same time not die laughing.

*   *   *

The atmosphere at some of those Caribbean grounds was unbelievable, none more so than the Old Recreation Ground in Antigua. Nasser Hussain identified it as the place where you really knew you were in the Caribbean, and he was absolutely right. It was always absolutely jumping, those old timber-framed double-decker stands looking like they might collapse beneath the sheer weight of unbridled enjoyment.

The Rec was unique for having its very own cast of characters, none bigger than 'Gravy', a bloke who would spend the entire match dancing and jumping around the seats and stanchions while displaying some truly remarkable dresses. You never knew how he'd look from one day to the next. I don't think I'm mistaken when I say he once even turned up as Margaret Thatcher, complete with cricket bat and handbag. It was an insane spectacle and, for a lot of the England boys, especially when Brian Lara was compiling his then world record 375, made better viewing than the cricket. Brian would smack another boundary and there'd be Maggie, even sometimes the Queen, bedecked in pearls, going mad in the crowd.

It was impossible not to be swept up in the atmosphere, especially if you happened to be fielding on that side of the ground. Gravy had rock-star status. You'd hear this massive roar, as if a really huge rock band had arrived on stage. You'd look round and there he'd be, bedecked in a crimplene Marks & Spencer number, entering the stand.

At the same time there'd be all these songs blaring out from Chickie's Disco – Chickie being another famed Rec character – some of which you didn't always particularly want to hear. I recall one, possibly called 'Dust in Your Face' which went something along the lines of, 'Ambrose – if Ambrose don't getcha – Walshy – Walshy's coming for ya.' All to a Calypso beat. You'd be stood there tapping your feet and then realise that actually this little song was about two fast bowlers getting ready to knock your head off. As a bowler, for me, it would more likely be, 'Tufnell – Brian's gonna getcha. Tufnell – Brian's coming at ya.' I mean, what happened to 'Sweet Caroline'?

Chickie had been doing this for years. The Rec was where local hero Viv Richards, who grew up not far from the ground, smashed the England attack for a 56-ball hundred in 1986. As Viv reached the milestone, Chickie stuck on 'Captain, the Ship is Sinking' for the benefit of England skipper David Gower.

Look at what's happened to cricket in the years since, and Chickie and Gravy really were ahead of their time. Chickie would launch into a tune between balls, overs, wickets and at drinks breaks. Gravy was a pioneer in exotic fancy dress. Now that happens all over the world. They essentially came up with the off-pitch formula for T20.

The Rec really was a place where anyone could be anything, including the criminal fraternity. The island's whitewashed prison was right next to the ground and inmates would be let out to help prepare the pitch and generally tidy the place up a bit. No wonder the stands were falling down. They'd probably nicked all the lead off the roof. Maybe one day they'll let a few old lags from the Scrubs loose on the heavy roller at Lord's.

When Lara did finally beat Sir Garfield Sobers' record Test score of 365, even Chickie's tunes were drowned out. The place went mental. Everyone came over from the stands, including Sir Garfield himself who strolled serenely to the middle to congratulate Brian. The place was absolutely swarming. I was fielding down at third man as hundreds of people ran past me. The coppers made a cursory attempt to stop one or two but when they saw how pointless it was they gave up. The result was a 20-minute party. I swear there were people setting up food and merchandise stalls on the field. Others were kissing the pitch, a few were coming up to me, 'Hey Tuffers! Thanks man for serving it up!'

A few years later there was a terrible fuss when the American team invaded the 17th green after Justin Leonard holed a long putt at Brookline in the Ryder Cup, and here we were with hundreds of people mid-game having a party. For all the madness of the moment, it was amazing to be part of sporting history. Even now, nearly 30 years on, it's one of my strongest cricketing memories; an incredible thing to unfold in front of your eyes. Lara's innings had been going on for three days by the time he reached the target. On day one, when he was in the 70s, outside the ground they were already printing T-shirts with 'Brian Lara – World Record Breaker!' written on them. We were thinking, 'Hang on a minute. He's still got three hundred to go!' Although I think Athers, ever astute, knew something was afoot. I'd just finished my first over when he sauntered over to me and professed, 'Brian's batting well. I reckon he could break Sobers' record.' Athers had a very good eye on a cricket pitch and unfortunately on this occasion he was right.

No matter what stage of my career, I always felt I had a chance of getting a wicket as my radar was always there or thereabouts. I was also a good second-guesser. I had a quite a good sixth sense, able to jump into the batsman's mind a little bit. The only time I didn't feel like that was now. The ball was old, the wicket was flat and the best batsman in the world was in the form of his life. He just didn't play a false shot. Angus Fraser was bowling at him and the ball kept flying through the gap between second slip and gulley. To plug the gap, Gus opted for one slip and two gullies. He then continued to bowl his immaculate line and length just outside off stump only for Brian to start edging it through second slip. Gus wasn't to be beaten. 'I'm not having this,' he said. 'I'll have a first slip, a third slip and a gully.' Again Lara missed the fielder every time. It was only then that the penny dropped. Gus looked at us. He could see from our faces that we'd just not had the heart to tell him. 'Oh, I see. He's not edging it. He's steering it.' Lara played the ball so late it made Angus look like he was bowling at my pace, and naturally that slowing down of the world also extended to me. I couldn't rush him, get the ball through him. It was as if I was bowling at 20 miles an hour. He made time stand still with his brilliance to the point where it felt like the ball would never reach him. Even when Chris Lewis ramped it up with the new ball, Lara tapped it around like he was playing back-garden cricket. He'd add a hundred runs and you'd think, 'He's barely tried. Where did that come from?' He was the best I ever saw, the angles, the power, the flexibility in his wrists. I'd put a deep square leg and deep midwicket out in case he fancied coming down the pitch and he'd bisect them perfectly for a one-bounce four. I'd think, 'Well, is that luck? Is it? Really?' After he'd done it ten more times, I concluded, 'Probably not!' I've never seen a team not field the ball so many times. Time and again it went past us to the boundary. There's probably a couple of the lads who never touched it the whole time he was out there other than to throw it back from the fence.

As Lara's score got bigger and bigger, so the story got bigger and bigger too. It was the only thing on the news – 'Is he going to get there?' It had become this huge dam of expectation and emotion and when finally it broke there was mayhem. What people generally don't know, however, is just how close, right at the very last, the record came to not happening. With Lara level with Sobers on 365, Lewis turned to me at mid-on and said, 'What should I bowl him?' I mean, of all the questions to ask. There's easier answers on *University Challenge*.

'Listen,' I said. 'I don't know. You might as well make it hard for him and stick it up his hooter. Anything but a half-volley.'

Chris seemed to take my advice because the ball climbed and as Lara swung round to hit it he also brushed a stump with his foot. It was enough to make the bail wobble. There's actually a great picture of Lara, heart in mouth, watching the bail flip up slightly in the air. I have to say, even if he had knocked it off I certainly wouldn't have been the one to point it out. Imagine that, after the 20-minute pitch invasion had finished, all the celebrations done, wandering casually up to the umpire. 'Er, you do know he actually knocked the bail off there?' I'd have been chased out the ground. They'd still be burning effigies of me now.

An oft-forgotten element of that celebration is that a Liat island-hopper aircraft deviated from the nearby airport and gave a little tip of the wings over the ground. Robin Smith, meanwhile, happened to know the pilot of a jumbo jet. When he made his own hundred later in the game, said pilot repeated the trick – in the jumbo. It didn't impress his bosses. Actually, I think the same bloke was renowned for landing his plane naked. Which probably didn't impress them much either.

I'm glad I was in the England team for that Lara master-class and not his 400 ten years later. Compared to the 375, that innings seemed a lot more dour. The England boys appeared sick to the back teeth as the innings went on and on, dragging themselves round the hot and dusty field over after over, whereas we were able to see it, yes as not an ideal situation, but as a celebration of genius talent. If anything, we got quite into it! In fact, if I'd thought about it I'd have bought one of those T-shirts on the first day! Thing was, the pitch at the Rec, hard and flat, was perfect for a big score. Although it did me no favours. I got exactly 375 runs less than BL.*

In the Nineties, it felt like pretty much everyone was breaking records against England. It became a regular occurrence. In Mumbai, when Vinod Kambli, in just his third Test, scored 224 in ten hours, in so doing making the highest individual score by an Indian against England, I'm pretty sure the announcer went through three bags of throat sweets he was piping up so much. It felt like every ball there was something, and prior to each announcement there'd be a Hi-de-Hi!-esque ping over the speaker. 'Oh no,' we'd think. 'What now?' There'd be a little cough and then this very well-spoken Indian voice would start up. 'And there we have it, the highest score by an Indian on a Wednesday during the blossoming season of the hibiscus.'

By the end we were begging someone to please shut him up, but he wasn't alone in revelling in his moment in the limelight. Usually, announcers had little else to do than give the name of the new batsman or bowler. A Test match was their chance to shine. Overnight they became Laurence Olivier, projecting to the back of the arena, delivering a great soliloquy about the 17th fastest fifty on this ground since the pitch had a welcome injection of loam.

There was another pitch invasion when Shivnarine Chanderpaul made a ton at Georgetown in 1998. Being

---

* I was in the mood for a big score but got a dodgy LBW decision.

from Guyana himself, it was always going to be a moment of huge celebration and it was during this particular melee that one of the locals took the chance to tell me, 'Tufnell, you shit, man!' He was running so fast that the sound of the comment was influenced by the Doppler effect, like an ambulance, but I still got the message loud and clear.

Another feature of invasions, aside from the odd insult, was that someone would nick your sunhat. After a while I got fed up of this and, at the first sign of the crowd coming on, would stick my hat down the front of my underpants. Anyone who wanted it after it had been down there was welcome to it. Thing is, I became attached to hats. Losing them would spark instant panic. 'Where's my hat? I can't go out there without my hat.' I wasn't alone, the most extreme example of hat-love being (it's that man again) Jack Russell. Jack had worn the same hat, patched up, re-stitched, even surviving a severe scorching when once he tried to dry it in an oven, all his career. When, on our tour to the West Indies in 1997/98, England and Wales Cricket Board (ECB) chair Lord MacLaurin insisted England cricketers should walk out on to the field wearing the traditional blue England cap, Jack was having none of it. He told the ECB if he wasn't allowed to wear it, he wasn't playing. While MacLaurin, understandably, was trying to build a more professional looking team, it hardly seemed worth a conflict. As Athers, the captain, pointed out, 'I really couldn't have cared less if Jack wanted to wear a dustbin on his head so long as he caught the ball.'

Crazy thing was there could never be anyone more patriotic than Jack Russell. He has a massive interest in military history and has captured several scenes of great heroism on canvas down the years, such as the Cockleshell Heroes, the Second World War Royal Marines who canoed 70 miles behind enemy lines to blow up enemy ships at Bordeaux, as well as visiting numerous Boer and Anglo-Zulu battlefields during trips to South Africa. As far as he was concerned his hat had an England badge, he felt comfortable playing in it and that was the end of the conversation.

If it wasn't opposition fans, or the upper echelons of our own management, giving us jip, it was animals. At our Guyana base of the Pegasus Hotel, Georgetown, there was a parrot. Robin Smith took a shine to the bird and would talk to it, feed it the odd peanut. It was touching to see his kindness towards this be-feathered specimen, eerily reminiscent of *The Birdman of Alcatraz*. And yet his thanks for this benevolence? The parrot waited its chance, lunged and nearly took his eye out. I wouldn't have been surprised if it had squawked, 'England are shit!' while it did it.

The press, meanwhile, had claws as long as any animal. On arrival in the Caribbean in 1994 I walked past a newsstand which welcomingly declared in huge letters, 'ENGLAND HAVE NO CHANCE!' Mind you, in those days I don't necessarily think we were ever given a chance anywhere, something which actually was very good for team spirit. We believed in ourselves even if no one else did. We had to, otherwise we'd never have got on the bloody plane. Once we were on the way that was it. All we could do was band together and get on with it.

I did actually manage to win something out in the West Indies – *TMS*'s daily Champagne Moment, incredibly for my batting. In the fourth Test at Guyana in 1998, I went in with 13 still required to save the follow-on. At this point, Carl Hooper decided to bring Curtly and Courtney back on. Anyone would think I had a reputation for not fancying fast bowlers. Of the first 12 balls I received, 11 were at my head. The odd one out, a 90mph yorker, nearly flattened several toes.

It was an inauspicious shot which got us past the follow-on. By now, having had a decent sight of the bouncing ball, I actually deigned to have a hook at one – well, more of a waft really, like I was trying to get rid of a moody bee. The result was the ball took a top edge and looped over the wicketkeeper. Certain I'd be caught, I just stood there. Ramps called me through for a run. I did as he implored but carried straight on to the pavilion. It was only when I saw the rest of the team gesticulating from the balcony that I realised the catch had gone begging. 'Run! Run!' they were shouting. I legged it back down the length of the pitch, dived home and that was it – follow-on saved. OK, more of a Lambrini moment than Champagne, but when it comes to batting I'll take anything that's going.

*   *   *

When it came to experiencing cricket in the Caribbean, I really did play at the best time. OK, some of the grounds might not have been in the best nick – the Rec was actually a wreck – but when the islands built pristine new stadiums all too often they took away the atmosphere with the rubble. So often the old venues were bang in the middle of town. Getting there would be amazing. All these people around, lots of noise and flags. It would remind me of when I used to watch the FA Cup final build-up on TV and they'd have a camera on the coach as it inched through the crowds towards Wembley.

Those central positions meant people could also make a spur-of-the-moment decision to go along. If, or rather when, Brian Lara got to fifty, the locals would start streaming in. Sometimes it would take you a bit by surprise. The morning would be pretty quiet and then all of a sudden after lunch there'd be thousands piling in. It would be electric. The smell of weed would fill the air. If the wind direction was favourable and you were in the right fielding position at the right time you had a lovely afternoon.* Out-of-town stadiums have taken that lovely kind of community spontaneity away.

I was glad that the Rec made one last hurrah when Antigua's new Sir Vivian Richards Stadium was deemed to have an unsafe outfield just ten balls into the Test match against England in 2009. I felt for the people who'd been

* Quick tip for any touring cricketers – always try to get on the boundary in the Caribbean.

inconvenienced but it was great to relive those memories of the Rec one last time. Brass instruments blaring out, drums going, spectators singing in the stands.

Character is in a stadium's bones. The flesh on top then comes from the people who come through the gates. Trinidad's Queen's Park Oval, for instance, had famed peanut seller Jumbo. What an arm he had. Jumbo could pick out a customer at 60 yards and ping a bag of peanuts straight into their hands. If only we could have had him as a substitute fielder.

He wasn't the only one with a good arm. At the Kensington Oval, in Barbados, word I was a smoker had obviously got around. Fielding on the boundary, the crowd would throw fags at me, I expect in the hope I'd light one up. 'Thank you very much,' I used to think, putting them by the boundary for later use – even I knew that lighting up during play was unlikely to be greeted with a slap on the back from the captain. The other boys would go in for lunch and I'd be out there another ten minutes collecting them all up. I wouldn't need to buy any for a month. Mind you, you did have to watch where those fags landed – they would occasionally graze goats on the outfield.

The thing about the West Indies is it's a disparate group of islands and subsequently each one is very different culturally. On any tour, taking for granted that you're au fait with the local customs is a risk. There was one particularly memorable incident with the Middlesex opener Michael Roseberry in the St Lucia capital, Castries. While the rest of the team wore shorts, Michael favoured budgie smugglers. We were on the coach going back to the hotel at the end of play, height of rush hour, when he stated that he'd like to stop off and get a couple of bottles of Coke. He jumped off the bus in the middle of a bustling street, sticking out like a sore thumb because of his blond hair, dressed only in his flip-flops and ultra-tight trunks. Straight away we could see he was getting a few strange looks. He disappeared into the throng, only to reappear two minutes later, running at speed with what seemed to be a blood-thirsty mob in hot pursuit. There were women waving umbrellas, blokes chasing him, drivers shouting at him. He was banging on the coach door – 'Let me in! Let me in!' The driver opened up and got him inside. The door flew shut again just as two women with frying pans slammed against it. The driver explained something to the bright purple and breathless Michael – in Castries it was highly offensive to be out in public in such a state of undress, basically the same as walking down the street with no clothes. Michael had effectively gravely insulted half the city.

I got back to my hotel room and set fire to my leop-ard-print thong.

7

AN INNOCENT ABROAD

Thankfully, aside from the occasional near-nude misunderstanding, when playing overseas the stick we got abroad was done in jest – I think. OK, everywhere you went people were giving you serves, but that was because they wanted to have a bit of fun. That never-ending back and forth was a lovely thing to be part of, and that's why, even now, I smile when before every Ashes series a bunch of Aussies tell me that the Poms are going to lose 5–0. A genuine smile. No gritted teeth, honest.

Despite the abuse,* I have always had a great affection for Australia. These days, of course, that abuse is not nearly so prevalent anyway. Only one in four doormen calls me a Pommie bastard.

My relationship with the continent goes right back to my late teenage years when, during the close season in England, instead of freezing to death in London, I'd jump on a plane and head south to play for Queensland

* And *Prisoner Cell Block H.*

University. It was a very good education – in independence as well as cricket. I went over there on my own, lived in digs and learned how to look after myself – or at least the way to the nearest pizzeria. You were totally left to your own devices and it made you grow up, quick. While some of that was a bit of a shock,* I did have a wonderful time over there. The Queensland guys were a great bunch and I got on really well with them all. Together we managed to reach the final of a one-day tournament, playing at the famous Gabba Test match ground, where I can still vividly remember taking a magnificent catch at deep midwicket to win us the game.

This was tough cricket. I turned up to one game and asked a bloke the directions to the changing rooms. 'There!' he said, pointing to the back of a car. Some places you'd actually get changed in the middle, the idea being it was about as far from the spectators as possible. I'm pleased to say that Australian temperatures are significantly higher than those in England. I wouldn't have fancied doing the same at Headingley in April.

It was during those early trips Down Under that I also met a player known as Gelignite Jim. One side of his face was a bit messed up, and initially I thought his nickname referred to an accident with an explosive. Actually, he had a habit of passing out after a few drinks, and the marks were the result of him falling face-first onto a hotplate at a barbecue. With barbies being a commonplace event in

* Who knew cricket sweaters shrunk?

Australia, and not wanting him to do the same to the other side, from that point on teammates would follow Jim in a slip cordon at such gatherings to make sure it never happened again.

Going back to Australia a few years later with the England team, making my Test debut in the vast bowl of the Melbourne Cricket Ground (MCG), I thought I knew what to expect. But those early years in the game were such a steep learning curve. I had to find out how to act in difficult situations and sometimes made the wrong choice, partly because no one ever told me what to do. At no point did anyone say, 'Phil, just be prepared for how different this is going to be. Melbourne's huge, everything's a blur of sights and sounds, and the crowd will try to get a rise from you.' Talk about being thrown in at the deep end. Up until then, I'd played in front of one man and his dog in county cricket. Now here I was, England versus Australia, the Ashes, in front of 100,000.

Mainly I was saved by naivety, which kept me from overthinking and the anxiety that so often accompanies it. In that rainbow whirl of the MCG, for instance, I wandered out for the Aussies' first innings and only then was struck by a thought that would surely have been nagging away in another player's mind for months – 'What the hell do I do now?' It seemed odd to take up my position at mid-off just like any other of the hundreds of games I'd played up to that point. I certainly didn't think to try to impress with a bit of determined body language or a sprint onto the outfield. I just sort of moseyed out there, like it was the third day of a county match at Taunton. Looking back on it now, be it consciously or subconsciously, I think I understood that just because it was a Test match I wasn't going to try and be anything I'm not. I was going to be myself.

Bowling also was a totally alien experience. At Lord's, your ring field on the offside almost felt impenetrable. Everyone seemed so close together. At the MCG, on the other hand, mid-off and cover point were about 100 yards away from each other. Fine leg to long-off – dial a taxi. Everything felt so far apart and created the illusion that the gaps in the field were huge and undefendable.

Now every commentator and observer would be all over that scenario – 'What were the selectors thinking? Why would they do that to a young impressionable player?' But actually I've never been one for holding young players back. You've got to do it some time. There will always be that sink or swim moment whoever the opposition is. Yes, people say it can scar a cricketer if they have a bad experience, but equally they can do too much preparation, to the point where the debut itself becomes a huge and unmanageable event rather than something that just happens. You can't be an England cricketer but only against certain teams and in front of crowds of less than two thousand. Thankfully, if anything, I loved a packed stadium. It added to the excitement. If I bowled poorly, it was never because of that. Also, as a bowler you get six balls. Bowl a bad one and you can just go back to your mark and start again. Make a mistake as a batsman and you're back in the pavilion. My view was simple – 'Well, I might as well have a go – it's not going to get any better than this.'

The one thing nothing can adequately prepare you for is the experience of playing in front of huge crowds under lights. The annual Tri-Series had come into existence after the Kerry Packer-inspired World Series Cricket revolution of the late Seventies when breakaway national teams representing the best talent in the world competed under floodlights. It was a whole new way of presenting the game, attracting thousands of spectators to what became not just a cricket match but an event in its own right. When World Series Cricket ended and normal service was resumed, the Tri-Series continued to produce many a memorable moment of both a cricketing and non-cricketing nature, such as when the infamous Bay 13 mob at Melbourne sent a rotund pig – smuggled into the ground under anaesthetic – wobbling onto the pitch with 'Beefy' written on one side and 'Eddie' (Hemmings, the England spinner) on the other.*

It was also the Tri-Series which produced one of cricket's all-time most explosive incidents when, with New Zealand needing a six off the last ball, the Aussie skipper Greg Chappell demanded that his brother Trevor bowl a

---

* Modern-day bag checks mean the chances of repeating such an act are minimal. You could potentially get a hamster in but the same level of impact is unlikely.

daisy-cutter underarm along the ground, prompting bats-man Brian McKechnie to hurl his bat away in disgust. Underarm bowling was banned as a direct result.*

For an English cricketer, the Tri-Series would be the first time they played any sort of night cricket. Well, there was the short-lived Lambert & Butler competition in the early Eighties, six-a-side on artificial pitches at football grounds, with the final at Stamford Bridge – decent-sized bounda-ries at each end, it's just the ones at the sides were 20 yards. In England, one-day cricket meant a lot of cup and Sunday games. The Benson & Hedges Cup, for instance, while being a favourite of smokers due to the sheer body-weight of fags the sponsors would chuck into the dressing room, involved a round-robin zonal group of 55-over games (later reduced to 50) before the knockout stages even began. Then there was the mammoth 60-over NatWest Cup (again later reduced to 50) and the John Player League (JPL), the 40-over-a-side Sunday afternoon competition. Of these, the JPL was taken the least seri-ously† – unless as the games went by it looked like you might be in with a sniff of the silverware.

The problem with the JPL was that not only could it feel like a knockabout but a bizarre, even for cricket, fixture list would often see a team dragged away from a Championship match running Friday, Saturday and

---

* My own view was that it should have been made compulsory in the West Indies.

† By me especially as I didn't smoke them.

Monday, to play a Sunday League fixture 150 miles away, and then have to drive back again for the final day. I'll freely admit I wasn't the best at the Sunday League. I never really pushed myself, and I got the feeling that quite a few county pros were the same. If your name didn't appear on the team sheet you were quite relieved. With a full season of championship fixtures, plus three one-day competitions, a day off could be a real rarity.*

The Tri-Series was the antithesis of English one-day cricket. Full-on, floodlit, it also offered another first – the opportunity to play cricket in 'pyjamas' – the term the media used to describe the coloured kit donned by each country. This was, naturally, deemed an outrage by the purists, still outraged that the ladies at Wimbledon were no longer wearing long-sleeved blouses and wicker-framed skirts. But for us it was great. It was always very exciting when you got your kit. Instead of the traditional whites you'd been wearing since you were a kid, here was this multi-coloured stuff with 'ENGLAND' emblazoned on the back. It did somehow make you feel more of a team; everyone in it together.

Floodlit cricket was a game absolutely made for me. Like a sleek jungle jaguar,† I used to come alive at night. This was my witching hour, so to then be able to play as well was just fantastic. The entire day would be heavenly – lie-in, late breakfast, bit of practice, leisurely relax and

---

* When I was supposed to get my dusting done, I don't know.

† Or a moth.

then all wander down to the ground just as the light began to disappear.

The Aussie stadiums were made for night cricket. The MCG, Sydney Cricket Ground, Adelaide Oval – so many of them had that feeling of being in a huge bowl. Floodlights would magnify the colour of the crowd's clothes, their eyes, even the whiteness of their teeth, like being in a nightclub when they stick the ultra-violet light on. And then you'd look up and the sky would be full of the most amazing stars. All this on a beautiful balmy evening, just the slightest of cooling breezes. It really did feel like something magical, made even more so by it being so, so different from anything in England. Forget a few soggy sandwiches, people would bring along the most amazing grub – great sides of ham, fried potatoes, wonderful salads – and they found the most inventive ways to have a good few slurps of booze, the vodka-injected water melon being the most infamous example. They'd also chant – proper chants – like it was football. For a lad stepping straight off the county circuit it was a truly incredible experience. For those few hours you really were part of something special. Utterly electrifying. Today, this stuff is just part of cricket across the world – T20, the IPL, it's all about colour, glamour and noise. Back then the one-day revolution was in its infancy. Every game was another 'Wow!' moment.

With the adrenalin still flowing through your veins, the fact the games finished about ten o'clock also meant you could walk out the ground straight into a great night out.

Obviously, you'd change out of your 'pyjamas' first. Walking into a bar with grass stains on your backside is never a great look. If we'd actually won, being able to enjoy that buzz late at night in the middle of an incredible city like Sydney or Melbourne was unbelievable.

The England team had traditionally been a little bit conservative when it came to the one-day game, pretty much sticking to the Test line-up – in the 1979 World Cup Final my old TMS colleague Geoffrey Boycott used up 39 overs to make 57. The West Indian captain Clive Lloyd later claimed he deliberately dropped Geoffrey on purpose to keep him out there. Competitions like the Tri-Series were waking teams up to a different way of doing things, using specialists and all-rounders instead of simply picking the old guard. When the 1992 World Cup came round, England realised that they could actually take the game to the opposition rather than adopt the natural defensiveness that comes from having limited personnel. By the early Nineties, England had developed proven one-day specialists like the all-rounder Chris Lewis and 'finisher' Neil Fairbrother, a player adept at keeping the scoreboard ticking over and steering his side home. The biggest innovation was bringing Beefy in as a pinch-hitter, something that hadn't really been tried at that time. For once, though, the selectors had actually given it a bit of thought. Having said that, a good number of that '92 team were already over there for the preceding tour of New Zealand. I do think I only made the World Cup side because I'd done so well in bowling the Kiwis out. The original World Cup plan had been to use only the Worcestershire left-arm spinner Richard Illingworth. Whatever the origins of that England side, it's undeniable that the best teams always have someone who'll come to the fore in any given situation. Once you have that you are a potent force. Only very rarely do those planets properly align, and for once that's exactly what happened. In any given situation we always had someone who could go out and deliver.

Sadly, I missed out on the semi-final against South Africa – a rain-affected game legendary for a pre-tournament formula which left our opponents needing 22 runs from one ball, having required the same score from 13 deliveries before a short squall descended on Sydney.

When this ridiculous new target came up on the board, we were just as dumbfounded as the South Africans were next door. Lamb and Gooch and a couple of the other senior players went off to find out if it was right and returned minutes later with a bemused confirmation. Obviously, everyone in both camps thought that was the end of it, but I'll be honest I thought they still might get it! You just never knew with England. Wins were never handed out on a plate. There just had to be a sting in the tail. From where I was sitting, 21 no balls in a row wasn't impossible.

To be fair, we'd been on the wrong end of the tournament's dodgy rules too. In the group stages, we'd bundled Pakistan out for 74, only for the match to be abandoned because of rain. With no spare day scheduled, the match was declared a draw. The two points Pakistan earned was what saw them through to the next stage. They then became the 'cornered tigers' of legend and went on to win the trophy – against us.

There was a massive hoo-ha about the South Africa calculation, and rightly so, but this was how random rain rules could be. Nowadays, weather-affected targets are all worked out by computer but back then, to understand what would get you over the line, over by over, you needed a Cambridge University mathematician in your side. More than once I wondered if 'run-rate expert' might become a specialist position, like wicketkeeper. 'He might not have got many with the bat, but once again Bamber Gascoigne came good for England in the end.' As it was, endless bits of scribbled-on paper would be ferried out from dressing rooms or kept crumpled in the bottom of a grubby pocket. It literally was back of a fag packet stuff. I recall once watching Graeme Hick pulling sweaty gloves off with his teeth, struggling to release his thigh pad, so he could get in his pocket to look at some horrible sweaty screwed-up piece of paper to know what he needed to keep up with the rate.

Other times, twelfth man would be coming up behind the boundary rope with messages that would instantly be forgotten. At the end of the over, Gooch would ask, 'What's the latest Phil?' And I'd splutter, '45 runs off 18 balls in 68 minutes. Oh, hang on. Actually it might have been 75 off 28 in 49.' Why they told me to take the message out I don't know. I can't even remember directions – 'First left, right at the roundabout and then right again at the lights.' It's disappearing out my head as they're saying it. I think half the time I gave my captains Sam Fox's vital statistics. Professional, it most definitely wasn't.

That tournament, even though we got beaten in the final, was an amazing little journey. We had a great feeling of belief that we could win – one of the few times that we really felt we could go out and do something really special. It was a great example of how trusting players, treating them like adults who can work out how to get the best out of themselves, rather than constantly being told what to do, does actually work. It showed that treating sport as something that should be relished, be fun, can actually pay dividends, just like it did when Brendon McCullum and Ben Stokes did exactly the same thing with the England Test team. Previously, the side was weighed down with fear of failure. Brendon came in, with Ben at his side, with a different message – 'Life's too short. Just get out there and enjoy yourselves.' As a sportsperson, it's easy to forget sometimes that this is what you wanted to do more than anything. This was your childhood dream – to play cricket for England all over the world. It should never be made into something, by you or anyone else, that wears you down. Everyone in that 1992 squad got on with one another and one of the main reasons for that was we were enjoying ourselves. More than 30 years on and I've still got a couple of those lovely light-blue England shirts from that World Cup. Not only do they hold great memories but it was the best kit England ever had. Much better than the New Zealanders' brown. They went retro far too soon!

There was another thing about that World Cup – we may have finished runners-up but for once we'd finished ahead of the Aussies, who would be the dominant force in world cricket for years to come.

It was an unfortunate manner in which I first met that much-revered team. I was playing a prank on a couple of the England lads early on in my first tour and in order to effect this hilarious jape had concealed myself in a wheelie bin where we'd gathered at the side of the ground. The idea was I'd pop up jack-in-a-box style and give them a bit of a scare. I got myself in there and after about three minutes came bursting out, fag in one hand, beer in the other. Little did I know that in the intervening period the Aussie lads had come over to say hello. They were all there – Shane Warne, Glenn McGrath, the lot. As ever, I tried to style it out. 'Oh, hello! The name's Tufnell. I'm going to be playing against you for the next three months.' A gentlemanly greeting doesn't quite work when you're stood in a bin pulling lettuce from your hair.

A more traditional form of socialising was the post-match drink but, for me at least, it was always a little bit tricky to let your hair down and feel totally comfortable after being pummelled day after day. More than that, the Aussies were vicious with the abuse – the art of 'mental disintegration' as their long-time captain Steve Waugh so pleasantly used to put it. I know there's a difference between on the pitch and off it but if someone's been in your face non-stop telling you you're useless it can be a little bit hard just to switch off and let it go. OK, we'd have a drink with them at the end of a Test but even then they'd come in our dressing room and start taking the piss a bit and I wasn't really up for that. I've been beaten in three days and now the other team are all sitting there giggling? I'm sorry but I'm not getting much from that situation.

All that, of course, is very much in the past. Now I go Down Under either as a pundit with TMS or as a tourist like everyone else. Australia's cities are as wonderful as ever, with Sydney remaining a particular favourite of mine. The harbour area is incredible with its amazing fish restaurants. But all those Aussie cities have their own little feel, their own vibe. Melbourne is forever lively, with its amazing nightlife and mix of culture. Adelaide has the most incredible mix of architecture, taking you from the mid-1800s to the 21st century and everything in between in a matter of footsteps. And Perth, by virtue of being the most isolated city on Earth, with thousands of miles of nothing between it and the next major centre of population, has a vibe all of its own – lively, sunny, sandy and surrounded by great natural beauty.

Being an ex-cricketer is handy because, wherever I find myself, I've got pretty good knowledge of the best places to go – this bar, this restaurant, this beach. You can call on your little black book, so to speak, of spots that you remember. Whenever I go to Sydney now, for instance, I like to get up early and do the seven kilometre walk from Coogee to Bondi Beach. It's well known because it's such a beautiful coastal path, a lot of it actually a boardwalk which threads past the beaches at Clovelly, Bronte and Tamarama, and also takes in the famous old graveyard at Waverley where the headstones overlook the sea. You can stop anywhere along that route and have the most incredible salads. In Britain a salad is lettuce, tomato and cucumber, the sort of thing you'd have with a plate of steak and chips. In Australia, salads are things of beauty, full of lovely fruits, and presented pretty much like a main meal. Everyone in Australia these days seems to be really healthy. Whereas before it always had a reputation as a bit of a party place, these days the pubs shut at half ten and you have to go and stand in a designated cross-hatched area if you want a cigarette. Take more than a couple of beers to the beach and you'll be turfed out. It's become a place where you feel healthier almost by osmosis. Before you know it you're renting bikes or ringing up a tour guide. The weather doesn't hurt of course. In England, try as you might, there will always be days when you're more likely to end up in the pub, having a pint of bitter and watching the rain fall.*

When I reach Bondi Beach, I won't hang around. Yes, it's iconic, but to be honest the thing I most remember about it is losing my trunks. On one England tour, half a

---

* The national pastime as it's otherwise known.

dozen of us had gone down there only to find the place absolutely mobbed. There were gangs of teenage kids roaming around, litter everywhere, coppers arresting people for being drunk. We didn't stay long, mainly because when I did finally manage to battle my way through the crowds to the sea I ended up getting attacked by a rogue wave which dumped me into a sandbank and relieved me of my swimming shorts. I spent the next 15 minutes chasing them round the surf until finally I saw someone very tentatively fish them out on the end of their finger a bit further up the beach. I managed to attract their attention – not hard when you're stark bollock naked on one of the most famous beaches in the world.

'Are you Phil Tufnell?' he enquired.

'Yes – any chance I could have my shorts back?'

He threw them to me, and I was glad to make the catch. Standing there in my birthday suit was bad enough without copping a load of stick for having butterfingers.

Since it had been duly noted that there was a bunch of England cricketers on the beach, we thought we'd head off before someone thought it was a good idea to feed the Poms to the sharks.

Fifteen minutes I'd spent at Bondi, during which time I'd been debagged, half drowned and sandblasted by the surf. I had grazes all over my hands, elbows and knees, and the rest of me had gone through an extreme exfoliation, soft as a baby's bottom all over. We headed off to a gentler spot up the road where I had a pleasant lunch washed down with half a bottle of calamine lotion.

Overhearing reports of my travails, the owner did actually inform us that Bondi beach used to have beach-wear inspectors who would go round measuring the dimensions of people's trunks and bikinis. Quite what they'd have made of my totally non-existent ensemble, who knows?

On any walk in an Australian city, it's only a matter of time before you come across a botanical garden with strange exotic birds strutting around, or stunning multi-coloured parrots. In England, on the other hand, we've got one-legged pigeons hanging around outside Greggs.* If it's not pigeons, it's magpies fighting with crows over a bit of old roadkill. I know we have peacocks, but word is they're actually Indian.

I like seeing a fox snuffling through the bins as much as the next man but our wildlife can, in the context of the wider world, be a little underwhelming. I've seen *Springwatch* and an awful lot of it is hedgehogs.† And so much of our stuff only comes out at night. The only people who regularly get to see native British wildlife are those poor sods who are up and about at four in the morning for work. I'm pretty sure if I went snooping around the bushes in my local park at four in the morning I'd be arrested. Down Under, they have proper wildlife – snakes, sharks,

* False legs for pigeons really is the business to be in.

† Sometimes slugs.

spiders and the deadliest 's' of them all, Steve Smith, the Aussie batsman. I've never seen a snake in England. Obviously, I wouldn't want to find one in a welly but something a little bit exciting would be nice.

The only slightly odd bit of wildlife I've seen in Britain is the massive one-eyed bunny rabbit that appeared in our downstairs toilet. We'd had a bit of a party and next morning I heard a Hammer Horror-esque shriek. Initially, I thought it was just Dawn's way of getting me out of bed to join in the tidying up. But I was halfway down the stairs when I saw her, a funny shade of pale, pointing into the toilet.

'What? What is it?'

I opened the door and there was this massive manky old rabbit looking at me, all beaten-up with its one eye. It seemed our cat Oscar had been in a punch-up with it and dragged it into the house. From the look of it, I'm pretty sure it was half dead when he found it. It looked like it was laden with myxomatosis it was that bad.

'Get rid of it!' Dawn cried. Well, I was as scared as she was. This thing looked like it was radioactive. One wrong move and it could have had my hand off. In the end I went to get our neighbour, a woman made of sterner stuff having used to be a farmer. In one fell swoop she picked it up, cracked its neck and that was the end of that. Rest assured, it didn't go in the pot.

In Britain, a spider – or a rabbit – might turn up in the bath once in a while but places like Australia, South Africa and India are absolutely jumping with them. You'd always have a little look under the bench in the dressing room before you sat down in case there was some hairy little blighter waiting to sink its teeth into your rump. There always seemed to be something knocking around wanting to give you a nibble, and for some reason our eight-legged friends have always liked the taste of me.

Take the first time I did *I'm a Celebrity* – I was actually bitten on the bollocks by one. I was sat round the campfire when I suddenly felt a nipping sensation on one of my nuts. Initially I thought maybe I was sitting a bit funny or had been prodded by an errant thistle. I had a bit of an adjustment but the pain soon became truly excruciating. I could feel my testes swelling up in the manner of the *Viz* magazine character Buster Gonad. I was jumping around a bit by now. There was only one explanation – there had to be something in my shorts. I lowered them and was having a hunt around, but as always happens you never find these things. It really was a mystery. I was wearing quite tight underpants* but it had clearly found an escape route. It's what these things do – they have a quick chomp and clear off before you can do anything about it. In the end I was in such agony that I had to go and see the show's resident medic, Doctor Bob. I was there lying on my back – 'Look at the size of them, Bob! What's happening to me?'

He reached for his magnifying glass and soon identified a puncture wound. Next thing I knew the rubber gloves

---

* Too much information, I know.

were going on and he was rubbing ointment all over my testicles. The cream did the trick, and I suppose it was better than having them lanced, but it was a desperately unpleasant experience.

It's the same with mozzies. They've always liked a bit of my blood. Even when I'm cocooned in a net they'll find a way in and treat themselves to the mozzie equivalent of a slap-up grill. These insects just seem to love us Brits. I was on a gondola in Venice once when I couldn't help but notice a fellow passenger's legs. She'd obviously been feasted upon – I think word must have got round the mozzie community that her blood was the equivalent of a good Chianti – and she had big lumps, not dissimilar to mint imperials, all over her legs. She'd seen me having a gander and so I felt I had to acknowledge her plight.

'Ooh! That looks nasty,' I noted.

'Yes,' she replied. 'I don't usually get bitten.' (It's always the ones whose legs look like Vesuvius that say that.)

'Well, something's taken a liking to you,' I said.

She just nodded. By now half a dozen other passengers had started staring at her legs. I think she just wanted me to shut up. But I blundered on.

'They're like a climbing wall for ants,' I added, trying to lighten the mood.

It really is a surprise I ended that little voyage not hurled overboard.

To be fair, we do have the wasp, the true English menace, especially towards the end of the season when they get a bit dopey. There was a particularly vicious gang of wasps who liked to hang around Edgbaston.* It was only when, as a young player, three of these hooligans disappeared up my trouser leg that I looked round and saw that all the more experienced lads had tucked their own strides into their socks as a precaution. No one had told me! The wasps got to work just as Angus Fraser was halfway up his run-in, at which point I gave out a terrific yelp, and the umpire's arm went out to stop play. Forget walking in, I was running around trying to get my trousers off. It was as if, with just a few days left to live, these black and yellow fools had gone up there for a last hurrah. And that's exactly what they ending up having. A terrific time for them. Utterly horrendous for me.

I've been stung by bees too down the years but I've never met a bee that's been vindictive. They never look for trouble. It's always an accident – wrong place, wrong time. Wasps? They can't wait to get stuck in. They've got anger-management issues. They're out for anyone they can get and seem especially fond of the inhabitants of the *Test Match Special* commentary box. I suspect it's the sheer bodyweight of cakes knocking about, but they'll always be in there. There'll be cups of tea going over. Absolute bedlam. I don't know why but everyone always feels the need to stand up when there's a wasp around. I think subliminally we're trying to intimidate them through size.

It isn't just the fauna that's epic in Australia. The flora's not bad too. More than once I've found myself sat on a

* You can't ASBO a wasp.

bench staring intently at a flower or a tree. 'Well,' I'll say to Dawn, 'this is rather lovely, isn't it? Shall we sit here a bit longer?' I never knew sitting on benches could be so good. Don't get me wrong, we have some lovely parks in Britain, but at the same time I don't think I've ever slid in dog muck in a botanical gardens or feared for my life when 20 youths in hoodies sped past on skateboards. We do though have better ducks. And crazy golf.

I agree that Australia isn't the easiest place to get to. Unless you really like planes, I wouldn't advise heading to Sydney for a weekend break. Take two weeks to criss-cross the country, however, and you will never ever forget it.* It's tempting just to stick to the big cities, but for me there was nothing quite like the one-street mining towns that pepper the wilderness; places where you'd swing open the pub door and everyone would stare at you like an alien has just landed† before remembering the England cricket town was in town for a couple of days for a warm-up. Then, so long as Steve Waugh wasn't sat at the bar, you were guaranteed a warm‡ welcome.

As an England player, an Ashes tour will always be a giant moment in your career. I was lucky enough to go on two of them. I'd like to have made it a hat-trick, but

* Especially if you run out of petrol in the outback.

† Traveller tip: In this situation, never ask for a Babycham.

‡ -ish.

regardless I knew Australia was somewhere I'd always revisit – the ultimate escape from the long dark English winter. Better still, nowadays I can return from an Aussie break without an awful feeling in my bones. As a player, barely would I have unpacked my suitcases than I'd be reporting for pre-season training. The county season was just around the corner.

Oh blimey! Really?

8

BLIGHTY

After a few months away touring, it was always nice to go home and just chill out. And yet the relaxation never lasted quite as long as I'd have liked. Ideally, I'd have had a few weeks enjoying a few pints, the occasional pot of whelks and a gentle stroll to the Wimpy. Sadly, however, the domestic season was pointing a finger in my direction. 'Come here,' it was saying, 'I've got some work for you.'

You might think getting back on the county circuit would be a nice break from the fast men of the international scene, especially the legendary West Indian quicks. Sadly not. Curtly played for Northamptonshire and Courtney at Gloucestershire. And it wasn't just them. Pretty much every county had a lightning-fast overseas bowler, many of them also hailing from the Caribbean. I had the intense pleasure of facing Michael 'Whispering Death'* Holding on a green one at Derby, getting a very

---

* So-called because of his silent run-up.

good look at the maker's name as the ball whizzed past my heavily sweating forehead. Lancashire had Patrick Patterson, roundly considered to be the fastest of them all, while Leicestershire had the lesser-celebrated but extremely potent George Ferris. Over the water at Surrey they had the truly intimidating Sylvester Clarke, who the great Viv Richards once revealed had made even him feel uncomfortable. Thing was, Sylvester, a gentle character off the pitch, was a different kettle of fish once he crossed the white line. If a batsman got under his skin, they knew about it. And the crowd weren't always safe either. So fed up was Sylvester of being on the receiving end of missiles thrown by spectators at a ground in Pakistan that he chucked a brick in the opposite direction and hit someone on the head. My Middlesex teammate Phil Edmonds expressed the belief that it was Sylvester's vicious late swing that did for the spectator. At the Oval, Surrey recently opened Sylvester's Bar. I'm assuming that five ounces of red leather flies past your nose on the way in.

It wasn't just the West Indians. Surrey also had the ultimate toe-breaker in Pakistan's Waqar Younis, whose in-swinging yorker would follow you like a heat-seeking missile as you backed away to square leg, and Lancashire had Wasim Akram, his equally potent countryman. At Sussex, meanwhile, there was the South African Garth Le Roux. His fellow South African Allan Donald plied his trade for Warwickshire. The list went on and on. Every week you jumped from the frying pan into the fire and back again.

Of course, these boys were really there to inflict damage on the top order, but they would sense blood, and a few easy wickets, when the likes of me tottered to the middle. That meant a couple of short balls to let you know they meant business, another fired in at your (and I'll use the polite term) inner thigh, and then the coup de grace, the one that sent your off-stump cartwheeling to the boundary. Pretty much always the last man out, at that point everyone disappeared while I was left standing there like a lemon. I'd check myself for the correct number of fingers, toes and limbs, and then slope invisibly back to the pavilion.

Look at the county game now, and there's very few real quicks knocking about, whereas players like me would step straight out of club or age-group cricket to quite literally facing the best fast bowler in the world in Hampshire's Malcolm Marshall. Malcolm was a truly lovely man and, after his premature death from cancer in 1999, I was privileged to play for an International PCA Bunbury XI against a Malcolm Marshall XI in a charity match in his honour.

When it came to me and the quick men, I was always left wondering if the manufacturers of cricket protection couldn't have gone just that little bit further. Before, infamously, the Sabina Park Test in Jamaica was called off after ten overs in 1998, with England on 17–3 on a pitch with more peaks and troughs than the Himalayas, balls flying through at head height off a length, and a physio seemingly on an elasticated rope between the pavilion and middle, I had made the early decision that I wasn't treading anywhere near that wicket unless I had every inch of me clad in padding. On top of my normal collection of thigh, inner thigh, inner inner thigh, chest pad and arm guards, I embarked on an increasingly desperate search for any item of soft furnishing that might double as protection. With the dressing room already picked clean by teammates, I ended up in the members' suite where I spotted a very nice Chesterfield settee, the only issue being there was an elderly chap sitting on it. You can't exactly tear the arm off a Chesterfield settee and stuff it down your trousers without the person occupying it failing to notice. In the end, I came up with a cunning plan. I would appear at the gentleman's side and tell him there was a phone call for him in the other bar. By the time he'd hobbled over there, looked around for the phone and come back, I would have stripped this elegant period piece (the settee not the elderly gentleman) down to the springs and be back in the dressing room with enough protection to see off a 15-over spell of 90-mile-an-hour cannonballs. As it turned out, a hubbub indicated there might have been an on-pitch development. I looked over and everyone was walking off. Relief doesn't even begin to describe it. Even so, from that point on, before any tour, I always made a point of looking in skips round the back of DFS.

It didn't get much better with the batters waiting to pounce. Starting out bowling for Middlesex I walked straight into a barrage of big hitters like Lancashire's Clive

Lloyd, Somerset's Jimmy Cook and Northamptonshire's Allan Lamb. Standing 22 yards from Clive Lloyd was perturbing enough – the man was a giant – without then plopping a 50mph ball down to him. I came up against him on a flat pitch, the sort where you wouldn't fancy bowling at anybody, let alone Clive, and actually did OK at keeping him quiet. Then again, I never escaped the feeling that any time he liked he could casually bop me into the stand, which is exactly what he did – twice.*

Thankfully, the early season games at Oxford or Cambridge University were devoid of such monstrous talent. For some reason, crazed fast bowlers and outlandishly violent batters never seemed to get three As in their A-Levels. The downside was those games were always freezing. As you got a little bit more experienced, you tried to avoid these trips to the nation's esteemed seats of learning. Perhaps there'd be a slight niggle you wouldn't want to aggravate. Maybe you'd be afflicted by a sudden cold. Or a friendly doctor would confirm your allergy to intellectuals. Occasionally you'd state loudly that this was a match where it might be of benefit to give a run-out to one of the newer lads, a chance to get a few overs under his belt and see what he could do. If this tactic failed to work and you were picked, you could guarantee the following few days would be deeply miserable. After a morning in

---

* I once had a nosey in the Lancashire dressing room and found he had eight rubbers on his bat. He was basically batting with a lamppost.

the field, the cold would get in your bones. You'd then go in for lunch hoping for a hot stew or pie and chips and be faced with a slice of ham through which you could see the pattern of the plate.

I lost count how many times I stood in the outfield for two hours in temperatures of five degrees watching the clock make its snail-like progress to the next opportunity to run back to the pavilion and stand by the radiator – before remembering there wasn't one. At Oxford, our scorers Mike Smith and Harry Sharp kept urging me to get some thermal long johns and in the end I headed down to M&S and did just that. Absolute luxury. I couldn't believe I'd spent so many early season games freezing my nuts off, especially when those new wafer-thin cricket trousers had come in. They might have been light as a feather and easy to wash but I might as well have spent the day at third man in my underpants. Up top, I'd have five T-shirts and half a dozen jumpers, and downstairs my legs were like ice cubes.

We actually got beaten by Oxford one year. None of us wanted to be there. It had been raining on and off all game and we were stuck in that horrible cold dressing room sat on wooden slats with nails sticking out. It was a three-day game and on the second evening the Oxford lads kindly invited us to what was termed 'drinks on the lawn' – not, as I'd imagined, a few cans of Skol in someone's back garden, but a smart do at some ancient college where people were wandering round in cloaks and black ties. We appreciated the offer, shoved on our blazers and headed down there. As part of this gathering there were big plastic containers, basically bins, dotted around, each one brimming with punch. As can happen in situations where temptation is laid in their path, suddenly a cricketer's most treasured piece of information isn't how to get the opposition's star batsman out, it's the weather forecast. Sometimes, Michael Fish would predict three days of rain, at which point we'd push the 'G' for Gamble button and head off down to the pub for the day. But then, with meteorology not being hugely reliable at the time, next morning, inevitably, the sun would be cracking the flags on the pavement.

This meant that often the soothsayers' guide to weather forecasting came into play. There was a lot of amateur meteorology at that time. Captains would judge whether to bat or bowl after seeing a cow sat down in a field on the way to the ground. At Lancashire they'd make the call based on whether it was 'raining o'er Bill's mother's' – some spot in the distance five miles away. This was professional sport by the way, making vital judgements on climatic conditions in pretty much the way the Vikings did twelve hundred years ago. You might as well have had a witch in the dressing room. Someone out the back making sacrifices to the gods. And so, based on someone seeing a white rabbit earlier that day, it was decided that the final day's play at Oxford would almost certainly be lost entirely to rain. Therefore, it was safe to get absolutely smashed.

Of course, when I hauled myself from my bed and pulled back the hotel curtains the next day, I was met with nothing but a mildly overcast sky. My heart sank. On the plus side the match was going nowhere and we were about to start our second innings, and so with any luck I'd spend the day nursing my hangover while a few of our lads had a bit of batting practice. Sadly, Mike Gatting had other ideas.

'Listen,' he told his grey and bleary bunch, 'we haven't come up here for nothing. This is an important warm-up game and we need to get something out of it.'

I was sat there, trying to keep my breakfast down, thinking, 'Oh, bloody hell!'

Gatt made a deal with the Oxford captain that we'd score some quick runs and then they could chase down 200-odd in about 50 overs. Not only were we going to spend two sessions in the field but they'd be competitive – so much for standing down at fine leg with a raspberry ripple.

The temperature plummeted throughout the day. When we went out to field I had so many jumpers on the only surprise was I didn't sign any autographs as Giant Haystacks. Despite me not being able to feel my fingers, Gatt seemed to think I was our best chance of victory. And thus I bowled 17 overs into a strong wind and took a grand total of zero wickets as Oxford reached their target with ease.*

* * *

* Funnily enough, most of the teams I played for became rather good at playing hangover cricket. I always thought it would be a good idea to have a pre-match agreement with your opposite number. You had to keep up with each other off the pitch and then you'd cancel each other out on it. Sadly, this particular plan never did quite make it into the laws of cricket. Or the laws of Gatt.

Unless it came at a key point of a game, and denied you obvious victory, a proper rain-affected day was greeted by a lot of players with joy whether a booze-up was planned or not. That might sound bad, but truth is there was a lot of cricket being played at that point and so the odd day with your feet up in the pavilion was far from a bad thing. This is why, in an ideal world, a dressing room would be fitted with four-poster beds, instead of, as at Old Trafford, three rows of stalls seats from an abandoned cinema.

While I did manage to sleep in most dressing rooms – there's usually a physio's bed or an ironing board knocking around – inevitably a lot of the time was spent just sitting around chatting, having a laugh, reading the paper, putting a bet on a horse, or maybe having a wander out to chat to a few spectators whose own comforts extended to little more than a cast-iron bench and an umbrella. So long as there was a bit of heating it was actually a very nice way to spend a day. Not to mention the fact you were getting paid for doing nothing. On the subject of which, a main turnaround in English cricket was when Graham Gooch pointed out that one of the reasons why it was so in the doldrums was because most of the professionals were quite happy not to play! And there was definitely an element of truth in that. More than a few players would have to admit they'd pulled back the curtains in the morning and rejoiced at the sight of a slate-grey sky with stair-rods battering down from it. When a game between Derbyshire and Lancashire at Buxton fell foul of snow in

June 1975, you can bet the rest of the county pros were deeply, deeply envious.

Snow did come my way once. Early on in my career we went up to play Durham at Chester-le-Street, quite an open ground, easily accessible to the elements – lovely views but absolutely freezing in the wrong weather. A gale was blowing as I got changed. Before we'd even stepped out of the pavilion I was frozen to the bone. And then the snow came in. Not just a dusting, but inches of it. The great Aussie batsman David Boon, a Tasmanian, was at the club at the time and it was first time he'd ever seen the white stuff. There's a famous picture of him with a woolly hat and a snowball. Driving from London to Durham always felt like you were entering a different world – and this proved it.

Even in the serene warmth of the West Indies, when a really big storm settles in it can cause a lot of excitement among cricketers. These things can last for days which means lie-ins, long lunches and the serious curtailment of training. You know that, even when the rain stops, the covers won't be coming off for 48 hours at least.

For the first two weeks of our 1997/98 tour, we found ourselves holed up in the abject luxury of a five-star hotel while it belted down incessantly. This is the place about which Lord MacLaurin uttered the famous words, 'Just because it's free, Phil, doesn't mean you have to drink it.' A more futile sentence can never have been delivered in the history of English cricket.

To be fair, we did still practice, albeit in the car park. We paced out 22 yards, Jack Russell put his gloves on, and off we went. It wasn't easy for Jack as most of the deliveries bounced over his head, but us bowlers felt like gods – 'It's coming out well. I've got a feeling about this tour. I'm going to take a stack of wickets here.' At 10.45 a.m., like clockwork, the daily monsoon started and so that was that.

I used to love it in the Caribbean when you'd see a storm gathering off the beach. Initially, everyone would retreat under their sunshades, but then the rain would really start in earnest and you'd leg it into a seafront bar. Well, once you were there …

Skiving aside, I do like a bit of rain and a brooding sky anyway. I'm one of those people who will stand at the window for ages, captivated by the drama; how everywhere suddenly looks so changed. And now I don't even have to worry about it stopping and having to play cricket.

Whatever the situation with the weather – sun, rain or meteor shower – batting first was always the desired option, so much so that when Gatt went out to toss most of the team would be peering desperately out the window. Binoculars might even be used. It was, of course, a 50/50 chance, but if Gatt lost the toss we'd take it very personally sometimes.

'You lost? We're bowling? How have you managed that? You're useless. Rubbish. I can't believe you've come in here and told us that.'

It was an affront to common decency. 'You've done that on purpose, haven't you? You have – you've done it on purpose. Just because you want to make me go out there and bowl.' All after a completely random flip of a coin.

If a captain won the toss and actually chose to bowl, they were in serious trouble. 'You what? You've chosen to bowl? Why on earth have you done that?' People would be looking at the bloke like something they'd scraped off their shoe. 'Well, you'd better hope they're all out before dinner or else there'll be hell to pay, I'll tell you.'

Admittedly, it would be perfect bowling conditions – overcast and a green seamer – but still the bowlers would be adamant – 'We should definitely have had a bat.'

The toss was always a big event of the day. On a serious level, you'd be on the edge of your seat sometimes, not only because you could see what the pitch was going to do, but the fact that decades of statistics show that if you lose the toss you've only got a 30 per cent chance of winning the game.* No wonder we'd all be at the window hoping it went our way. The toss meant so much. It wasn't like football where they flip a coin to see who attacks which end. Lose the majority of tosses and it could affect your whole championship season. One-day cricket was different, but again the toss carried a huge influence. There were a number of Lord's finals where the team bowling first skittled the opposition with a swinging

---

* Unless it was against Australia in the Nineties when winning or losing the toss didn't really matter.

ball under grey skies. Of course, nowadays, with cricket less attritional and more attacking, and players who do actually want to go out there and have a game, maybe the toss isn't such a big thing. Also, the shorter the format the less it matters. And weather forecasts are accurate to the minute. The 'G' for gamble button, it seems, is no more. Unless it's a call for a card game, again not always the best idea.

We used to play cards in the dressing room, but in the end had to stop. Things were starting to get a little bit lively. On a rainy day at Middlesex once we had a game with some of the rival boys from Surrey. It was like something out of a film – 'There's your grand – and I'll raise you another.'

'I'll take your grand – and raise you my car.'

'OK, pal – how's about this, I'll take your car and raise you my Alsatian, house and grandmother.'

I don't know who was sweating more, the people playing or watching. When the game reached its conclusion, which inevitably meant a fair few quid had gone down the pan, there could be a measure of ill-feeling. People had basically lost the best part of a week's wages, and there'd be no sympathy from the winner. A cheque, or cash payment, for the full amount would have to be produced there and then. This could be troublesome at Lord's. St John's Wood is a posh part of town. The lack of pawn shops meant you couldn't trade in your watch, earrings or socks. You could approach a gentleman of the road, but they tended not to offer a realistic figure.

It was friction central. A player would lose five hundred quid and be left eating pork scratchings at the bar while watching a now loaded colleague throwing steak and bubbly down his neck. Similarly, during the 'any other business' part of a team meeting, tempers could flare if a batsman pointed at his opening partner and asked, 'Oi! When are you going to stump up that five hundred quid then?'

More often than not, anger was directed at yourself. You'd be running into bowl mentally telling yourself off. 'Why didn't I just stop when I had a chance?' The batsman version of that is having the same concentration-wrecking conversation while some six-foot-seven man-mountain is steaming in trying to knock your head off. It's very much not an ideal scenario. In the end we turned the heat down by setting a limit on the dough. Having said that, with the vagaries of the British summer wiping out entire matches, I did wonder if the cricketing authorities had ever thought of making a rainy-day victory over the opposition at poker worth a County Championship bonus point.

Funnily enough, in retirement I would become a commentator on *The Great British Poker Tournament*, a job which isn't as easy as it sounds. After all, there's only so much you can say about a bunch of people sat around playing cards – 'Ooh! Look! He's got a king and a queen!' I even had a DVD out – *Win at Poker with Phil Tufnell* – 'If you want to become a card shark to beat them all, Phil's here to teach you the ropes.' I've just looked and it's available for 75p on Amazon. I think all in all I'm better suited to *TMS*.

Thing is, you definitely do need something to pass the time. In the morning you'll have a flick through a stray magazine, wondering why a copy of *You and Your Goldfish* has ended up in the Lord's dressing room, and then gorge on half a dozen lamb chops for dinner, but if it's still hammering down on the covers, what do you do then?

This is one of the reasons I always liked playing outgrounds, away from county HQs. There's a bit of an old romantic in me, and outgrounds represent a lovely upbeat festival-style cricket experience, a social as well as sporting occasion. While a wander round Lord's might result in an impromptu ten minutes hiding in a broom cupboard to avoid an irate committee member, outgrounds offered friendly chats and a go on the bouncy castle.

On the downside, they were rarely the best facilities. Even with a bit of a spruce-up, the showers never worked, and even if they (or it) did, they would release a dribble of water as if from the chin of a thirsty man at an oasis, and be surrounded by a shower curtain held together by Amazonian-grade mildew. Grouting would veer between unedifying shades of brown and grey. In other hygiene news, never was there a toilet seat.

Thing is, these places are meant for games which last a few hours on a Saturday afternoon. They're not set up for 15 big blokes to take up residence for four days, with all their old socks and bits of sweaty kit hanging around.

Tripping over someone's case and banging your head on a slatted bench might look funny* – but it really isn't.

A batting collapse would be mayhem. Suddenly, three of the chaps would come rushing in, spikes going everywhere, trying to find their pads and what have you in the volcano of kit on the floor. It would be like hopscotch just to get out of the door, jumping over coffins, bags and piles of clothes.

A wet game on an outground meant there was no chance of getting your stuff dry. All you could do was stick your bits and pieces on the parcel shelf of your car in the hope they might get a bit of sun. At the end of the game, you'd drive home in something smelling like a mouldy laundry basket.†

Your spot in a dressing room like this very much depended on where you were in the playing hierarchy. In your first year you'd be 100 per cent guaranteed the seat with 2cms of rotting plywood between you and a 15-stone man on a toilet. Three years on and you might have graduated to the bench with the silverfish infestation. A year after that and you'd have the one by the window where every time you got changed the entire ground could see

---

* Have a look on TikTok.

† Thinking about it, playing at an outground was actually very much like camping. If someone had started heating up a tin of soup on a portable gas stove, I'd have been in no way surprised. The only real difference between an outground dressing room and camping was that every now and then you'd have to get up and go and do something which vaguely resembled being a professional cricketer.

your backside. Once again, everybody, I give you English professional cricket.

To escape the squalor of the dressing room, you'd sit out on the little veranda. Depending where you were, and how rarely they staged first-class cricket, this could mean being stared at like some sort of exotic creature, like a mariner might a mermaid on a rock. A rope would have been strung across the side and front of the pavilion so people couldn't approach, stroke or feed the players.

To escape these confines, I was always more than happy to have a wander round, have a chat with the locals and check the age limit on the swing boats. Other times I'd nip out the back of the pavilion for a crafty fag. It's strange, whatever age you are, wherever you might be, when you go out the back of somewhere – pub, bike shed, pavilion, whatever – you always end up with the same mob of characters. I've been out the back of pavilions for a fag in my pads while waiting to bat. I was one of the few players whose batting gloves had nicotine stains.

It would always be the same – 'It's Tuffers! Here you are, mate, have a fag!' Occasionally it would be followed up with, 'Fancy a beer to go with it?'

'Well, no. Thanks for the fag but I think I'd better pass on the beer. I might be batting in a couple of minutes.'

Of course, you can guess what their reply was to that. Something along the lines of, 'Come off it, mate! It can only make you better!'

It's remarkable now to think that us smokers didn't always step out for a fag. There'd be Athers and Stewie waiting to go out to bat in a haze of fog. I mean, what were we thinking? I used to be sitting in the corner with a fag on and someone would say, 'Tuffers, can't you take that outside on the balcony?'

'I'm allowed to smoke in here,' I'd reply. 'It's a free country.'

But then I did start to realise that it might be slightly inappropriate and antisocial. There's Graeme Hick sitting next to me, trying to get in the zone while coughing and spluttering and his gear all stinking of Embassy Number 1. To be fair, some of the smoking was probably nerves. Waiting to bat against the West Indies is not the time to give up nicotine.

Sadly, first-class games on outgrounds are becoming fewer and fewer. Time was when you'd play five or six games a year on either your own outgrounds or those of another county. At Middlesex, we had Uxbridge, Richmond and Southgate, where I actually started my club career, exploiting what was a nice little turner, and bowling up the hill from the beautifully named Waterfall Road End or down the hill from the Adelaide End. There again, it was the whole atmosphere that appealed. You'd turn up in the morning, wander into the clubhouse for a bacon sandwich, lean on the wall outside and watch as all the marquees were readied for the gates opening. There'd be people arranging wine glasses, setting deckchairs out and the ground staff would be making the field absolutely immaculate. If you were batting and a collapse wasn't imminent, you'd go for a little walk round and have an ice cream with a flake. There just isn't any other sport where a Mr Whippy forms part of a day's play.

In a funny sort of way I enjoyed playing at outgrounds more than I did the big Test match county venues. Trent Bridge, for instance, is a great ground, but a thousand people rattling round a 15,000-seat stadium could never match a packed festival ground for atmosphere. The pitches tended to offer a bit too. You would sometimes feel for an opposition batsman as our West Indies quick Wayne Daniel steamed in, firing it down at 90 miles an hour on what was essentially a club wicket. If it was a turner, meanwhile, they'd be up against John Emburey or me. Green-top? Let me introduce you to Angus Fraser! We had all angles covered.

Away from Middlesex, you might find yourself at Scarborough, one of the great festivals in English cricket, with 3,000 spectators and double the amount of seagulls, or on the other side of the country on a windswept outcrop off the Lancashire coast. As a curious chap, there was always something about stepping out of a hotel into a strange new town and having a wander round, bumping into people, having a little chat. Everyone talks about the big overseas tours and what an incredible experience it must have been – which it was – but I genuinely think I've also been incredibly lucky to see so much of my own country. In fact, it was travelling the circuit of county grounds that finally, after three or four years, made me realise I actually was a professional cricketer. Sounds daft, but until then I'd never really thought about it. But as I spent more and more time in the first team, it reinforced in me how fortunate I was to do what I did. It really was a wonderful existence. I'd look around on a lovely summer's day and there'd be the little fella on the paper stand, a chap rooting around in his bag for a sandwich, a couple of kids knocking a ball about on the outfield. There's not many sports where everything is so chilled out.

Subconsciously or otherwise, being a cricketer developed a love for Britain that one hundred per cent remains to this day, another reason I'm so glad to put in a word on our outgrounds' behalf. They're definitely a key element of the English county cricket experience, for players and spectators, and it would be very sad to lose them.

The one big outground missing from my CV is Blackpool. I never played there – possibly a good job considering the temptations on the doorstep. I did, however, still compete in the town – as a contestant on *Strictly Come Dancing*. In 2009, I made it to the iconic Tower Ballroom where myself and dance partner Katya Virshilas performed a rumba to 'Maybe I'm Amazed' by Paul McCartney. Believe me, nobody was more amazed than me that I was still in the competition at that point!

Afterwards, me and Dawn went for a little look around. Probably not my greatest idea. It was November, dark, freezing cold and blowing a howling gale – not exactly sandcastle weather. If there was a Golden Mile out there I never saw it. Nevertheless, I'd always quite fancied having a look at the town's famous Illuminations and so we headed for the promenade. Well, I very nearly got an unscheduled close-up when they started blowing around. An extra-big gust and I'd have had a thousand-bulb representation of Ken Barlow on top of my head.

Dawn will always remember Blackpool for another reason. While we were there she set out from the hotel to find somewhere to have her hair done. A couple of hours later she returned sporting the oddest hairdo I've ever seen. Back-combed and heavily sprayed it was as if she'd been transported back to the 1960s. There were bits all over the place, like she'd been attacked by gulls. After a pint and a bag of chips we weren't too sorry to head back down south. I need to go back in the summer to get the proper Blackpool experience.

That won't include any rollercoasters. I had enough of that when I took part in the rather odd quiz show *Scream if You Know the Answer!*, in which various celebrities were tasked with answering general knowledge questions while being slung around on various horrific rides at Thorpe Park. Have you ever tried to remember the capital of Hungary while plunging towards the ground at what feels like 100mph? Give me a seat on *Blankety Blank* any day.

No, it's for its serenity that I most love Britain. I know – serenity? Tuffers? You must think I've gone mad. But remember, once that little sojourn around the county grounds of England was over for another season, the madness of the overseas tour loomed once again. And one tour in particular would be the craziest of them all.

9
A TOUR LIKE NO OTHER

As September arrived and the domestic season wound down, thoughts would turn once again to the winter. If your name came up on Ceefax page 340 – no chance of a one-on-one phone call with the selectors in those days – it meant you were touring. I came into the international set-up just at a point of crossover. It was towards the end of the Beefy era when, as we've seen, if you played your cards right, you could have a right old time, and just on the cusp of a new regime of ultra-fitness. At this point, the powers that be were testing the water as to the right way to go about turning the England cricket team into the kind of stars deemed fit to adorn the front cover of *Sports Illustrated*. In the past, we were more likely to be asked to do a photoshoot for the *Pig Farmers' Gazette*.

Prior to the New Zealand and India tours, the National Sports Centre at Lilleshall was the option our bosses chose. This was a multi-sports training facility with a track record of transforming results. Already it had taken the women's shot-putt team from 18th to 17th in the world.

Lilleshall itself is near Telford in Shropshire, no doubt a very pleasant and interesting place if you live there, but better known as 'the middle of nowhere' to the rest of us. In the early Nineties, the biggest challenge Lilleshall presented to most professional sportspeople was just finding it. When you did, you immediately wished you hadn't.

Problem was that England cricketers in the Nineties, for the most part, were used to doing things a certain way. While admittedly the team had seen the arrival of new more fitness-minded individuals, there were others who preferred to keep themselves athletic, at least borderline mobile, in the more traditional manner, such as walking 500 yards to the nearest pub, and lifting a naan bread. I think this might have been why the fitness instructors we encountered at Lilleshall would not have been out of place on an army parade ground.

It was very much, 'Right, you 'orrible little man. Going on an England cricket tour? Think that makes you somebody do you? We'll soon knock that out of you. You won't enjoy a single second of this!'

And I'd be, 'What have I done? I've only just got out of my car!'

It was like turning up at borstal for a month of the short, sharp shock. I'd just keep thinking, 'But hang on. I just want to play a bit of cricket,' while at the same time wondering if I was going be accosted by an inmate with two pool balls in a sock.

At the same time I could see that things did need to be a little bit better regulated. When I started out with

England, you'd have a 20-minute net in your shorts and then pile in the Mini Moke and head off down to the beach bar. The problem was the regime then went a hundred miles in the opposite direction. I'd be bowling for 90 minutes in 40-degree heat in the nets. That kind of thing does you no good as a bowler. You've found your rhythm after 25 minutes and the rest of the session is just physically draining and mind-numbingly pointless. You end up bowling with your wrong hand or running up backwards with your tongue hanging out just to make it mildly interesting.

Thing is, I'm not entirely sure Lilleshall was the best answer. Bearing in mind that in 1993 we were preparing for three months in the scorching heat of India, it was hardly perfect to be in a freezing cold sports hall in Shropshire while frost covered the grass outside. Let's face it, England tours pretty much always are to a place of hellish heat, so much so that cooling breezes were given almost godlike status. In Perth, you had the old Fremantle Doctor which would start up about two in the afternoon. The downside was it usually signalled the introduction of Terry Alderman into the Aussie attack to get the ball swinging sideways.

To combat such heat, Jack Russell would make his own pre-tour arrangements. He'd sit in a red-hot sauna fully kitted-up. Others saw that as plain nuts but I saw it as dedication. He's not putting two jumpers on, full batting gear, and a helmet and sitting in a sauna for an hour just to be weird. That's a very uncomfortable thing to do. He's

171

trying to become accustomed to what's coming, to replicate the situations he's going to be playing in. But it was easier for some to portray it as 'mad old Jack', a big laugh and a joke. Obviously, the image of him sat in there with all his gear on is funny, but on the other hand he was doing that because properly organised preparation was lacking, same as how, on one occasion before we were off to Australia, we had a golf outing to Barrington's at Vale do Lobo in Portugal. All very nice, but what the hell has that got to do with facing a mystery spinner in 95-degree heat? As you've probably realised, I liked Jack. It didn't need a sauna for me to warm to him as someone who did things his own way.

Similarly, I'm not sure other Test-playing countries' tour preparation made provision for not upsetting the bowlers community. It was reported that extra padding on the indoor surface, cushioning the stress that goes through fast bowlers' legs at point of delivery, had been removed because it sent balls off course. The pitches at Lilleshall were so hard we absolutely smashed ourselves to pieces. They were like concrete, which also meant I didn't spin a single ball the whole time I was there. It was simply impossible to do so. Have a bat, meanwhile, and the ball would be whistling past your ear. The colder it was, the faster it went. I sometimes wondered if the coaches had been handed the wrong itinerary; if instead of India they thought we were going to South Africa for three months on the hardest, bounciest and nippiest of wickets. Bear in mind that at this point India would generally field the ageing Kapil Dev, who bowled at the speed of a Morris Minor, and four spinners – practice against extreme pace was most definitely not what we needed.

In the end, sore knees were the last thing on my mind in India. The place was such an assault on the senses that I was pretty much rendered numb all over. On the first day of the opening Test match, we got off the bus and the crowd converged from everywhere, like being at the centre of a giant rugby scrum. If that was a shock, then the way the police officers dealt with it was even more so. Basically, they beat the living hell out of them with great big bamboo canes. Essentially, you were walking into the ground with grievous bodily harm going on all around you. I did actually ask our security liaison officer why it had to be like that.

'We do this all the time,' he said. 'It's the only way you can get any sort of order.' But to me it looked like some of those officers were enjoying it a little bit. They were giving people a proper thrashing. The nearest I'd come to anything like that was that old 'game' at school where kids lined a corridor and you had to run past while everyone gave you a punch or a kick – 'chicken run' I think it was called. It was about a thousand times less violent than what I was witnessing here.

The crowd were treated like a completely separate entity to what was happening on the pitch. We existed in our world, they existed in theirs. I'd look into the stands, packed with spectators, and it was like looking into a human cement mixer – heads, bodies, arms, legs, constantly on the move. When an Indian player reached a century, the crowd would start fires. Sometimes the police would move in and start whipping people again. I'd be down at third man and look round and behind this mass of barbed wire there'd be absolute bedlam. Literally thousands of people moving and swaying in every conceivable direction. It wasn't like Lord's that's for sure. There was no one reaching into a Fortnum & Mason hamper for an egg and cress sandwich and another bottle of Champagne; no murmur getting progressively louder throughout the day. The noise, at all times, was like nothing I've ever heard. Absolutely insane. And that was the same inside and outside the ground. The only quiet you ever heard was when you woke up in your hotel room. You'd then head down to the hotel lobby and the second the lift doors opened, that was it – like someone turned the volume up to ten. On the drive to the ground it would hit 11. Policemen shouting. Sirens blaring. People getting knocked off bikes. Our bus would send two or three cyclists head-first into a ditch every morning.

Remember, at this point I had toured only Australia and New Zealand. I mean, the Aussies could get a bit unruly sometimes. Bay 13 at the MCG was a place you fielded in front of under only the most extreme duress. Even the Aussies themselves weren't keen on heading down there. On one occasion, Shane Warne went across to Bay 13 in a helmet to ask its occupants to stop pelting players. A suit of armour would have been more befitting.

It's always difficult to know how to interact with a crowd. Ignore them and you look like a miserable git. Turn round and have a chat and a wave and you can guarantee that will be the exact moment a top edge comes your way. In England, crowd interaction often meant signing a few autographs between balls. As a player, once you've got a bunch of kids gathered by the advertising boards you're stuck between a rock and a hard place. Ignore them and you look plain mean. Sign and you've got the captain glaring at you for not concentrating on the game. Throughout my career I always tried to sign as many autographs as I could if kids were waiting for me by the pavilion. Of course, the one time you couldn't do everyone because you had to head off – for a team talk or something – was the one that would get all the publicity. Next day in the paper, it would be, 'This England team have got a bad attitude – all they think about is themselves.' And I'd think, 'Well, hang on, I've come off the pitch after bowling 30 overs in 90-degree heat, signed 500 hundred autographs, my hand's hanging off, and now I'm getting jip for being a selfish git?' If I hadn't got in that pavilion there was a very good chance I'd have passed out!

Spectators in New Zealand, compared to Australia, were generally very quiet. They had their moments but if there wasn't much happening it was like being in an episode of *Gardeners' World*. Compare that to India where crowds were often ordered not to carry sticks and glass bottles into the ground.* Quaintly, 'looking-glasses' were also banned, which was a bonus – the last thing you want after 150 overs in the field is to get a glimpse of what you look like in a mirror.

On the pitch, life was equally tumultuous. We lost that series 3–0, with the Indians racking up some pretty hefty scores. England's cause wasn't helped by the selectors picking bowling attacks that would have been OK for a green-top at Headingley but were somewhat ill-suited to the likes of Eden Gardens, Kolkata. The Indians fielded four spinners and we were going in with pacemen. Theirs was a thankless task. Before the final Test, at Mumbai, Phil DeFreitas, still wicketless for the entire tour, claimed to have worked out how to dislodge the prolific Vinod Kambli. He was on 223 when Gatt walked past Phil in the field – 'Er, any chance you could get him out now?'

It seemed the only thing we were adept at was shooting ourselves in the foot. In a warm-up game, dribbling out to a draw on the last afternoon, and with the threatening Navjot Sidhu at the crease, our skipper Graham Gooch turned down the standard option of an early finish, believing we needed more practice. Sidhu was singularly unimpressed with this decision. I expect he was looking forward to a bath and an evening meal, as were the rest of us. He needed something on which to focus his frustra-

---

* What the rule was on six-inch bolts, I'm unsure, but Devon Malcolm actually had one thrown at him in a one-day international at Jamshedpur.

tion, and that something would be a 40-year-old off-spinner from Peckham. John Emburey was known for his miserliness with the ball. But Sidhu was no respecter of reputation, at least not when he was being made to wait for his dinner. He proceeded to run down the wicket and smash Embers again and again out of the ground. At the same time he smashed the confidence of one of the few men on the tour in a genuine position to take a few wickets. The pay-off for that extra practice was huge.

Having said that, getting wickets in India as an England spinner was borderline impossible. Hit a batsman on the back pad two inches in front of and halfway up middle stump and you'd be lucky to get so much as a shake of the head for an LBW appeal. These things just weren't given. How I wish my career had coincided with DRS.

The thing about that India tour was that so much of it, on and off the pitch, was so bad, that after a while the whole thing became absolutely hysterical. Planes nearly crashing, hideous illnesses, vast journeys on rat-riddled trains – after a while we stopped trying to fight the situation and actually started to embrace it, like we were starring in our very own Carry On film – Carry On Dropping Catches, Carry On Being Hammered by the Media, Carry On Losing Two Stones a Week. Every now and again you'd hear maniacal laughter, like that of the slowly disintegrating Inspector Dreyfus in the Pink Panther films, coming from a player's room. It was like people were gradually being possessed, so that even the most professional of the boys – the ones who'd go through hell to get a few throw-downs or go for a run – would find themselves grinning, or more likely gurning, inanely into mirrors.

Thing is, life's too short to be sitting on the sidelines being miserable. That's why, after being battered in the second Test, when every England team member was, rather bizarrely, given a bike at the presentation, I was more than happy to sling my leg over the saddle and head off round the ground. That behaviour earned me a few disapproving looks when finally I got back to the dressing room. Presumably I should have been moping around with a face like stone. But me sobbing in the corner wasn't going to change the result. Sport is entertainment, and as I rode round the boundary, pulling the odd wheelie, doing some top-class skids, I thought about the kind of lives some of these multitudes of people would have. They weren't being paid to play cricket. They weren't going back to a plush hotel. And so if someone was going to give me a bike at the end of a match I wasn't going to ignore it and walk off, I was going to have a bit of fun with the crowd. What did I have to complain about? I had all my arms and legs – the sight of limbless beggars on the streets was truly shocking – and was living my dream life as an England cricketer. I knew I was lucky and I was going to crack on and enjoy myself. Any frowning at that little bike ride was totally wasted on me.

The way I saw it I was right. Laugh in the face of discomfort and you take others with you. Plus it's an attitude that frees you up mentally. Look at it this way: to get to play competitive sport at the highest level, and feel like you've succeeded, that you've contributed, that you've come out on top against some bloke trying to knock your head off or smash you out the ground, is an incredible feeling. It's such an adrenalin rush. And you want to keep that going. People would always say, take the good times and the bad times in the same way, then you won't get too up or too down. Essentially, they meant your mood and demeanour should always remain at some kind of medium level. But I was never really one for that. In cricket, like most sports, there'll be more lows than highs. And when the good times came I was always going to celebrate. Of course, the question is then, how do you deal with the lows? My answer was to try to go out and have a good time anyway. What else are you going to do? Lock yourself away? That's when things do start going wrong. If I fumbled a catch at an important point of a cricket match, I couldn't just hole up in my hotel room thinking, 'Why did I drop it? Oh my God, the world's a terrible place.' Much better to be out with other people, try to find something to laugh about – get the whole sorry episode out of your system. I was actually very good at drawing a line under something and moving on from it.

Remember, 11 of the 17 players on that trip had never been to India – the selectors weren't, it seems, going for experience! – and so, almost as a group, we were the classic fish out of water. Just the same as it was a massive culture shock for me, a boy from north London, the same could be said of Richard Blakey from Huddersfield, Neil Fairbrother from Warrington, Ian Salisbury from Northampton and a load of the other young lads. If they were anything like me they would have had no idea that anywhere like this – anywhere so, so different – existed, and actually an England cricket tour is a very surreal way to discover it. There's a time when the madness of what you're seeing – people lying in the street after being run over by a passing truck, or a report in the paper that hundreds have died in a rubbish dump fire – makes you question whether any of what you're seeing or doing is truly real, or if maybe that old 'theory' that we're all just tiny particles under a giant's thumbnail is actually true.

Ultimately, it was that level of separateness from anything that could ever be termed, in our limited experience, 'normal life' that brought us so close together. Yes, we were beaten out of sight, and yes it felt like everything was against us, but ask every single bloke who was on that trip what was the best tour they ever went on and they'd all say 'India 1993' because no other overseas series came near it for feeling that we were living something as one.

That emotion would never happen now because the England Lions (a set-up for emerging players) introduce young players to different conditions across the world as much as they can. Most players picked for the England senior team now will have been to, and played, in India to some degree. They should feel relatively confident and prepared. Our preparation for the Indian summer was to practise in rural Shropshire in winter. The average March temperature in India is 29 degrees. In Shropshire it's 20 degrees lower. It's like the England football team preparing for the Qatar World Cup in Iceland.

On the subject of the football blokes – they always looked significantly fresher than their cricketing counterparts. Then again, England's footballers never had to undergo a nine-hour train journey from Bhubaneswar to Kolkata with a rat running around the floor. Because of a pilots' strike, we had several epically long train journeys on that trip, but again, instead of staring bleakly out the window, all they did was bring us closer together. I mean, don't get me wrong, no one mistook us for The Railway Children, but on a good day someone would produce a bottle of Johnnie Walker, generally pilfered from the High Commission. Someone else would then haul on board two crates of Boddingtons, purloined from a similar source. Foreign fags might be a little bit on the strong side, occasionally removing the roof of your mouth. Again, the good news was, wherever you went, you could always find a bloke who could get you some black market Benson & Hedges. However, getting hold of these kind of goodies wasn't always easy and in a squad of players you always needed a couple of characters who wouldn't have been out of place in Colditz. A plea for a bottle of the hard stuff would entail a call to the 'scrounger', who would then make arrangements for the acquisition of the booze, and relay its location, possibly via the back of some rice paper which would be seen once, memorised and eaten, to the designated collector who would slip off into the darkness and retrieve the goods.

Often the people who are most adept at this sort of below-the-radar behaviour are the ones who'd attended what is commonly known as the 'University of Life'. While the average dressing room will feature a liberal smattering of well-educated types, the sort of people who've filled in *The Times* cryptic crossword while you're wiping a tea stain off your trousers, a lot of the time these people will have absolutely no common sense. OK, they'd be able to read a map of Kolkata standing on their head, understand time travel and know the Latin name for a dormouse, but could they hail a taxi? No chance. Ask an Oxbridge graduate to get you a 99 Flake and a can of Irn-Bru from the ice-cream van and they wouldn't know where to start. But again, in this England changing room, we somehow all fitted together. Our characters gave us roles. The tough one would look out for the group and intervene if anything kicked off; the wise one would show us the way forward; and the one with the mate at Watneys brewery would provide the beer. In some ways, it was like being in *The Magnificent Seven*, not mathematically of course,* but definitely in terms of that mix of young hotheads, surly bandits and moustachioed old gunslingers. We were the sum of our parts. OK, we didn't rescue many victimised

* We were more 'The Fetid Fifteen'.

villagers, but we did know how to get hold of some Hamlet cigars.

I guess if I had a role in Colditz, it would be as leader of the escape committee. Even now I can give you chapter and verse on hidden staircases and laundry lifts in virtually any major hotel in a Test-playing country. But, like everyone else, I was totally reliant on the alternative skills of those around me. Take Andy Caddick – he could fix anything you put in front of him, helmet strap, Walkman, in-growing toenail, you name it. Some people thought Caddy was slightly geeky but I always liked people who were a bit different, didn't necessarily fit the mould that everyone else thought they should. Dressing rooms would be very dull if we all behaved and thought the same.

When it came to kit maintenance, I was certainly reliant on those around me. I was never very adept at sorting my gear out. Changing a batting grip was one thing I never got used to, possibly because my bat got so little use I rarely needed to. On tour, however, I was prone occasionally to pick up my bat with sun cream on my hands. When it then came time for me to have a little wander out to the middle, my bat would slide straight of my hands. Play my traditional slog and the square-leg umpire would end up wearing it. I'd be panicking only for Lamby or Robin Smith to have the rubber whipped off and another on in a matter of seconds. It was like watching an F1 tyre change. The tool they used, a round thick wooden rod, was officially called a cone, but more commonly known as a donkey's dick. In the England dressing room, there were three donkey's dicks of different sizes.* I can't remember who they belonged to. You see, contrary to popular opinion, everyone in that Nineties England dressing room had a skill. It's just that it wasn't always playing cricket.

That lack of results on the pitch always got people searching for reasons why. Those reasons were never poor preparation, lack of selection consistency or dearth of long-term planning. In India, according to some observers, we had failed because we looked scruffy and unprofessional. Truth was it really was very hard not to, for me especially. There are players who walk off the pitch at the end of the day and look like they've never been on it. I wasn't one of them. Even now, after nine holes of golf, I walk into the clubhouse looking shattered, bedraggled, shirt hanging out, hair messy. After a long day in the field in 35 degrees I was a physical wreck. I'd look at Alec Stewart, as ever, pristine. 'Hang on, have you actually been out there the same amount of time as me?'

When we did actually win a match, against what was basically an Indian Railways XI,† we were castigated not only for our play but also our supposedly slovenly appearance, and it's true to say that by the time we bumbled into Mumbai for the third and final Test most of us looked like we felt: absolutely shit. To be fair, we'd actually been advised not to take a razor to our chins because diving around in the dusty outfields of India in that heat could

---

* Fill in your own punchline.

† Why British Rail never took on touring teams I'll never know.

cause skin infections, but no one bothered to write about that when they were discussing what chairman of selectors, the late Ted Dexter, called 'the whole issue of facial hair'.*

Ironically, the demands made on us to be immaculately dressed in multiple different outfits per day made us even scruffier. The 1993 India tour was the first time I can remember where England's day-to-day clothing, as well as our playing gear, was sponsored. Nothing wrong with that – all sponsorship gratefully received. In fact, at Middlesex our shirts had been sponsored by the high-street tailor Austin Reed, which meant piling down to Regent Street for the big unveiling of the new design. It was an occasion where many of us put on a few pounds, not because of some grand buffet, rather due to the jumpers, socks, trilbies and various other garb-based paraphernalia we 'added' to the free goodies. We'd walk out of there wearing four jackets and shoes upon shoes. Middlesex also had a deal with Siemens Nixdorf for a while, but it didn't interest me too much. How can you walk out of a meet-and-greet with a fax machine?

Anyway, out in India our clothing sponsor had got so carried away that we didn't know what we were supposed to be wearing from one minute to the next. On a Monday, for example, for a training run we'd have the yellow T-shirt with the yellow shorts and the white socks, then change into our pale-blue evening clothes for a visit to the High Commission. Tuesday, we'd need to wear our cream

* It never seemed an issue with W.G. Grace.

breakfast outfits as a photographer was expected. There'd be another photo-op in the afternoon so please could we then change into our smart maroon afternoon gear. It almost became more important than trying to take wickets and score runs. There Robin Smith would be, arriving at the nets in 100-degree heat, only for a PR bloke to suddenly appear – 'Excuse me, Robin, you couldn't just change into the red? The blue is really just for warm-ups on match days.' The poor bloke would have dragged himself down there after three days of extreme nausea and vomiting and now he was being asked to go all the way back again.

We had about seven different coloured shirts, tops, trousers and shorts to suit particular occasions. Well, as you can imagine, travelling round India for three months, and relying on not terribly efficient hotel laundries, this amount of kit could cause serious problems. After a few weeks you'd have Neil Fairbrother's yellow top, John Emburey's brown socks and Phil DeFreitas's pale-blue shorts. On days when sponsor-wear was required, there'd be maroon tracksuit bottoms paired with lime-green penny-collar shirts, glow-in-the dark pink socks paired with slate-grey blazers, and white slacks matched with orange bodywarmers. I wouldn't have been surprised to see the scorer in a sarong. You'd be asking for advice from a teammate – 'Do this top and these trousers go together?' Really, we needed Jeff Banks along.

The same issue applied to your playing gear. You'd hand it to the hotel three days before a Test to be dry-cleaned

but then there'd be times when on the eve of the match it
hadn't come back. On one occasion in India, the entire
England squad was down in our accommodation's laun-
dry area rooting through washing bags. 'Is this anybody's?
Hang on, it's got some initials on it. AJS – who's that?
Anybody know who that is?'

'Alec Stewart.'

'Oh right! Over here, Stewie! I've found your trousers.'

We were down there until about two in the morning
sorting it out. Even then it wasn't right. I was walking out
on to the grass when I realised I was wearing Devon
Malcolm's socks. I pulled them up and they were thigh-
high. I looked like I was wearing stockings.

The fact that in India our leisure time was essentially as
diaried as our playing time I found especially difficult.
Look at the great ton that our all-rounder Chris Lewis,
more complex a character than many realised, and, like
one or two others, burdened with the 'next Botham' label,
made at Chennai (then called Madras), smashing 15 fours
and two sixes along the way. The story always goes that
he did that after a few drinks at a nightclub. This makes it
sound like he spent half the night at Stringfellows, but a
nightclub essentially meant a small bar with a bit of music
in one of the plusher hotels, part of a weekly circuit of
venues – Monday High Commission, Tuesday such and
such a hotel, Wednesday a different commission, etc. –
which, as a bit of a free spirit, I found quite hard to get
used to. Having said that, the High Commission was a
better night out than it sounds. They had Boddingtons, did

187

egg and chips and had a snooker table. For an England touring side in India in 1993, that was a fantastic combination.

It's amazing the turnaround there's been in India in the years since that infamous 'Spinwash',* as it came to be termed, tour. Very quickly, in the space of no more than a decade really, India changed immensely. It became a lot more cosmopolitan and the infrastructure a great deal more user-friendly.

That massive improvement extended to the cricket stadiums. No exaggeration to say that the facilities for spectators used to be non-existent. You'd enter the Wankhede Stadium in Mumbai and literally be ankle deep in urine. Half a dozen toilets for 60,000 people. Even in the better parts of the ground, washing facilities would be a copper pipe sticking out of a wall.

To tour India now would, I'm sure, be seen as one of the great highlights of a career – as it was for me, but just in a different way. The country is an economic powerhouse, easy to get around and home to the IPL, the biggest and most successful T20 franchise in the world. Crowds watch the action unfold from ultra-modern stadiums and are an integral part of the occasion. The days of police officers with sticks treating people like cattle are gone, and a night out for a visiting cricketer tends to be a bit more than a

* We should have been sponsored by Indesit.

fry-up down the High Commission and a clumsy game of billiards. I wonder if there's a veterans' scene over there ...

In many ways, however, I'm glad I toured India in 1993 not 2023. The other-worldly feel of that trip made everyone very, very close, as seen on the behind-the-scenes footage captured by our all-rounder Dermot Reeve who had the foresight to bring along a little hand-held video recorder. In the age of camera phones, people take this kind of stuff for granted, but back then a camcorder was something totally new. Considering we spent so much of that trip puking up, on the toilet or getting hammered by India, Dermot did pretty well to get any usable footage, and yet there I am in a hotel gym with a fag on, while on several other occasions we're seen having a laugh against the odds in the dressing room.

Dermot's film says it all about how hard we worked not to disappear down a hole on that tour. Yes, we were stuck in hotels, but we'd have games of table tennis and pool, and just get to know each other in a way that might otherwise never have happened. Sitting on trains and funny old aeroplanes for months on end, with accompanying adventures, also created a closeness that maybe doesn't happen in other sports.

I get the appeal of being away for a shorter period, but now England's cricketers seem to play three tours a winter. They're back and forth, in and out of different places, different tournaments, different formats, different squads, all the time. There's pluses and downsides to everything but the itinerary for cricket now is bonkers. I'm not sure now you could have a night out even if you wanted one. If every day is either training or playing, where is that time to relax? To go and wander about the Victoria Falls? To have a look at the crocodiles? Go on safari? Simply to get a glimpse how normal people live?

Whereas modern tours are in and out,* we were almost ambassadors for our country. We'd meet civic dignitaries and travel around. There was an element of bringing cricket to the shires, so to speak. You'd find yourself in some remote old places, and the great thing was that everyone who lived there would down tools for the day and come down to the ground.

Those old tours went on so long they almost became a world within a world. It was like being in a story and waking up each day not quite knowing what was going to happen. We had those precious days, those endless laughs and japes, but now players just seem to have so much to do. If we're not careful we'll end up with a generation of burnt-out cricketers who forgot why it was they wanted to play the sport in the first place. A tour should always mean exactly what it says on the tin.

Oh, and one last thing.† While, like everyone, I might have struggled for wickets on that tour, my batting aver-

---

* I don't know why they don't just build a ground at ten international airports and have done.

† Always liked *Columbo*.

age of 28 was higher than Gooch, Stewart, Smith and Atherton, and included my Test top score of 22 not out. Why bat sponsors so rarely wanted a slice of me, I don't know. I mean what self-respecting bat manufacturer wouldn't want to be associated with a player of my calibre? No one got more widespread coverage for the label on the splice than me. As the last man out in whatever Test match we were losing, the image of me looking forlornly at my bat would be the photo used in all the papers to illustrate the parlous state of English cricket. I should have got more money than any of them.

I suppose what I'm trying to say is had I been pushed up the order, that series could well have been a very different story.*

* Even worse.

10

WHICH END?

In India, togetherness got us through another challenge – at any given point half the squad were nursing one illness or another. If you felt about 60 per cent OK, it was pretty good. At times, so bad were these runs* of illnesses that people who had merely travelled over to watch a couple of games found themselves in the England mix. When our scorer Clem Driver took to his sickbed, none other than Dermot Reeve's mother took over his pen. Had the Barmy Army been up and running, anyone who could hold a bat would have had a decent chance of featuring in the end-of-tour averages.

That's actually not as mad as it might sound. Players would literally disappear. Athers, Agatha Christie-esque, vanished for a week in India. The rest of us literally thought he'd gone off the tour. You'd be asking round, 'Has anyone seen Athers?' And the physio would pipe up, 'Well, yes, we're monitoring the situation.'

* No pun intended.

'The situation?' You'd start to worry that a benign presence, the evil dead, had started taking players in the middle of the night.

'Well, can you just tell me if he's going to be OK?'

A week later this grey husk of a man would appear at breakfast. Players would age 15 years in seven days. They'd hobble on to the coach and just sit there, perspiring.

Make no mistake, people would lose phenomenal amounts of weight through illness on tours. It wouldn't be 'til they passed you in the corridor that you realised who they were.

'Athers? Is that you? I thought it was the ghost of Denis Compton.'

These things happened a lot, especially back in the day. It didn't matter what country you were in, if you were going to some place up country where the water wasn't great, or just different to what your body was used to, people would be dropping like flies. It didn't just happen in India. It happened to me in Lancashire and parts of coastal Yorkshire. I used to lose loads of weight – and that's someone with not very much weight on there to begin with. My dad said he didn't recognise me when I came back from a couple of tours. Cricket fans waiting to greet us at Heathrow would be shocked as a series of wizened figures appeared. It was terrible. On occasions I was barely able to carry my duty free.

In places where a dodgy stomach was a bit more likely, some players would try to sort their own food. Alec

Stewart, for instance, had been known to source his own breasts* – and Jack Russell, famously, would live off Weetabix, soaked in cold milk for exactly 15 minutes. To this day, Jack's one of the few people with the blood group semi-skimmed.

Clearly, some of the guys worked very hard to avoid any type of stomach upset but I always felt it was a battle, no matter what provisions you made, that was virtually impossible to win. For quite long stretches you would end up surviving on chicken and rice. Later, I'd yearn for such a dish when I was staring at the hideous bleakness of raw ostrich anus on *I'm a Celebrity ... Get Me Out of Here!*.

At least in the privacy of your own hotel room you were shielded from the public humiliation of the on-pitch emergency. It didn't surprise me at all to hear that Joe Root had need to fashion a makeshift nappy while on tour in Pakistan. My TMS colleague Jonathan Agnew, meanwhile, tells a great story about the late Alf Gover, an England bowler of the Thirties and Forties who coached him in his early days. Alf was playing in India, opening the bowling, and, as the umpire announced 'Play!', set off on his long run. At that very moment he felt a terrible gripe and, rather than deliver the ball, hared straight on down the pitch, past the slips, over the outfield on the other side and into the dressing room. According to Aggers, Alf was short

* Chicken.

by six yards. The batsman was left standing there wondering what on earth was going on.

On the whole, a stomach upset was no laughing matter, adding another level to that other great touring issue – dehydration. Some of this was, admittedly, self-inflicted. Whereas today's players will rehydrate on isotonic sports drinks, replacing vital lost minerals, in the Eighties and Nineties, after playing in blistering heat, chances were, depending where you found yourself, you refuelled on either lager or rum. That's not to say there wasn't some key rehydration advice available. It's just you learnt from the senior players rather than a doctor. 'Have a couple of pints of water before bed,' they'd say, 'and you'll be fine.' It was like a batting net for drinking.

I took that advice on board – well, sometimes – but it never seemed to make much difference. You'd wake up and it would be stinking hot, no air-con and you'd have been baking away all night. If you'd been a cake, someone would have opened the door and found a mound of ashes. You'd then have to try to force a plate of scrambled eggs down to give you some energy for the day. At that point I did sometimes think, 'I wonder if this really is the right preparation for a Test match cricketer,' because I felt like death. But then slowly, throughout the day, I'd work my way through the unpleasantness, and then, by the evening, I'd be back out and about – if you're in Barbados, you're not going to stay in – and so the whole cycle would start again.

* * *

WHICH END?

On an England U-19 trip to St Lucia I got very bad sunstroke. We were staying at a hotel called the Green Parrot, tucked away up in the hills surrounded by vegetation. For me, a hotel called the Green Parrot was never going to indicate luxury, and I wasn't wrong. I'm not sure if the green parrot was the receptionist or what we had for dinner every night. What I do know is I was soon feeling green, if not like a parrot.

To be fair, this malady was nothing to do with the hotel. It came from my own lack of attention to the need for sun protection. This being an U-19 trip all we wanted to do was get a tan and look good for the beach. Sun cream and a hat? I really don't think so.

The result, predictably enough, was a very bad case of sunstroke. Me and another bloke were confined to a wing of the Green Parrot, if you see what I mean, while we recovered, tethered to a drip. This sort of nurse lady attended to us. She'd pop in and give us a few paracetamol every four hours but otherwise we were just left there, forgotten, groaning and feeling terrible. I later saw the film *Misery* with Kathy Bates and it brought back the most awful memories.

Eventually, we emerged with towels over our heads, mere shadows of the young men who'd been taken there days earlier. Sympathy was thin on the ground. The management weren't too happy we'd got ourselves into such a mess. Bob Willis, who was in charge of that trip, had warned us to wear protection and keep our hats on, but at that age we were wandering round clad in nothing but blissful ignorance and a pair of Speedos. Same with hydration. In the Caribbean, who's going to be drinking three litres of water every night when there's rum punch on tap?

What does happen is that slowly – in my case very slowly – you learn from your mistakes. As a young cricketer these kind of balls-ups end up logged in your memory bank. Occasionally you learn from other people's errors. For instance, after watching a few players wearing jewellery on the pitch, chains smashing them in the face as they went for a caught and bowled, and earlobes nearly being ripped off when diving for the ball, I realised that particular fashion statement wasn't for me.*

Point is, you learn how to look after yourself, what to do and what not to do. By the time your last tour comes round you just about know where you're at. With that point still some way off, drips would continue to be a feature of my career, to the extent where I really should have thought about incorporating one into my kit.

'Right, I'll just go through my checklist. Bat, pads, gloves – drip.'

I could have hung it up on my locker ready and waiting for the inevitable moment when I'd need medical attention. Fielding down at long leg? I'd have had one of those

---

* An urban myth also used to do the rounds about wedding rings – someone had gone for a low catch and as his hand hit the ground, the ring had caught in the turf and ripped half his finger off. It would have made a great clip for the 'What happened next?' segment on A Question of Sport.

hospital drips on little wheels, an extra-long line in case I needed to chase the ball.

I was hooked up again when England met Australia at Sydney in the early stages of the 1992 World Cup. Australia batted first and Beefy, fresh from a stint in pantomime, took four wickets as we bowled them out for 171. He then went out and smashed a half-century as we cruised to victory. I played in that game, a great triumph – which I listened to at Sydney Royal Infirmary. I'd not felt great before the match but had done OK and bowled their danger man Tom Moody out. Then, I'm not quite sure what happened. Back in the dressing room at the break between innings I just couldn't stop throwing up. Gooch gave his team talk to the echoes of me hurling my guts up in the toilet.

'Now, lads, we're in a strong position, let's be professional in the field and not throw it away.' HURRRPP!

I began to faint and was lain flat on a bench with my feet above my head. Sometimes when things like this happen, a kindly teammate will take advantage of your incapacity to shave your eyebrows off or draw a pair of glasses on your face with a marker pen. On this occasion, some blokes arrived and took me off by ambulance to the hospital where I was attached to my old pal. From here, England's number eleven listened to the run chase on the radio surrounded by people screaming in pain from burst appendixes and minor limb breaks. One of the greatest moments in England World Cup history – and I spent it on a drip.

One time I definitely should have been attached to a drip was a brief three days in Bangladesh when me and Andy Caddick flew out to Dhaka as part of a Rest of the World team playing a one-day game against an Asian XI. I've an idea Shane Warne was injured so they needed a left-arm spinner – hence the invite. It was a fairly relaxed affair. There was a practice day which no one took very seriously, then the game and then back to the airport. Perhaps unsurprisingly, my first five overs went for about ten each, but then I pulled it back with the wickets of Sachin Tendulkar and Sourav Ganguly. The heat, however, was oppressive, and by the time it came to my last over I was feeling very odd indeed. The colour – of which there wasn't much anyway – had drained from my face and I'd adopted a dull-eyed stare.

The Aussie Mark Waugh was captaining the Rest of the World. He came over for a chat. 'What's the matter, Tuffers? I don't think I've ever seen anyone look like that before.'

'I can see pink elephants,' I told him. 'Pink elephants floating around the sky.'

'Pink elephants, Tuffers? You sure?' The Aussie boys had always thought I was a bit unorthodox but this was something else.

'Yes, and there's little stars everywhere too. Can you see them, Mark?'

Mark couldn't. He advised I go off and get a bit of attention. I didn't really get what he was saying and so was half helped, half dragged from the field. I wobbled straight into the dressing room and spent the rest of the game sat under a cold shower. I'm pretty sure the only reason I didn't end up on a drip was that the flight was straight after the game. Faced with a hospital drip or British Airways Club Class I opted for the recuperative qualities of the latter.

The more I think about it, the more surreal that trip was. It felt like three days all rolled into one – no day, no night. Plane – jet lag – practice – game – pink elephants – cold shower – plane. It was like an out-of-body experience.

To be honest, there were many times I nearly fainted on the field. Inevitable, considering the intense heat of places like Sri Lanka, India and Australia. Think about it: you're stood roasting in direct sunlight, no shelter, for hour after hour. The difference between the temperature on an air-conditioned team bus and the oppressiveness outside could be monstrous. The second you disembarked you were willing the captain to win the toss and bat so then at least you could lie on the cool tiled floor of the dressing room. The alternative was to be out there at fine leg, the sun draining away your energy. More than once I had a woozy five minutes.

Finally, you'd head inside at lunch, desperate for an ice-cold drink, and what would be waiting – a hot cup of tea. Forget isotonic sports drinks, if you wanted something cool and recuperative, you stuck your head under the tap and hoped for the best.

Only later in my career did England start taking a designated doctor on tour to deal with, amongst other things, the day-to-day issues of playing in extreme climates. Otherwise, it was a bit like that famous theatre cry – 'Is there a doctor in the ground?' At which point, a frail gentleman in a monocle who stopped practising 30 years ago would appear. It didn't really matter who they were, I knew what they were going to say – 'Oh, yes, he's a little bit dehydrated – stick him on a drip.'

The worst part of the whole drip experience was having it put in. I've never been a fan of needles. I've tried to give it the big one and look like I'm not bothered, but those kind of things always get to me. The only thing I looked forward to when I needed a little operation here or there was the soothing effect of the pre-meds. I remember a nurse once coming to get me to wheel me down to theatre.

'Hang on,' I said, 'where's the pre-meds?'

'Oh, we don't do that anymore.'

'What? That's the only reason I've come!'

Cortisone injections, used to treat swollen or painful joints, were hugely unpleasant. These are particularly big needles and tend to go into parts where there's not much flesh. The first one I had, the bloke produced what can only be described as a sniper's gun case.

'Oh my God! What the hell is that?'

Next thing I knew, he'd clicked it open and was screwing this big needle together, like people do with snooker cues. My mouth had never been so dry. I needed hooking up to a drip just to get over the shock.

When they give you a cortisone injection, just as you're looking away in terror, they tend to deliver a get-out clause. 'This might not work,' they'll say, 'but you'll know when it does because it will hit the right spot.' That leaves you in a strange sort of hinterland. You don't know what's coming but you know if, and when, it does you're going to go through the roof. Part of you is hoping it doesn't work because the pain will be horrendous, and another part is hoping it does because you want to be able to play. It's a horrible thing to experience. I had about seven cortisone injections. I only found out the other day that you're only meant to have three or four in an entire career. Like most medication, the side effects, including long-term damage to the affected area, are something you really wish you'd not read about.

I was my own worst enemy when it came to the kind of niggling injuries that might attract the cortisone needle. I reckon I slept on more sofas and floors than your average professional sportsperson, often crashing at someone's place after a night out. Sleep on a sofa and get it wrong and you'd wake up, move and know immediately that you'd irritated an old injury or strain. You'd do a few exercises but you knew the issue wasn't going to disappear anytime soon, and so you'd be having another jab to get you through the game.

For me, a cortisone injection erased the fear not just of being unable to bowl, but also unable to throw. There's nothing worse as a professional cricketer than not being able to throw. I'd rather not be able to bat and bowl. It's just the humiliation and the embarrassment of plopping it in a few yards, the batsmen taking three on your arm, or someone having to run with you to the boundary to help you out. Even with a good arm you'd struggle on some grounds. Boundaries tend to have been brought in a bit now, but some, like the MCG, would be vast. It would take me a minute to reach the ball let alone throw it back in. If you were stood at midwicket at the MCG and the ball went square you'd have to put in a hundred-metre sprint to have any chance of stopping the four. After about 50 metres I'd be shattered, willing it to go over the rope. In many ways it was better to give it a little nudge into the advertising boards than the alternative – turning round, ball in hand, and seeing the wicket somewhere in the far distance. The crowd were typically unforgiving. The second you picked up the ball, they'd start a rising 'Whoooaaah!' as you wound up to throw it in – the 'skip of fear' as I call it. There'd then be a big cheer when it landed a third of the way back. From that distance, even the best throwers would have to double bounce it in. Well, that's what I like to tell myself!

I'm very glad never to have had any part of me snapped or manipulated back into place, like a dislocated thumb or shoulder. I saw it happen to the England all-rounder Adam Hollioake once. He had to have his shoulder put back in after landing awkwardly in the field. Adam's a tough, strong bloke but you could really see the pain he was in.

The physio did the deed back in the dressing room. No two ways about it, this was going to hurt, to the extent that Adam was actually given a bat to bite on,* like in an old film when they'd shove a stick in some poor devil's mouth before sawing his leg off with no anaesthetic. At that point there was a rush for the door. The rest of us were tripping over boots, bits of old kit, everything, in the stampede to get out of there.

I have dislocated fingers a couple of times – a hazard of fielding – but they're not so difficult to deal with. A worse feeling is getting your knee the wrong way round. This can happen occasionally when you're chasing a ball and don't notice a little incline. You put your foot down and your knee goes inside out like a flamingo's. It doesn't happen so much on a beautifully groomed ground like Lord's but on an outfield that's a little bit ropey it's a lot more common. You'd see someone chasing a ball and next thing you knew they'd gone down like there was a sniper in the crowd. It's a horrible feeling. Give me a 90-mile-an-hour ball in the bollocks any day of the week.

I would like to throw in one last particular malaise that affects cricket especially – superstition. I mention it in this section because it's as infectious as any disease known to man. Also, for many players, a cure has yet to be found.

* Somewhere out there is a bat with Adam Hollioake's teeth marks in it. If found, please forward to the MCC Museum.

The only time I succumbed to superstition was a short period when my routine extended to the number of fags I had to smoke before I went out on to the field. Over time I found this could be a difficult superstition to enforce. Arrive at a ground two hours before play and smoking ten B&H isn't that hard. Arrive half an hour before and you're sucking on three at once. In the end it seemed ridiculous to think that coughing my lungs up could make me play better on any given day and so I gave this particular bit of irrational buffoonery up.

Others, though, took their superstitions very seriously. Take Angus Fraser. At lunchtime, Gus would always have two cheese rolls. He'd want them ready and waiting because that 40-minute break rushes by in half the time. Routine soon turns to superstition. Wickets fall after lunch and suddenly it's not because of Gus's talent and skill, an amazing piece of fielding or a bad decision by the batsman, it's because those cheese rolls were where they should have been, when they should have been. Mind you, compared to South African opener Neil McKenzie, a couple of cheese rolls sat waiting, possibly facing magnetic north, is barely worth mentioning – McKenzie used to insist that all the seats in the dressing-room toilets were up. Presumably then, and only then, would he be flushed with confidence.

Superstition certainly does strange things to people. A couple of players would insist on – how shall I put this? – finding a little relief before they went out to bat. It became a bit of a thing with them to the extent they'd chalk off grounds where they'd done it, a bit like those people who feel inclined to visit all 92 league football clubs.

Even Athers, perhaps the most sensible man in cricket, a person who, had he not taken up the game, would surely now be delivering the Royal Institution Christmas Lectures, or at the very least be something high up at the Large Hadron Collider, had his peccadilloes. Athers always needed to be first on the pitch when batting. Unfortunately, when Marcus Trescothick became his England opening partner that was his superstition too. He was walking down the steps at Old Trafford to make his debut against West Indies when suddenly Athers came bombing past and knocked him sideways.

The best-known, and surely most mindless, superstition in cricket is staying in one place during a run chase. Just that scenario occurred when Dominic Cork and John Crawley were chasing an unlikely target of 300-plus in the third Test against New Zealand at Christchurch in 1997. Thankfully, on that occasion I'd chosen a good position, watching the game from a very comfortable sofa underneath the stand. Me, Darren Gough and Ronnie Irani were all down there while the rest of the boys were upstairs on the viewing gallery. We'd pop our heads up from time to time and they'd all go mad.

'**** off! Go and lie back down on that sofa.'

'Oh right – well, if you insist.'

Such scenarios weren't uncommon. If anyone left their position and a batsman got out, there would be hell to pay, which I always found a bit unfair. Especially since it was always me.

'What am I meant to do – sit there and wet myself?'

Then again, most things have been made my fault down the years – the weather, the state of the pitch, the umpires.

'Oi, Phil! If you hadn't worn your socks inside out we'd have got a good hotel.'

'What? It's nothing to do with me!'

It was as if I was thought of as a sorcerer, someone who had power over all things. I would like it confirmed for the record here and now that I have never been a character in *The Lord of the Rings*.

Superstition really can make dressing-room life very awkward. 'Don't touch his gloves, he doesn't like it.' 'Don't say good luck to him, he thinks it's bad luck.' 'Don't stem the bleeding from your broken nose – if the flow stops he's bound to get out.'

'Er, do you think someone could put a definitive list of superstitions on the dressing-room wall, then I could stop putting my foot in it?'

'No chance, Phil. Haven't you heard? That new bloke – he thinks lists are unlucky.'

I thought I might have escaped suspicion of being a practitioner of dark arts when I joined *TMS*, but no. There exists the invisible demon that is the commentator's curse. Over after over I've resisted lavishing praise on batsmen, only finally to give in.

'That's a fantastic shot. His feet are moving beautifully, his hands are in the right position, he looks in complete control. He's on for a big score here.' Two balls later the middle pole is out of the ground. And then the messages start.

'Tuffers! For Christ's sake, what were you thinking? You made that happen.'

To which I always reply, 'How can what I say in a commentary box possibly influence what happens on the pitch?'

I've tried to prove it. An innings by Rory Burns for England is a great example. Someone in the box mentioned the commentator's curse, to which I piped up, 'Look, there's no such thing. I do not have the power. None of us have the power. This is absolutely ridiculous. We cannot dictate the game from up here. I'll show you.

'Burns,' I predicted on air, 'is playing really beautifully. I fully expect him to go on and get a hundred.

'There you go,' I turned smugly to my fellow broadcast-ers. 'I assure you nothing will happen.'

Next thing I knew his middle stump had been uprooted. A previously unblemished innings lay in tatters. Initially there was stunned silence – and then everyone slaughtered me. I don't know why they don't drop 'Soul Limbo' as the *TMS* theme and replace it with the 'Doo-doo-doo-doo. Doo-doo-doo-doo' from *The Twilight Zone*.

I tried it again during the home Ashes of 2019 when Steve Smith was immovable. At Old Trafford I was throw-ing out commentators' curses left, right and centre. On that occasion, the witchcraft very definitely didn't work. He got 211. My guess is there's an unwritten edict that the commentator's curse only works on your own team. You can't put spells on the opposition because that would be unfair.

Just in case, though, before England's next Ashes tour, I'm checking out courses in wizardry at the University of Surrey.

11

AND HERE'S YOUR ROOM, SIR

Genuinely, I don't think there's any other sport in which participants are guaranteed to spend so much time in hotel rooms feeling deathly. That meant it became a significant factor in the eagerness to ensure you got the best room possible.

While the modern England cricketer has their every whim catered for, it was slightly different when I toured. You'd have six-foot-six bowlers crammed into a bed more befitting Ronnie Corbett. They'd come down to breakfast hunched like crabs, barely able to move. In search of a good night's sleep, one or two players might even take their own pillows on tour, although I never bothered with any of that. I was lucky to take a bat.

My modus operandi was to always try to be at the front of the queue on arrival at reception. Bearing in mind you were just one of a reasonably sized touring party – players, staff, and what have you – chances were there'd be rooms of varying standard. The trick was to get a key as quick as you possibly could and whip up quickly to your room. If it was a balcony room facing the sea, fine. If it was a shoe-box facing the car park, you'd nip straight back down and start bartering either with the receptionist or the other boys – 'Come on, mate, since when have you been bothered about a balcony? You're scared of heights!' Thankfully, as a smoker I did generally get assigned a balcony room. A teetotal vegetarian who worshipped his body, meanwhile, would be sharing a linen cupboard with three ironing boards on the bottom floor.

Generally speaking, however, you got what you were given and that was the end of it. That meant there was a mix of anticipation and dread every time you opened the door. It was always either, 'Oh, lovely! I'll have a slice of this!' or 'Oh come on! You've got to be joking!' If it was bad news, your heart would sink. Gingerly, you'd push open the toilet door, hoping against hope it wasn't two footpads and a hole. Not only would you be getting battered in the cricket but you couldn't even have a leisurely sit-down.

In India especially it was the ceiling fans that terrified me. They always seemed to have a terrific wobble going on. I never particularly wanted to appear on the scorecard as 'Phil Tufnell – retired decapitated – 0.' On another tour, one of the boys got bedbugs. He woke up in the morning virtually eaten alive. There are ways of losing a bit of weight and that's not one of them.

Out in the Caribbean, a lot of the hotel rooms had hurricane warnings on the wall. Again, a bit of a shock. It's just not something you find in a B&B in Broadstairs, a plan of action should the roof come off in the night. Even more concerning were the hotels with a hook concreted into the bedroom wall, the advice being that, in the event of disaster, should the fire escape be unreachable, you should tie the bedsheets together, perhaps add your dressing-room cord and the bathmat, attach them to the hook and shin down two dozen floors. I don't know why they didn't go the whole hog and provide a bungee cord.*

Luckily, for the England teams I played in, the team room was always a great place, which meant the necessity to spend a lot of time in a dodgy hotel bedroom wasn't necessarily there. Sometimes you're in a place where going out isn't advisable, or maybe you've blown your money for that week, and so the team room provides an alternative way to have a chat and a bit of a laugh. Certainly, in Australia in 1990/91 it was very much that way. With England sponsored by Tetley and the Aussies by Castlemaine XXXX – which found its way to us as well† – it was like having your own bar on tap. For those who liked something a little more refined, Lamby would get on the phone to one of his wine contacts and barely would he have put the receiver down than several cases of the finest reds and whites would be stacked up in the corner.

---

* Storm and flood warnings were everywhere in the Caribbean. What they didn't have was what to do if you're 75 for eight against the West Indies. That really would have been very helpful advice.

† At least the sponsors were nice to us.

Nowadays, bored players will sit around and play video games for hours. We didn't have any of that. We'd get excited if the hotel had KerPlunk. Remarkable to think in this time of WhatsApp and text messages, but we actually used to talk to one another, even if, by midnight, none of it made the slightest sense.

A bunch of people drinking in a hotel has been known to get out of hand, but in all honesty this was hardly rock 'n' roll excess. At no point was a Rolls-Royce driven into a swimming pool. At the very most a golf trolley might have been upended. I did once throw a television out of a hotel window, which does, admittedly, put me in a club more generally occupied by the rock-star community, but this was during the aforementioned mental breakdown in Perth. Also, it was only a portable. And I opened the window first and had a good look out for anybody down below. It's hardly Keith Moon is it?

If anything, the most memorable rock 'n' roll hotel moment I witnessed came after I'd retired from the game. It wasn't long after I'd come out of the jungle the first time and was co-hosting a show called *Simply the Best* with Kirsty Gallacher, which entailed filming a big arena show, basically *It's a Knockout* meets *Gladiators*, in the Jersey capital, St Helier, on alternate days for a month. The fact we filmed every other day meant that after a recording the crew would get back to the hotel, pile in the bar and get smashed without worrying about an early start. I get that it wasn't strictly necessary to adhere to that regime, but in some ways that show echoed my cricket career.

Aside from the jungle, *Simply the Best* was my first big venture into primetime TV as a presenter. An entire show, with all the investment and infrastructure that goes with it, had been built and I wanted to do my best by it. That meant, once each show was wrapped, the adrenalin coursing through the veins was something unreal. It sounds daft for a TV show, but there was definitely a euphoric kind of high. Switching off, having a cup of tea and retiring for the night was never going to happen. Like sport, everyone piles down the pub or into the bar and feeds off the excitement that together you've created. You have to enjoy your success because otherwise your body can't shut off. It needs a release.

Anyway, in Jersey, the hotel management were rubbing their hands with glee at the prospect of some truly rip-roaring bar takings, but as time went on they wearied of our presence. In all honesty, those late-night drinks did lead occasionally to a little mischief – sliding down bannisters, running around corridors in your underpants, that kind of thing. I expect it's quite similar to what happens at the annual Women's Institute get-together.

As if the management weren't losing enough hair, the situation wasn't helped when an English professional rugby team came across to play a benefit match and booked into the same venue. That particular night was absolute carnage and by the next morning the bar pretty much looked like it had been through an earthquake. It also happened to be the first time I met my future *A Question of Sport* counterpart Matt Dawson.

215

It was towards the end of this little Channel Islands adventure that a baby grand piano somehow managed to make its way down a flight of stairs. The noise was unbelievable. Like the one in the famous Laurel and Hardy short *The Music Box*, only louder. Forget Jersey, I reckon it woke people in Guernsey 27 miles away.

Next day, the inquest started. There were knocks on doors, people being quizzed in the lobby. I had – for some reason – been identified as a suspect and my whereabouts had become of great interest to the hotel management. The only surprise was that sniffer dogs weren't handed one of my socks and told to get on the trail. I spent about a week sleeping on the floor in different people's rooms as the hotel hierarchy tried to find me. It did occur to me that not a lot had changed since my touring days with England.

Eventually, filming came to an end and I was able to escape unnoticed back to the mainland. Whether this incident remains in the 'Unsolved' file of the Jersey Hoteliers' Association I don't know. I will, however, say here and now that, just as then, I have no clear memory of exactly what happened that night. As far as I'm concerned, that piano went down those stairs accidentally. Potentially it was the work of a poltergeist. Whatever the cause, *Simply the Best* never got a second season.

I'd like to point out that I'm now the model hotel guest. No more pianos have accidentally careered down staircases and I always leave the Corby trouser press intact. Very occasionally nowadays it's actually me doing the complaining. Take this one hotel me and Dawn stayed at in Jamaica. We'd found what looked a great place online and pushed the boat out for a real treat. Sometimes, however, the advert just doesn't quite encapsulate the reality.

We checked in late at night and immediately thought the place didn't look quite like how we thought it would. Never mind, it was dark. It might look completely different in the morning. We found our room and crawled into bed. It was then that Dawn piped up – 'Phil, there's something funny at the bottom of the bed!' I had a feel round with my foot and she was right, there was definitely something there that shouldn't be. I reached down and felt a small bundle. Pulling it out, we both stared at this rolled-up thong. You didn't need to be Miss Marple to conclude what had been going on where we were now lying. We called up reception and they insisted fresh sheets had gone on that day. Fresh sheets or not, there was someone else's pants in our bed and so we asked to be moved.

The new room was equally interesting, its main feature being a corrugated iron roof. It then started raining. The result was like being inside an ocean-going liner in a shipyard at the riveting stage. No way were we going to get any sleep. We almost wished we'd stayed in the knicker room. To make matters worse, about 4 a.m. an endless torrent of lorries started using the road outside at a decibel level not generally heard outside the average F1 circuit.

By the time it got light we hadn't slept a wink but thought maybe we'd just been a bit unlucky on that first night and things would improve. We made it down to breakfast – all very nice – and then had a lounge by the pool. Things were definitely looking up. It was then that the roar of jet engines began. Thirty seconds later a 747 took off from what appeared to be a runway directly behind the hotel wall. The plane was so low I could distinctly see the faces of the people inside. They were waving at us. I think one of them, possibly a previous guest, was gesticulating with their thumb as if to say, 'Get the hell out of there!'

Again I thought I'd give the place the benefit of the doubt – 'Never mind, Dawn, maybe these planes are only every couple of hours. That's not so bad.' No such luck. Twenty minutes later another jumbo came into land. As it screeched overhead, landing gear down, I swear it created a wave on the swimming pool. That was it then – they were every ten minutes. The thing that made me laugh through my tears was that no one else around that pool seemed in the least bit bothered. They didn't even look up. Not me. I'd come out to Jamaica for a welcome bit of peace and quiet. The corrugated roof, lorries and low-flying aircraft had put paid to that. We left that evening. I've never been one for taking towels and robes with me, but in a small act of revenge I did use all the free body lotion and shampoo. For the rest of the holiday, every time I went in the pool my hair would involuntarily lather up.

Perhaps the most unnerving hotel experience I ever had was at Georgetown, Guyana. Touring with England, I discovered that, with political discontent raging, bombs and grenades had previously been found where we were meant to be staying. As you can see, I survived to tell the tale, although explosives did become a bit of a theme in Guyana. On that same trip we had to temporarily evacuate the dressing room after the ground received a bomb threat. As if dealing with the West Indies quicks wasn't bad enough.

It did feel like in a lot of places we toured there was an underlying element of threat. I don't know whether it had anything to do with me – 'Tufnell's arrived – let's riot!' – but there was always something going on, always a good chance of being called into a room and have an officious bloke in a pink shirt with greased-back grey hair attempt to put our minds at rest or, more likely, relay the message from Lord's that if we didn't like being trapped in the middle of civil unrest, they'd soon find someone else. We didn't really have a choice. This was before the era of central contracts. You did what people said or you lost your winter money and couldn't pay the mortgage next year. To be fair, it wasn't like we were short of security – we had a scorer, a physio and, for a short period, a cleric. It seemed to me that the only place you could guarantee a smooth ride as an England cricketer was New Zealand. Even in Australia you'd hear about possible protests from republicans or some kind of kangaroo uprising.

A lot of issues that arise on England cricket tours are of course to do with history and empire. But you never turn on the telly and hear that the England netball team has been blockaded in their hotel. When was the last time the hockey team was escorted to a ground by outriders with machine guns? By the time we turned up at some venues we'd be nervous wrecks. And then even when the game started there was the ever-present threat of pitch invasions or someone throwing a Pot Noodle at the back of your head. Say what you like, but I've never seen that in squash.

As a cricketer, even if you never went near a trouble spot you were still sure to spend thousands upon thousands of hours in hotel rooms. I realised after a while it was always worth acquainting yourself with the layout of a room before you went out for the evening. That way you might have a chance of finding the bathroom in the middle of the night rather than wake in the morning to find your room-mate staring up at the ceiling, wondering how the next floor up had leaked into the wardrobe. Possibly it's a little late now, but apologies to those affected.

Some hotels, however, are so utterly illogical that no amount of homework can ever make a difference. The Trinidad Hilton was a case in point. The first time I stayed there I thought I'd stumbled on to the set of *Thunderbirds*. Set into the side of a cliff, I half-expected the palm trees to separate and Virgil to jet off on an emergency mission. Bizarrely, reception was on the top floor. The higher the number the floor you wanted, the more levels down you went. Anyone thinking a twelfth-floor room would guarantee a fantastic view of the surrounding bay would in fact discover they'd booked a direct view of the service gate.

This fascination with things being the wrong way round extended to the bar. No joke, instead of being something you lean on, the bar at the Trinidad Hilton was sunk three feet into the floor. It was the only bar I ever went to where you were on your knees at the start of the night.

The main joy of the Hilton was that it wasn't the dressing room at the island's Queen's Park Oval cricket ground where there was barely room to swing a jockstrap. Indeed, if you weren't careful, you'd be sat there for 20 minutes before you realised you had someone else's on. It reached the stage where we had to sling out anyone who wasn't actually playing. It really could be quite dangerous when someone got out. If they were a bat-thrower, you just had to duck and hope for the best.

Meanwhile, at all times, socks and underpants would be whizzing round the overhead fan. Think about it, you've got 11 blokes, all with five sets of trousers, shirts, socks, vests, the lot, to get them through the Test. That amount of gear soon mounts up. It was like the men's department of Primark in there, or, in Alec Stewart's case, C&A.

I was actually pretty tidy compared to most of the boys. Thankfully, unless you really are *Stig of the Dump*, there is always someone worse than you in any cricket environment. Athers, for instance, literally didn't have a sense of smell and so would quite happily stick the same shirt on for five days. After 72 hours the rest of us could take no more. 'Come on, Athers, sort it out!' It was a question of what walked out the door first, us or the shirt.

If there was one player who the Queen's Park Oval really wasn't designed for it was – yep! – Jack Russell, another who had never come to terms with the concept of tidiness. Wicket-keeping glove inners were often the worst offenders in terms of stench and his would be strewn everywhere. On top of that, as the game went on, Jack's surrounds would increasingly resemble an old man's workshop. He'd endlessly be cutting bits off (or adding bits on) to his gloves and shaving bits off bats. There'd be tins of glue, sandpaper, even Stanley knives. Jack didn't need a dressing room so much as a shed. I saw my kit as nothing more than functional but his was like an extension of both body and character. His batting gloves really were something to behold. I wasn't picked for the infamous Queen's Park Oval match when West Indies bundled us out for 46 in just 19 overs, but like everyone I was in shock as the wickets kept tumbling, even more so when Jack was hit by Curtly Ambrose and his entire hand was torn off. At least that's what it looked like. In fact his glove had disintegrated on impact. Good job for the next bloke in really. Last thing you want is to take guard next to a teammate's dismembered appendage.

On the subject of dismemberments, at another Caribbean hotel we shared our accommodation with the cast of *Jaws*. They actually had miniature sharks in pools dotted around the complex. You'd be walking across to the restaurant for breakfast and one would pop its head out and have a little stare. After falling down a hole earlier in the trip, it worried me considerably that I might slip and plunge into one of these pools after a couple of glasses of wine. I did make this point to a waiter.

'Not to worry,' he said, 'we've taken all their teeth out.'

'Fine,' I said, 'but I'm still not too keen on being gummed.'

That was slightly hypocritical of me as in New Zealand on a previous trip I'd been sea fishing with our paceman Alan Mullally when he'd caught a shark. We'd taken the beast back to the hotel, accessed Athers' empty room, and put it in his bed.* To be fair, Athers took the jape in good stead. I suspect, however, even to this day, there are still guests wondering why room 6G smells like a tuna-canning factory.

* Well, as a cricketer on tour you have to seize your chance. Opportunities to put sharks in the captain's bed are few and far between. Play against Essex at Southend, for instance, and it's unlikely you'll encounter a Great White in the shallows – 'We're going to need a bigger pedalo.'

12

BACK IN THE JUNGLE

Sometimes you'd do anything for a night in even the most basic hotel. It was this exact thought that crossed my mind as I watched holistic nutritionist Gillian McKeith empty the contents of her knickers on to a log. It wasn't quite how I'd envisaged spending the day, but there you go.

I'd been to South Africa on my last England tour, and, if I'm honest, had found it a bit weird. There remained a hangover from apartheid and the visible sign of that segregation still existed in the form of the townships, such as Cape Flats in Cape Town, we'd pass on the way to the grounds. The fact that on one side of the road you had so much hardship and on the other was a beautiful modern city didn't sit well with me.

As an England cricketer of course, we only saw the good life, and if you know where to go in South Africa there are some amazing places, but the inequality I witnessed did tarnish my initial opinion.

Then there was the crime. In South Africa, we had a security detail. Or a bloke with a gun as it's otherwise

225

known. In the city of East London, our hotel was on a patch of wasteland (maybe not how it was described in the brochure) with a load of shops somewhere in the middle distance. One night a couple of us fancied a bit of KFC and were just about to head over there when the bloke with the gun appeared. He was about seven-foot tall and six-foot wide so was hard to miss. I believe he'd had a previous job as a wall.

'No, you mustn't go over there on your own,' he told us. 'It's not safe. You stay here and I'll go.' This seemed very reasonable of him. And so, armed not just with his weapon but an order for a party bucket and some hot wings, off he went while we sat in the hotel lobby and waited. And waited. About two hours had passed when out of the gloom we saw a dishevelled figure staggering towards the hotel. As he got nearer, we could see blood coming from his nose. Naturally, we were concerned – we couldn't see the KFC.

He pushed against the revolving door and stumbled into the lobby.

'What happened?' we asked.

'I got mugged,' he said. 'They stole my gun.'

There was 30 seconds of awkward silence.

'So does that mean we've got to get the Kentucky?'

* * *

I'd also been out to cover the 2003 World Cup in South Africa with TMS. I was reminded of that trip when I travelled round New Zealand with Brendon McCullum for *This Could Go Anywhere*. Baz was a great travel companion with a real knowledge of his home country. Again and again he said to me that the key to seeing the real New Zealand is to get out of the cities. Only then, he'd tell me, do you get a feeling for the real essence of the place – its heart and soul. And South Africa was exactly the same. You don't come to understand a country by wandering round its shopping malls or spending endless nights at the cinema. You have to get out of that urban environment and really experience it. In South Africa that means the most immensely beautiful landscapes, dramatic mountain regions, tumbling waterfalls and rivers, and incredible wildlife.

In 2023, came an unexpected offer to see a bit more of all that. Did I want to go on a 'legends' version of *I'm a Celebrity*? Except instead of the Aussie jungle, where I'd been crowned king in 2003, we'd be based in South Africa's Kruger National Park. The name rang a bell, and then I remembered. On that England tour I'd done a little bit of safari with my fellow spinner Graeme Swann. While I'd dressed reasonably sensibly, Swanny had turned up in the shirt of his favourite football team, Newcastle United. It was only when every lion in a three-mile vicinity started making a beeline for our 4×4 that we realised his choice of top might have been a mistake. Newcastle famously play in black-and-white stripes. Your average lion knows nothing about football, but it does know a lot about zebras. Everyone dreams of seeing a lion close up – just not that close up! Swanny was lucky his England career wasn't ended before it had barely begun.

With this in mind, I had a little think about ITV's offer. In the Australian camp we'd seen snakes, spiders and lizards. In Kruger there's leopards, cheetahs, lions, rhinos, hippos, buffalos and African wild dogs.* I made a mental note to check if any of the trials involved big cats before I signed up. Being entombed with a thousand cockroaches is one thing, spending ten minutes in a cave with a leopard entirely another. I was assured that nothing with incisors would be involved in the show – Janet Street-Porter hadn't been invited back – and so was happy to go with it. The original *I'm a Celebrity* had been an incredible experience, fun and maggots all the way, and if this new version was anything like that I was sure I'd be in for a treat. At the very least a mashed worm sundae.

The South Africa series would take place over two weeks, with another week of Covid quarantine at the start. Thankfully, Dawn came with me for that first week and then stayed while I went into the camp. We flew out to Johannesburg and then boarded a little plane, which I'm never too fond of,† towards Kruger. It was all a little bit nerve-racking, especially since I couldn't even anaesthetise

---

* Essentially, anything that can eat you is there.

† If you're going to make a plane at least make it something that will survive an impact with a pigeon.

my anxiety. The in-flight service comprised a glass of water and a bag of crisps. It made Ryanair look like Qatar Airways.

Anyway, we plopped down in what seemed to be an old army base. It was red hot, right in the middle of the bush. The sort of place you could fry an egg on the pavement, if there'd been a pavement – or an egg. It really was quite a primitive set-up. The baggage pick-up consisted of a bloke slamming your stuff on a table. I felt the chances of picking up some Christian Dior after-shave in the duty free was pretty slim.

No sooner had we got our bearings than another chap in full ranger gear turned up, ushered us into the back of a Land Rover, and off we went. Straight away we saw a giraffe out for a stroll, which in itself was very exciting, and then we turned into an enclosure full of huts, the sort of thing you might get in a high-end garden centre, giving it an admiring glance as you head across to the compost bags.

We'd be here, alone, for a week and, to satisfy the quarantine restrictions, wouldn't be allowed out of our own designated area. Food and refreshments would be dropped at the door. I suspected the other contestants must have been there too but there was sufficient distance between each hut that it was impossible to see who they were.

It was very nicely done – with a little pool and everything – but also a bit basic for a week's stay. Immediately we noticed a high concentration of bugs, which aren't my favourite holiday companions.* I was just flicking some weird-looking insect off the end of my nose when the ranger arrived to give us a few pointers.

'Shake out your shoes before you put them on,' he advised. 'And if you see a leopard don't approach it.' The first part was good advice. When it comes to leopards, however, I have to say my first instinct, even as a cat-lover, would never have been to tickle it behind the ear.

Anyway, off he went and so we thought we'd get into the swing of things by having a relax in the pool. We were in for a shock. There were so many creepy-crawlies having a leisurely dip we could hardly get in there. Including a bloody great scorpion!

I phoned up the ranger and over he came. 'Oh,' he said, 'don't worry about that. That's not a scorpion.' Now I'm not daft. I know what a scorpion looks like. It's got a bendy tail and looks very angry all the time.

'Mate,' I said, 'don't try to tell me that's not a scorpion. That's the most scorpion-like scorpion I think I've ever seen.'

He kept insisting it wasn't. I kept saying it was. I reminded him that he'd actually warned us about scorpions beforehand. Eventually, he scooped it up. I assumed we'd be reunited in a Bush Tucker Trial.

Thing was, there was no avoiding this kind of stuff. No sooner had we got in the pool than some other big horri-

---

* No one ticks the box for cockroaches when booking a room.

ble thing rocked up.* There was just stuff everywhere. First time I went to the toilet, there was a frog in there. He stayed for the duration. You'd give the pan a flush and think that must have done for him but then you'd return two hours later and he'd be back. I mean, fair play to him but surely there must be better places, with better views, to live. At night, meanwhile, there was a light on by the door to keep the leopard away, the downside being the sheer bodyweight of moths it attracted. I could barely see the end of my fag. The alternative was to go down a bit nearer the road but then the hippos or the crocs might have a slice of you. The place was in the middle of the bush. We were in their home. They weren't in ours.

In the morning we'd wake to the sight of little warthogs snuffling about by the pool, and some incredible-looking deer with big horns. There'd be monkeys running all over the roof. I'm no expert but they seemed permanently to be having it away with one another. At one point, me and Dawn were lying on our sunbeds and a big male appeared in a tree up above. All I can say is that it appeared to have taken a very big shine to Dawn. I'm not sure if she was flattered or not.

What with rogue scorpions and amorous baboons, when the time came for me to go into camp it felt like quite a lot had happened already. It was emotional saying goodbye to Dawn. They say absence makes the heart grow

---

* Note to the BBC: I'm always available for expert narration of nature documentaries.

fonder, but I don't really see it like that. If I'm going away anywhere, I'd rather be doing it with Dawn than without her, and vice-versa. No matter the newness and excitement of whatever I'm doing, I'll always be worrying if everyone's all right back home. Despite all the bugs and what have you, we'd had a really lovely week, just the two of us, sat around reading and chatting, looking up to see a giraffe sticking its head over the fence. For two people from London it was quite an amazing thing and I couldn't help wishing it could go on longer.

Anyway, a jeep with blacked-out windows turned up and that was that. The last thing I said to Dawn was, 'Watch out for the leopard.' She's good at looking after herself but I could see even she was putting a bit of a brave face on it. I mean, it was very nice there, but being spied on by a flange of amorous monkeys and knowing there's a big cat wandering around is bound to create at least a degree of nervousness. Thankfully, once the quarantine was up she could go for a bit of food with the other partners and families, but even so she did admit that lying awake at night listening to all these screeches and howls was a little bit blood-curdling. One time she tried to soothe the anxiety with a chocolate brownie. She bit into it and straight away hit something crunchy. She thought it was a pecan nut only to find on further inspection it was a cockroach. She still can't look at a chocolate brownie now.

Eventually, the car reached an opening with three helicopters. Me and two other contestants, javelin champion Fatima Whitbread and *Coronation Street* actor Helen

Flanagan, were in one and the rest in the others. At this stage I still didn't know who the other celebrities were going to be, although like everyone I'd seen the rumours in the papers. My only clue had been a distant hut where occasionally I'd spotted a huge man pumping massive weights. There were weights at our hut too. I'd done a few kilogrammes to keep myself ticking over. The chap in the distance was lifting the whole lot. I felt like a little bloke on one of those old seaside postcards, having sand kicked in his face by some be-muscled oaf. If he was my opposition in any of the challenges, I'd had it. Once in camp, I reasoned this giant must have been the street dancer Jordan Banjo, who not only was a big bloke but about as ripped as they come.

The helicopters transported us to a huge escarpment, like the Grand Canyon, swooping in near the sides. I found that mildly unnerving. 'Look out!' I kept telling the driver. 'You're too close!'

'Mr Tufnell,' he replied, 'I can reassure you I'm a very competent pilot.'

That changed nothing from my point of view. 'There's a rock on my side! Watch out!'

All three helicopters then peeled away and began to fly in formation to create a great shot for the cameras. I looked sideways and the blades were virtually touching. It felt like one good gust and we'd had it. The only camera shot I was envisaging was the one of us lying in a heap of metal on the valley floor. I don't like helicopters. I don't like flying close to rocks. And I don't like flying close to other aircraft. Forget the bugs and all that stuff, I was a nervous wreck before we'd even landed.

Eventually, we touched down near the escarpment, by which time I was feeling a level of nausea matched only by my first appearance on the show when I had to swallow a witchetty grub.*

Straight away we were into a trial. It entailed being winched out to four giant balls hanging above a 500-foot drop, the idea being that you jumped from one to the other and then made a leap for a star which would secure a meal for camp. Fatima's a no-nonsense kind of person and was up for going first, no bother. 'Well, if you insist,' I said. It would have been rude of me, after all, to stand in the way of someone who really wanted to do something.

Off she went in the harness while me and Helen shouted encouragement from the side. 'Go on, Fatima! You can do it, Fatima! Great stuff, Fatima!' Well, she was out there for about an hour and a half. I mean, you can't encourage for an hour and a half. By the end it was more like, 'How's it going, Fatima? Are you nearly done? You do know what time it goes dark?' To be fair, she was 61 at the time, which really is no age to be hurling yourself around on giant swinging balls. Most 61-year-olds I know are happy with a pub lunch and a copy of *The People's Friend*.†

---

* For some reason still not available in most high-street delicatessens.

† You and Your Teeth is also popular with this age group.

A deeply nervous Helen was next. I was doing my best to cajole her. 'Look, Helen, it would be good if you could at least have a try. That is why we're here.' I was talking to her for what felt like ages. 'Think how proud all your family at home will be.' All this kind of stuff. I think I'd have qualified for some sort of counselling degree by the end.

With Helen adamant she wasn't doing it, I set out across the balls myself. I'm not big on heights but they do make sure you're well tied on, and if the worst did happen there was every chance my fall would be broken by a hippo. I was quite getting into the whole leaping from ball-to-ball thing when I got my timing wrong on the third one, face-planted it and went tumbling towards the ravine floor. Why on earth didn't I stay in England and do *Celebrity Mastermind*?

We then had an hour's walk into camp. While the other contestants were great, I was keen to introduce myself to my bed, only to find all that was left for me was a hammock. My heart sank. I couldn't be sleeping in a hammock. I've got a bad back. Being a left-arm spinner for 20 years isn't good for you. There's Jenga towers stronger than my vertebrae. I have to sleep on my side, and that position just isn't hammock-compatible. I tried, and every time I fell out the side. I didn't sleep a wink and by the morning had stiffened into a human horseshoe. I was walking about in the manner of that bloke from Notre

Dame, and wasn't the only one. Even the bed-dwellers were in trouble. Janice Dickinson, the American model, was screaming for her meds, while Shaun Ryder, the Happy Mondays singer, got up and immediately dislocated his hip. It was only because he could do a half decent Shakin' Stevens impression that he managed to snap it back in. This wasn't I'm a Celebrity, it was a jungle care home. I was half expecting a singer to come in and start doing 'The White Cliffs of Dover'.

I couldn't do the hammock again and so slept the next couple of nights on a log before *Made in Chelsea* star Georgia Toffolo saw my anguish and offered me her bed for a night. I was very grateful. I'd been waiting for a couple of days for one of the more youthful contestants to do so. Clearly, that whole thing of young people making way for older people, such as on the bus, has all gone. Thankfully, with me on painkillers and wondering if I was going to last the course, the show did finally give me a bed of my own.

Even then, sleep could be restless. Some of the noises you'd hear in the middle of night were astonishing. You'd just be dropping off, something would emit an almighty squeal, and you'd nearly fall out of your bed. I'm talking really big shouts, the sort of noise you might hear at a city-centre taxi rank at 1 a.m. In the day you'd look into the trees and there'd be things with horns running around, stuff with big hairy faces, snakes nipping about. When you went for a little stroll you'd see baboons, but they never came into camp. Either the fire kept them away or the lack of deodorant. Coming from Surrey, where a vole is considered exotic, it really did come as a bit of a shock. It was particularly disturbing to find that vultures were watching us in our sleep. One night we were woken by this terrific screeching and in the morning Helen informed us that she'd seen them in the trees. There's something quite gruesome about being watched by scavengers in the night. I couldn't help thinking of those old cartoons where vultures would be pictured with napkins tucked under their chins, holding knives and forks while waiting for some poor unfortunate to breathe their last.

Then again, sleeping in a wood is going to be a little bit strange wherever you do it. It's not something I've gone out of my way to do in life.* Maybe that was why I'd generally be last to bed. I'd have a fag, a poke around with the fire, and a little mull over what had happened in the day, things people had said, maybe what I was missing about the outside – a glass of wine and a flapjack, that kind of thing.

The oddest thing that happened in the night involved Janice. In her late 60s, she was a little unstable, not made any better by the fact that, like all of us, she was clunking round in these big boots. For contestants of a certain age, me included, going for a wee in the night was a regular thing. The path to the dunny was dark but there were lights to show us the way. This particular night I nipped

* I've watched a few horror films and woods do seem to be a common place of sacrifice.

237

down there, with the monkeys screaming and God knows what rustling in the bushes, and was just getting back in bed, the only light coming from the embers of the fire, when I heard a thud, followed immediately by a groan, a bit like when Wayne Daniel used to hit someone on the head. It didn't sound at all good, and so I got up and had a little look around. Everyone else was spark out and so I shouted for a bit of help. All the lights went up and there was Janice. It looked like she'd tripped over a log and landed face first. We helped her up and could see straight away she'd smashed her face pretty hard, plus her arm and shoulder. We tried to comfort her and a couple of minutes later a paramedic appeared. Myleene Klass must have watched a lot of *Casualty* because she delivered all the details the paramedic needed in immaculate detail.

The medics carted Janice away and the showrunners, because we were all a bit shaken up by what we'd seen, then actually came down to have a little chat. I considered this a very good time to ask for the classic cure for shock – a nice cup of tea and some biscuits.

'Well, I don't think we can really do that,' they said.

'But I really do feel very shaken,' I insisted. 'My blood pressure's gone through the roof. I mean, what we really need is a drop of brandy.'

I think a few of the others could see what I was up to and started putting in their own orders. Since when a Big Mac and large fries has been a cure for shock I don't know. Sadly, none of it appeared.

I was sorry to see Janice leave in such circumstances. She was an open book. I never like it in these programmes when people start whispering to each other, having little one-on-ones, clearly saying something about someone else. It was something I didn't like in dressing rooms as a cricketer as all it does is create divisiveness and cliques. What you see with someone should also be what you get.

People like Janice, who have worked in a tough competitive business, have been around the block too many times to be bothered with faking it. She said whatever she wanted and didn't care who heard it.

I formed a lot of respect for Janice early on when, in the face of a truly hideous eating trial, she declared, in no uncertain terms, that she wasn't going to do it anymore. I totally got how she was feeling. I've done all sorts of trials on the show, locked in cupboards full of snakes, cockroaches crawling up my trousers, but when you realise it's an eating challenge your heart really does sink. On the one hand you want to show your steel and win a bit of grub for camp. On the other you're going to have to sit there and down half a litre of liquidised pig's arsehole with a cockroach cheesecake dessert. These things truly are disgusting and very hard to keep down. Eventually, you get that feeling in your chest of the whole lot coming back up, the most horrendous eruption about to happen.

A lot of the time the proper grub isn't much better. The last night I was there, they winched down our bag of food and inside we found an antelope's neck. I couldn't believe it. We'd done everything asked of us that day and that was our reward – these wobbling vertebrae that looked like they'd been half-gnawed and spat out by a lion. I drew the line at that. In fact, I even offered up a few words to the people up above – 'What? This is it, is it? This is what we get! A bunch of b*******, that's what you are. A bunch of b*******. You hear me?'

Fatima cooked it up but I couldn't be bothered eating it. She was a very good cook, Fatima, one of the few people who could turn a crocodile's foot into something edible, but at this I drew the line.

I myself was asked if I wanted to be the chef for a while but I turned down the offer. Some people are good at cooking, some people are good at emptying the dunny. I stuck to the dunny – believe me, an unenviable task. I'd literally have nightmares about it – tripping as I was carrying it away and being consumed by a cascading torrent of celebrity sewage.*

For once on an overseas trip, I'd followed all the rules. Before going into the jungle, you're put in a little room where a ranger checks your bags to make sure you're not

---

* A little secret here – the contestants remove the dunny, but don't actually empty it. They carry it down to a camouflaged wooden hut, tap on the door and clear off. It's basically an extreme version of that old knock-and-run game where you wrap a bit of dog muck in newspaper, set it on fire, drop it by someone's front door, ring the bell, and leg it. The householder emerges, sees the burning paper and stamps on it to put out the flames. I'd like to point out that I stopped doing this when I reached 40.

smuggling anything in – food, fags, inflatable en-suite bathroom, that kind of thing. I had nothing to declare and the warden neatly folded my underpants and put them back in the case.

Once in camp, however, it became clear others weren't quite so squeaky clean. Gillian McKeith, for one, had been acting a bit suspiciously. She seemed to like making her own drinks and could be a little furtive around food. I hadn't twigged but there'd been a bit of skulduggery going on. After a few days, a disembodied voice called for everyone to gather round the campfire. We assembled as requested, at which point the voice stated, 'There has been contraband smuggled in.' Not so much *I'm a Celebrity* as *Banged Up Abroad*. We were all looking at each other wondering who it could be. The voice stated that if the person responsible didn't own up we'd be denied our dinner. That wasn't good news. The evening meal, albeit it would probably end up being iguana nostrils or hyena nipples, was all we had to look forward to. Missing it would be very bad indeed.

After a little bit of discussion, Gillian went into her rucksack and pulled out a vast pair of knickers, the sort of thing used for landing operations by the Parachute Regiment. These 'spicy knickers', as she termed them, were the ones she'd been wearing on the way in, and therefore they had escaped the search. They weren't like any normal pair of knickers. They had pockets sewn in. She laid them out on a log. And then the contraband started tumbling out – Japanese miso soup powder, eight herbal stock cubes, rock salt, celery and garlic and cumin powder. It was like a mix between the conveyor belt on *The Generation Game* and *The Paul Daniels Magic Show*.* We watched, jaws agape – 'Is there more?'

Gillian looked at us. 'Well,' she said in her lilting Scottish brogue, 'there is a little bit more, yes.' Teabags, mints and almonds were tucked in her bra, and a herb shaker hidden in a toilet roll. I was just grateful she hadn't thought to bring a pepper pot. From that point on we called her either Gillian Escobar or Pablo McKeith.

When I realised what had been happening, my mind did switch back to a couple of days earlier when Gillian had asked me if I'd like to go for a walk with her to the shower area. I said no at the time, clearly having misconstrued what she meant. I've done all sorts of stuff on TV but showering with Gillian McKeith wasn't something I particularly wanted to add to the list. Later she slipped me a couple of leaves of mint and, on reflection, furnishing me with the odd herb might actually have been her motive for the shower trip.

The other very strange thing that happened was the mathematician Carol Vorderman finding a condom in the toilet. The main suspects were, of course, the blokes, and again I was keen to emphasise my own lack of involvement in the event. While Carol thought there might well have been some sort of shenanigans going on, my suspicion was that Condomgate, as it will forever be known,

* Also *Masterchef*.

was again something to do with Gillian's herb-smuggling operation.

Less surprising was that Shaun Ryder had also smuggled something in – a vape. More than once I'd had a drag on it only to find out that later that he'd got it past the ranger by sticking it up his arse.

'You could have said something,' I told him, 'before I sat there puffing on it for half an hour!'

I should have known Shaun would be a consummate smuggler when, somewhat startlingly, he revealed he'd been the resident DJ for a Mexican drugs cartel.

Shaun became my big mate in the jungle. When he wasn't flat on his back snoring, I spent some lovely hours with him looking for faces in the side of cliffs, talking about baboons and taking in his stories of his days back in Manchester with the Happy Mondays. There was no side to Shaun at all. He was happy just to sit there and be himself. He was great, great company, and I was sad when he was evicted early on, even if he wasn't. Cannily, Shaun had hooked up with Gillian for this particular eviction challenge. If losing meant going home earlier, then he was quite happy to be last. It made me laugh that Gillian felt a little slighted by Shaun's choice of her as his trial partner, as if he'd jeopardised her position in the camp, like she was some sort of warrior goddess destined to reach the final stages. While Gillian might have been a seasoned spice smuggler, she wasn't really cut out for the nuts and bolts of *I'm a Celebrity*. Forget cockroaches and snakes, she'd gasped when she'd seen the rice and beans.

It's funny how people have a strange perception of themselves.

The challenge entailed each pair of contestants putting
their tethered hands in various boxes full of creepy-crawlies to complete various tasks. Just as we were about to
start, Gillian piped up, 'Do you mind if I put my gloves
on?'

We were astonished. 'Gloves! Where's she had them
from?'

Off she went and produced a pair of what appeared to
be white snooker referees' gloves, the kind of thing worn
by Len Ganley – 'Gillian McKeith, foul and a miss.'

Our view was that gloves shouldn't be allowed. The
whole point of shoving your hand in a box full of horrible
things is that you can feel them against your skin. Gloves
or not, it made no difference. Gillian was wholly unable to
overcome her fear – 'I'm gonnae faint!' – and that was
that.

Shaun was absolutely delighted. Me not so much. I'd
lost my big mate, and his vape with the unusual taste. As
he was unlocked from his partner and walked away, even
with his bad hip I saw him do a little skip as he headed to
the hotel for a pint of lager and a good feed.

It really was disappointing to see Shaun go so early.
There are people in shows like this who always act so
determined, so up for it, although whether that's what
they're like on the inside I'm not so sure. Others are enthusiastic in a very prim and proper way, constantly fussing
about and doing endless needless jobs. Shaun was abso-

lutely just himself, completely up-front, and because of that I loved spending time with him. I could also see he was totally ready to go. There does come a point, usually when you're on your eighth consecutive day sat on a log, where you think, 'Actually, I've had enough of this now. I've done a few trials. I've had a bit of a laugh. But my bed isn't very comfy, my back hurts, I've eaten sod all and if I'm honest I'd like to go home.' At that point, if there's an eviction from camp, some people will say they're happy to go if it means other people can stay longer and enjoy the experience. They want it to look like a selfless act. Others are a bit more honest. 'Listen, I really couldn't care less. I've had enough and I just want to go home.'

Twenty years had passed since I was on *I'm a Celebrity* the first time, and when you get a bit older it's only natural you like your home comforts a bit more. A bit of nice food is one of life's great treats. Similarly, no one furnishes their home with logs. Somewhere out there is your lovely armchair, your ever-welcoming settee and your bath. Being in the jungle isn't genuine hardship, of course it isn't – everyone in there is being paid and are lucky to have lives where they're removed from the stress of the nine-to-five – but at the same time your mind does inevitably wander to how nice it would be to have a bacon sandwich and a cup of tea. Talk about paying a price – I must have missed 15 episodes of *Cowboy Builders* while I was in there.

*   *   *

With Shaun gone, I was glad when soap actors Joe Swash and Dean Gaffney turned up as late arrivals, two people with a bit of personality who gave the camp a new lease of life, because at that point it was getting a little bit dull. I was struggling to listen to another rendition of ex-royal butler Paul Burrell's Princess Diana stories and couldn't understand how seriously some people had reacted to the fact that Gillian had brought in a bit of salt. You'd think they'd been shown a video of her raiding the Royal Mint. More than once I had to stop myself screaming out loud, 'IT'S A TV SHOW! IT'S JUST A BIT OF FUN!' When you're in camp it does feel very real, but at the same time it's clearly a manufactured situation. You aren't actually cut off from civilisation. There's hundreds of cameras in the trees and the same amount of production people not that far away. We aren't like Tom Hanks washed up on a desert island. Nobody's best friend is a volleyball. There has to be a bit of order but at the same time the experience has to be something that everyone enjoys.

After two weeks, a scenario was created where contestants could save one another from a two-way eviction face-off. It was down to a last three of me, Dean Gaffney and Joe Swash. It was now Paul Burrell's turn to choose who to save. I'd been with Paul from the start, sleeping in the bed next to him and generally trying to help him through the whole *I'm a Celebrity* experience – he was missing home and was clearly nervous of the challenges. It seemed like at times he was a bit fragile and I hoped I'd gone some way to keeping his spirits up. Dean, on the other hand, had been there three days. Paul chose Dean. I couldn't help feeling a bit disappointed. I'd tried to help the bloke out and in return he threw me under the bus. Or, more literally, into a coffin full of snakes – which was the challenge now facing me and Joe.

While everyone knows it's only a TV show, before a trial you can't help but get a horrible feeling in the pit of your stomach. A real dread, such as you might get before a trip to the dentist. Everyone puts a brave face on it, but no one particularly likes doing these things. Don't get me wrong, it's exciting to know you're going to be doing something but they're all quite grisly in their own way. Let's face it, you never arrive at the jungle clearing to find a large pen of kittens that must be stroked relentlessly for three minutes. Anyway, the die had been cast and so off me and Joe went. Only one of these two former Kings of the Jungle would live to fight another day.

This time we arrived in the clearing to find two ready-dug tombs. I was instantly reminded to re-watch *The Godfather* trilogy when I got home. Gingerly, we lay down in the coffins, strapped in – again an experience I wouldn't recommend – with only our arms free. The lid was then slowly lowered down. It was pitch black in there aside from a very weak yellow bulb which gave everything an extremely bleak feel, like a particularly downbeat episode of *EastEnders*. For a few seconds, everything went quiet. It was then that I really started to worry – 'What if every-one's just ****ed off?' In my head I suddenly pictured the little brown mound that signifies a grave in cartoons. I was reminded also of times gone by when people would be buried with a bell just in case their death had been misdiagnosed. Hence the phrase 'saved by the bell'. Except in the cartoon image in my mind the bell was *on* the mound, not *in* the coffin!

During that trial, 55 snakes were dropped on each of our heads. That's a lot of snakes. These things are big, pure muscle and actually weigh a lot. In effect you're lying under a 15-tog snake duvet. The arrival of each reptile is a shock in its own right. Subsequently, your breathing becomes irregular and you start to shake. And then somehow, to win the trial, you've got to undo a load of fiddly combination locks, never the easiest thing at the best of times. As a kid I could never get the one off my bike in broad daylight. Now here I was trying to do the same thing with half a jungle's worth of reptiles crawling up my trouser leg.

My solution was to revert to my old cricketing persona. I decided to hate the snakes in the same way I'd hated batsmen* back in the day. I was shouting at them – 'You ****ing ****s! You're not going to stop me! You ****ing ****s!' The kind of expletives normally reserved for hardcore areas of football grounds.

It worked – finally I managed to finish the trial. 'Now get me out of this ****ing box!' One thing you don't get about *I'm a Celebrity* watching at home is just how bloody awful everything smells. There's a reason why none of the top

* And the occasional Australian umpire.

fragrance companies have produced a scent called 'Eau de Rat'. All those odours are only made ten times worse by the humidity and temperature. I can only compare it to high summer when your wheelie bin hasn't been emptied for a couple of weeks – and then someone says the only way you're getting your dinner is if you sit in it for 15 minutes.

Ant and Dec declared it the sweariest trial they'd seen in the show's entire 20 years. I wouldn't be surprised if the bloke on the bleeper button has since developed repetitive strain injury. It also convinced me of something I'd begun to suspect – the showrunners listen in on the contestants as they chat in camp. How else do they so often succeed in matching people's phobias so precisely to the tasks?

'Hang on – Carol Vorderman's just said she hates spiders! Quick, order two thousand tarantulas for her next challenge. And make sure it's one where they're dropped on her face.'

I say this because I vaguely remember mentioning I don't fancy snakes very much, and also that I'm not a fan of confined spaces. Had I understood this, I'd have manufactured an elaborate bluff. 'I really do love snakes you know,' I'd have idly dropped into a fireside conversation. 'And another thing you might not know about me is that for several years now I've slept in a coffin while buried alive. Sometimes I even try to undo combination locks hanging directly above.'

I dread to think what my heart rate was when I got out of that coffin. I'd hazard a guess that it was about the same as when I bumped into Graham Gooch in a hotel lift at 7 a.m. – the England skipper coming down to breakfast, me just in from a night out. I mean, if you think about it, in real life if you were buried in a tomb full of snakes it would stay with you for years. Decades later you'd wake bolt upright in bed trying to strangle your dressing-gown cord. In telly-land, however, you're expected to carry on like nothing's happened. In the meantime, your body's released so much adrenalin it feels like you've been plugged in at the mains. You can't blame it. It doesn't know you're on a TV show and none of these things can actually hurt you. As far as it's concerned, you're Stone Age man being chased by a sabre-toothed tiger. It needs to keep pumping the adrenalin out to give you any chance of making it back to your cave. While Captain Caveman then sits back with a well-deserved cup of nettle tea and a dinosaur thigh, all I get is a couple of medical blokes giving me a quick once-over and sending me straight back into camp. More than anything I wanted a lie-down, but barely had I slumped on my bed than the call came through that we were all off out again for another challenge. My back was in turmoil at this point. Two weeks of kipping in hammocks and camp beds had left me a wreck.* Now I found myself forced into a tea chest while several hundred biting ants were tipped over me. There was a lot of squirming around to complete the challenge, by the end of which my back had gone into spasm. The paramedics appeared and adminis-tered a muscle relaxant via a buttock injection. The good

* Every night I dreamt fitfully about Parker Knoll recliners.

news was that by this time I'd befriended a cameraman who took pity on me and gave me a fag. When Ant and Dec came down to camp later, Jordan Banjo was basically holding me upright as we gathered on the logs. It's the nearest I've come to being a ventriloquist's dummy. By the time I finally got to bed, I knew one thing – it was a day I'd neither forget nor particularly want to remember.

In the end, I came fourth, voted out just before the final. I was accused of not pulling my weight in camp, but I did my fair share. The problem was people kept inventing jobs that didn't need to be done. What was I supposed to do? Get the Mr Sheen out and start polishing the trees? I suspected Fatima thought I was lazy but then I'd look at her sweeping the jungle floor and think, 'Is that strictly necessary?' She was actually sweeping something that was made of dirt. It was like hoovering a wood.

I didn't hang around once they'd made their choice. Bag packed, I was gone in, at a conservative estimate, 12 seconds. I found the energy for one last sprint (well, hobble) into the arms of Dawn and we returned to our cabin where I had the best glass of cold lager I've ever had* while from a tree my old monkey pal gave me its traditional one-handed welcome. Watching the sunset with Dawn that night, hair shampooed, crevices scrubbed,

* Celebrities – it's worth doing the programme for this moment alone.

toenails manicured, was one of the best feelings I've ever had. I'd even moisturised.*

For sure, I didn't mind missing the final. Even on my very best day, I wouldn't have been able to match Myleene Klass, named the first ever *I'm a Celebrity* Legend after eating 60 mouse tails and 40 spoonfuls of fermented tofu, an incredible achievement and one which does make you wonder what future contestants might have to contend with as they try to keep the show moving along.

'How many stars did you get?'

'Five.'

'Right, OK. What did you have to do?'

'Well, first they put thumbscrews on me, then they pulled my fingernails out, and last up they stretched me on the rack.' (At this point, the other contestants walk disinterestedly away.)

We all returned to camp to watch that final trial, and I was delighted to be reunited with my buddy Shaun and also to see Janice again, replete with two big black eyes, a reminder that while from the outside the show looks very professional – and don't get me wrong, it is an amazing set-up, and everyone feels 100 per cent looked after and safe – every now and then something does happen where you realise in this kind of environment not everything can be controlled. Janice's fall was one of them, another was the biblical downpour that happened in the second week.

---

* Laboratoire Garnier – if you wish to discuss sponsorship opportunities, please contact my agent.

It's quite something to see a downpour like that. Occasionally I've witnessed them in Australia and the Caribbean, but this was particularly explosive, alternately hair-raising and exhilarating. Afterwards came the disembodied voice – 'Can everyone now please take cover as we implement our drainage procedures?' We were expecting a quite complex cleaning-up operation only for two blokes with scaffold poles to appear and start prodding the canopy until all the water had tumbled off the sides.

Just like the first time round, I enjoyed the show but think that's probably it for me and blended hog anus. *I'm a Celebrity* is a young man's game, and maybe the gap between my own appearances made me remember the exciting bits more than the other stuff, like the sleeping arrangements and waking up in the morning to a cup of stagnant water and a canteen of rice and beans. But then again once you start chatting to everyone and get used to the layout, you also remember that actually it's great fun; an odd situation but one where you get to spend time with amazing people who you'd never meet in normal life. It definitely reminded me of old dressing rooms – all these different characters forced together, trying to get on with one another and achieve something.

After a couple of days at the cabin, me and Dawn were picked up and whisked away to the airport. Amusingly, while two or three of us boarded our Virgin plane, everyone else, including Ant & Dec, was flying with British Airways. Their flight got cancelled.

Oh, well, there were still beds available in the jungle.

13

MISUNDERSTANDINGS

There was a bit of a narrative in *I'm a Celebrity* whereby some people said I was coasting through, hoping to go a little bit unnoticed in the background and avoid having any unpleasantries dropped on my head. Fatima actually referred to me as a sloth, which I found a little bit harsh. Sloths are so loath to move that they actually get covered in moss. OK, I'm renowned for liking a kip but I've never woken up adorned with greenery. Unless I've slept in a bush.

People who've shared dressing rooms with me might also point to the fact I was known occasionally as the Artful Dodger. This wasn't because I went round picking through personal items from teammates. The nearest I got to that was cutting the end off a pair of Ian Botham's socks. He put them on after a shower and was astonished to find they went straight up his legs. No, the Artful Dodger tag was more due to the fact that, when volunteers were sought for certain tasks – bowling at aging MCC members in the nets, fetching 20 portions of cod from the chippie, a pre-season friendly in Aberdeen – I had a habit of shrinking so far into my seat that pretty much only my ears were sticking out.

I don't think there's anything inherently wrong in not being desperate to spend every waking moment running around with a feather duster in both hands and a broom up your backside. It's why I never revelled in being twelfth man, not that many players do. Being twelfth man back in the day was awful. In a single swish of the coach's pen on the team sheet you went from privileged professional cricketer to mere skivvy. From Phil Tufnell to Hilda Ogden.

Nowadays, the England team seem to have five people in bibs running around after them at all times. When I was twelfth man I'd have to get lunches ready, ferry drinks round, make cups of tea, the lot. It was like being in *Upstairs, Downstairs*. The only thing they didn't give you was a butler's uniform. 'Phil, my good man, for tea I really would like the finest Outer Hebridean salmon on a bed of Welsh watercress drizzled with olive oil.'

'Yes, sir, of course, sir. And will sir be wanting it tipped on his head?'

How on earth I was meant to enjoy a little snooze in those circumstances I don't know.

Perhaps I'd been spoiled by my early days in the Middlesex dressing room. There we had Roy who looked after us. At the beginning of each day's play, he'd come round. 'Right, lads, what will you be wanting to drink after play?'

It was brilliant. All these drinks would be shouted up – 'Double scotch.' 'Large gin and tonic.' 'Two pints of lager.' And that was just me. At the end of play, all the drinks would be lined up on the lockers in the middle of the dressing room. Phil Edmonds would ask for a bottle of red wine, and there it would be, with the cork open and a glass. There'd be an ice bucket full of mixers. Rehydration drinks? Sports massages? Forget it.

Thing is, just because I didn't leap up from my seat every five minutes didn't mean I didn't have anything to offer. Some people could see that more than others. Nasser Hussain was one of them. Nasser was a captain who appreciated being able to talk through situations. If he asked an honest question he expected an honest answer, and he worked out early on that I had a very good cricket brain. As a spinner, that particular attribute is an absolute must. You're not one of the fast boys slinging it down at 90 miles an hour. Instead of using speed to get your wickets you have to rely on wit and guile. You're thinking, thinking, thinking, about length, flight, fielding positions, and a million and one other things. Like I've said, I also understood that switching off is as important as switching on, and so didn't want to be sat around talking about cricket 24 hours a day, but that knowledge was there, waiting to be tapped, at any time.

On several occasions on tour, Nasser came and knocked on my hotel room door. Nine times out of ten I wouldn't be in there, but it was worth a try. If I did happen to be at home and not dancing on a table at the

Rum Baba nightclub down the road, he'd come in and we'd have a couple of beers while chewing the fat about various issues.

Probably the most notable occasion he spoke to me was on the back of the team bus in the Caribbean just after he'd been offered the England captaincy.

'Phil, what do you think I should do?'

'Mate, take it – they can't drop you then! You're going to get another ten or 15 games minimum!' Well, I had to have a bit of a joke. More seriously, we talked about the stresses of the job, the commitments that come with it and how it might affect his form with the bat.

In my career, a lot of people saw me as someone who liked a bit of a laugh – a good-time boy – and that was it. That was the beginning and end of what I could offer. Only towards the end of my playing life did more than the occasional colleague start to understand that actually, just because someone likes to enjoy themselves, it doesn't mean that they don't have a good understanding of what's going on around them. In fact, the way their brain works might mean they see things from a completely different perspective. They might actually have an insight that's missing elsewhere. This is the thing with me – despite what people might say, I can take things seriously. I can discuss all sorts of things the same as anyone. I just choose not to for the majority of the time because life is for living and your own little innings is soon gone.

Also, I never saw the point of just telling people what they wanted to hear. It serves absolutely no purpose whatsoever and delivers precisely nothing for the person who's asked for your opinion – unless they're the sort of person who just wants to be told they're right, in which case a conversation is a complete waste of time anyway. OK, there were times when I was accused of not necessarily voicing my opinion in the right way, but then again, on too many occasions to mention, the only time I was asked what I was thinking – or more likely 'what on earth' I was thinking – was in a fines meeting.*

If people didn't like what I said, that wasn't me wanting to be troublesome. My answer would never come from a position of malice or trying to get one over on someone. It was more, 'You've asked me a straight-up question, you might not enjoy the answer, but this is what I think and I'm going to say it.' I don't honestly see what's wrong with

---

* In the end, I used to have a contingency plan for fines. I'd think of a tour fee like planning an extension on a house – factor in losing an extra 20 per cent for unexpected issues that might pop up along the way. With hindsight, I should have negotiated my fines in advance and paid a lump sum. It would probably have been cheaper. Thing is, everyone got fined, either by the management or the match referees. Wrong trousers, wrong shoes – someone had their hand in your wallet at every turn. Stewie was the one who got fined the least, but when he lost his rag after a clear-cut bat–pad catch off me was given not out in Australia, even he fell foul of the officials. Another time in Australia, Stewie and Athers had managed to avoid a penalty all the way through the tour, and then, on the morning of the last day of the last Test, they were caught, I think in flip-flops, getting on the bus. Four months of a clean record down the pan. It was so stressful getting dressed in the morning. Put the wrong socks on and there would go your steak and chips in the evening.

that. Nasser could see the value of that approach even if others couldn't.

Coming out of the game, I was lucky that the TMS producers could also see that I was more than some kind of court jester. Yes, I could be funny, but I was also able to offer incisive analysis of the game. The thing with TMS is choosing your time to switch from one to the other. From the start, I tried to go back to when I was a kid and remember what it was that me, Mum and Dad liked about the show when it was on in the car on summer days out. For me, it was the ability of everyone involved to encapsulate the big moments in a way that was as vivid and exciting as if you were there, and also to fill in the gaps in between with a lot of entertaining chat, mainly, but not always, about cricket.

For all the big moments we cover, a lot of people tell me their favourite part of *TMS* is when the action goes a little quiet and, as above, the conversation becomes, well, a little inane. This is good for me as inanity is my specialist subject. I've always had an interest in little-known facts, stuff that you pick up as you're going along in your everyday life, like a banana being a herb not a fruit, and dogs not being able to eat onions. I once sparked much interest, and possibly caused mild nausea in a lot of listeners, with my mention of a much-revered variety of cheese that contains live maggots, their poo delivering the distinctive taste which makes it an absolute delicacy.

I do beg your pardon if you're reading this over your dinner.

My work on *The One Show*, where I was oft dispatched to meet all kinds of weird and wonderful people, certainly helped on the niche information front, and while initially Aggers doubted a lot of my facts, over time he came to see that I was telling the truth – which was great because it meant I could then drop in stuff that might be completely made up. I once told Aggers that the tennis player Novak Djokovic was an avid collector of donkey cheese, Serbia being the epicentre of global donkey cheese production. Actually, there is a little kernel of truth in that one. Honest, guv.

Another story that sounds very unlikely, but is actually true, I learned from being dispatched to Ireland by *The One Show*. There I met the artist who created the famous Che Guevara image seen on a million T-shirts, having been serving in a bar when the Marxist revolutionary happened to step through the door. Again, a lovely little thing to take back to *TMS* where the topic of revolutionary Marxism rarely pops up during a passage of play.

Obscure knowledge can also come in useful in real life, like when I went to a tapas bar and felt convinced the waiter was putting on a Spanish accent. 'Do you know where the name "tapas" comes from?' I asked him as we sat down. He told me it meant little pieces of things to eat. But I'd watched Rick Stein on TV a couple of months earlier and he'd explained how in Spain, back in the day when a lot of people worked in the fields, they'd have a lump of bread, a bit of cheese and a glass of wine for lunch. Rick explained how if they needed to nip off for a wee they would put the lump of bread on top of their wine to stop the flies going in. 'Tapas,' he explained, means 'on top.' I pointed this out to the waiter, perhaps for a bit too long, because by the time I'd finished he'd got bored and was back in the kitchen. But I like the way that facts can stop people in their tracks and also start a little debate. You can't talk about the follow-on target forever.

Occasionally, an odd discussion point falls in your lap – maybe even drives into your living room. I've always hated being late and *TMS* is no different. The only time I've had to ring ahead was when a car arrived in my front room, a scenario which does take quite a lot of sorting out. At least I knew the person responsible. It wasn't like I was watching *Emmerdale* one night and a family of four pulled up by the settee. We'd had a bit of a party and a few cars were packed into the drive. I was saying cheerio to a few people by the door when my mate fired his car up, took the handbrake off, and promptly reversed straight through my bay window. He went through the wall, removed a radiator, and came to a halt next to a couple of blokes having a game of pool, one of whom was extremely annoyed as he was on the black at the time.

I had insurance and all sorts to deal with in the morning and so by the time I got to the *TMS* studio, my co-commentators were ready with the clever comments.

'Oh, you decided to come in after all have you? What was it, another dodgy curry?'

'No, I think you'll find actually that someone reversed into my house.'

'I've never heard that one before, Tuffers. Come on, what really happened?'

They only believed me when I showed them the CCTV. There was 30 seconds of dead air while they stared at me open-mouthed in disbelief.

It was perhaps the fact that I've never really compromised on being myself that helped me win *I'm a Celebrity* the first time round. In all honesty, if you're on TV solidly every night for two weeks, people are soon going to work out if you're being yourself or trying to be something you're not. Who knows why I won, but for me I think it was a case of seeing someone quietly getting on and enjoying themselves. Post-retirement, I would take tour parties of cricket fans to overseas Test matches, and I think a lot of the success of those trips also came from the fact that people saw me as being a bit like them; a normal sort of bloke who, through cricket, and eating the occasional cockroach, just happened to have done OK.

I enjoyed those little sojourns immensely and met some wonderful people but don't think I ever realised just how much work being a tour guide would be. It was ten times more gruelling than being on tour as a cricketer. There'd be groups of punters dotted around various hotels and I'd flit around between them saying hello, having a few drinks and doing little talks. I wasn't seeing my bed before four in the morning and then would be up again in no time for a breakfast gathering. One or two people also seemed to mistake my role as being one of administration. My phone would ring at some ungodly hour and it'd be someone complaining the bulb had gone in the bathroom or they were low on toilet paper. I'd gone from *I'm a Celebrity* to a very bad episode of *Crossroads*.

In India one time, the Test matches had come to an end and I was getting ready to go home, suitcases in the lobby, when I was approached by a bloke from the tour party.

'Where are you going, Phil?' he asked me.

'Well, I'm off home,' I replied, gesturing towards my baggage.

'What are you talking about?' he said. 'I booked an extra week. I thought you'd be staying here with me.'

Don't get me wrong, he was a very nice man, but I had things to do. I couldn't just spend a week sitting around a pool in Mumbai with him. Where does the arrangement end? I wondered if I needed to point out that he wasn't invited for Christmas dinner.

I've always been slightly nervous of giving out my home address for just this reason. But it was actually a Premier League footballer who made me regret it the most. I'd met the Millwall, Tottenham and Liverpool defender Neil 'Razor' Ruddock a couple of times while out and about and found him a really funny and genuine guy. One time we were having a couple of drinks and I wrote down my phone number and address. Immediately, he stopped dead.

'You shouldn't have done that,' he said.

'No, mate,' I said. 'It's fine. We get on well. Give me a call if ever you're in my area.'

He remained insistent. 'Really, that was a mistake.'

A few months later I was sat in the living room watching *The Sound of Music* on Christmas Eve when I heard bang, bang, bang on the back window. I nearly jumped out of my skin. It was past ten. Once I knew the Von Trapp Family Singers had safely reached Switzerland I was planning on heading to bed.

The banging happened again. I went to have a look. Initially, I couldn't see anything and then, out of the darkness, up popped a figure – 'Aaaghhh!'

Slowly, I realised it was Razor. I opened the back door. 'What's going on?'

'I told you – never give me your address.'

Turned out he was at a mate's party just down the road. He insisted I accompany him. And so off I went. One day, Razor Ruddock allowing, I will definitely get to see the end of *The Sound of Music*.

14
FOOD

In many ways, my desire not to take the most obvious path in life has led to my most memorable experiences. Food is a case in point.

In Guyana, for instance, I accidentally ate a rat. It was in a restaurant and, just to be clear, wasn't exhibited as rat on the menu. It was only afterwards when I commented to someone how much I'd enjoyed it that they informed me what it was. I've not been back.

I made a similar error elsewhere in the Caribbean when I ordered the 'mountain chicken'. It sounded lovely. Surely any chicken that's spent its days pecking mountain seeds and breathing in delightfully fresh air would be absolutely lovely. How free range can you get? What turned up on my plate was the remains of a massive frog. The mountain chicken is otherwise known as the giant ditch frog. I can see why they hadn't stuck that on the board outside.

* * *

Of course, there are other ways to find your stomach churning in the eateries of this world. Me and Dawn were over in Miami once, wandering around looking for a place to eat. Eventually, we asked a passer-by and he pointed us in the direction of a Japanese place. The minute we stepped through the door we realised this was somewhere very special indeed. Even to our untrained eye we could see it was full of the local glitterati – American football players, Russian oligarchs, high-class hookers, that kind of thing. I whispered to Dawn, 'Come on, we can do this. Style it out!'

We were taken to a table and handed a very fancy menu, one of those with no prices. I'll be honest, neither of us had any idea what any of it meant.

'Listen,' I said to Dawn, 'I've got a good idea. When the waiter comes over, I'll ask him for his recommendation.'

Over the bloke came, looking a little bit bored. When I asked the question, I sensed him perk up a bit.

'Oh, definitely this,' he said, pointing to something utterly incomprehensible.

'Oh, very good – yes, we'll go with that, thanks.'

As he walked away, out of the corner of my eye I saw him high-five the other waiter. Clearly, he was on commission.

Twenty minutes later, the background music stopped and was replaced by a fanfare. Out came several silver cloches, adorned with giant sparklers. The rest of the diners burst into a round of applause. I had a horrible feeling this little lot was destined for our table. Again, to myself more than anything, I muttered, 'Style it out!'

The cloches were indeed placed before us and then lifted, at which point a load of dry ice came pouring out. I wondered when exactly Heston Blumenthal had moved to Miami.

What we'd ordered was a tasting menu – course after course after course – and it was horrible. We ploughed our way through it, not wishing to look stupid, and asked for the bill. Over it came. I opened it up. If I wasn't feeling sick already, I sure was then. Fifteen. Hundred. Dollars.

At this point my ability to 'style it out' sadly stalled. While I'm sure everyone else in there was rocking American Express or Diners Club, I gingerly produced my battered old Barclaycard. The waiter's expression was the very embodiment of disdain.

It was McDonald's all the way from that point on.

Thing is, I'm not someone who's got ridiculous tastes with food. I've been to some of the best restaurants in the world and come out disappointed. As a kid, my favourite was lamb chops, boiled potatoes and peas. Like flares, the boiled potato went out of fashion. But I remain a fan.

I'm quite a simple man – I'm not keen on your foams and all that stuff. When we were growing up, it would be fish and chips on holiday. I'd have started crying if someone had covered my cod in foam. On the other hand, if I'm in an oyster restaurant overlooking Sydney Harbour I'm not going to call the waiter over and ask if they wouldn't mind doing me egg and chips.

Of all the places I've eaten, The Cliff in Barbados, overlooking the sea with the outdoor seating lit up by big

269

torches, is a definite favourite. If you want to make memories, these kind of epic sea-view restaurants are the place to do it. This, I should point out, is very much in retirement. As a cricketing tourist, dinner wasn't on my radar. I was a young bloke. I wasn't going to waste my evenings sat napkinned-up at a restaurant table discussing the new Austin Montego or how to string a tennis racquet. I wasn't going to waste my money either. Each day, we would be given our 'per diem', a few quid in the local currency for food. It was a far from significant amount. For all the talk about us trying to eat healthily and keep fit, we couldn't actually go out for a decent dinner because all we could afford was pizza and chips. I used to pick up a bit of food when it was free at grounds or at dos. That meant I could use my per diem down the pubs and clubs. Apart from the peanuts off the bar, the most I'd eat in the evening was the occasional bit of fried chicken on the way out. Thinking about it, I probably did most of my career on fast food. I should have replaced Colonel Sanders as the face of KFC. I got most of my vitamins from cocktails and iron from Guinness. On the advice of a senior pro, I did an entire English summer on the black stuff. It was one of the few tips that stuck with me. I very much took it to heart.

The way I saw it, playing sport for a living was an amazing thing in itself without the need for fancy fodder on top of it. Home or away, to be out there with all your mates was brilliant. To be in your early 20s and earning money doing something you love, which could in no way be described as work, there's no better feeling. No two ways about it, it was a fantastic life. I'd be there in my Middlesex blazer, driving around in a sponsored car. What's not to like? If you've won the game, got a few wickets and are on your way home on a lovely summer's evening, then really you have to pinch yourself. No way at that point was I going to lounge on the settee and put Coronation Street on. I'd be absolutely buzzing.

It wasn't just the socialising that affected my calorific intake. In a really hot climate, especially on a day when I was playing, I'd often find lunch difficult to eat. So again, breakfast was key – and that was the time, after a big night out, I always felt the worst. Depending where you were, breakfast could be anything from a full English to goat curry – try getting that down after a few too many the night before.

There's always an exception to the rule and for me that was the food in the Caribbean. I could eat it all day and all night. Wherever we played in the West Indies, I never used to have lunch in the pavilion. I'd find a great little vendor somewhere round the ground and come back with a tray of flying fish or a box of all sorts of stuff – jerk chicken, rice, peas, salad, macaroni cheese. I'll be honest, chicken's feet were a speciality I never warmed to but I loved everything else. The smell of this food sweeping across the ground was heavenly. Trouble was, if you were twelfth man, the rest of the boys just used to keep asking you to nip out for grub. On the plus side, twelfth-man duties didn't always last that long in the Caribbean. At Trinidad, for England's aforementioned infamous 46 all-out, I'd collected the lads' drinks at the start of the innings, thought I'd nip out and get some corn soup – Trinidad's was the absolute best – and when I came back we were about eight down. Like most things that went wrong on an England trip, even that collapse was laid at my door.

'Where the hell have you been? We've been waiting for drinks here!'

I couldn't believe what I was hearing. 'Waiting for drinks? You were only out there one ball.'

'And I wanted you to put my gloves to dry in the sunshine.'

'You were in them for precisely two minutes. What are you on about?'

Soul food was the Caribbean speciality, nourishment that lifted you both mentally and physically. Corn soup, for example, somehow felt like it gave you a bit of power. Unlike a cheese roll and a bottle of Panda pop at Grace Road, which just gave you indigestion. Or the chips, mushy peas and carrots that would appear at certain other grounds. Don't get me wrong, good food – so long as you're planning an afternoon in an armchair watching *The Guns of Navarone*. I'd look around at people on the county circuit and the amount they used to stick away was unbelievable. Some of them were proper troughers. The big fast bowlers, or – how shall I put this? – 'sizeable' batsmen, spent their lives like vast rodents, continuously looking for the next meal. On a night out, they'd rotate pints with kebabs. Had they rotated rum with flying fish – admittedly difficult in Worcester – they'd have been twice the player.

I wouldn't like people to think I'm someone who doesn't know his food. I do like a bit of the old cooking and in fact did make an appearance on *Masterchef*, to this day embittered that I was robbed. I rustled up this fantastic dish of scallops on a bed of celeriac mash with wilted greens and a salsa verde sauce, which, considering you don't know what ingredients you're getting, I was quite proud of. My mistake came with the follow-up dish, again with mash* but this time involving a piece of chicken so large it could just as easily have come off a pterodactyl. I cooked it OK but then forgot to take it off the bone and so it looked a little out of place on the plate, the kind of thing Henry VIII might have torn a few chunks off and hurled over his shoulder into the cleavage of a busty wench.

In the end I lost out to a spaghetti Bolognese made by Craig Revel Horwood. Having put a lot of love into both my dishes, I will admit I felt a little hard done by. Nothing against Craig, who I know from my time on *Strictly Come Dancing* is a lovely bloke, but spag bol is pretty standard fare. It's the sort of thing you rustle up on a Tuesday night when you haven't got much in. It's in the same league as chilli con carne, and the salt 'n' vinegar crisp sandwich. It

* If you want a potato beaten to a pulp I'm your man.

had been a very long day and after the recording, as is traditional, we had a few drinks, and I was having a chat with *Masterchef* judges Greg Wallace and John Torode. Still peeved, I raised the issue of losing out to the spag bol. They felt my seasoning was an issue, whereas I thought I'd got it spot on. I'll admit it's probably not a debate on the scale of what you'd hear on *Yesterday in Parliament* but I had my standpoint and I wasn't going to back down.

Matters got a little heated and in the end I was removed from the *Masterchef* environs and placed, unceremoniously, hand pressed on top of the head like in *The Bill*, in the backseat of the car that was to take me home. My final word on the subject, hurled in the direction of Torode, might have been influenced by one or two Ashes defeats down the years. 'You're just a burger chef! That's all – a burger chef! You Aussie ****.'

It was definitely one of those times when you wake up the next day and slowly bits of pieces come back to you about the night before. 'Hang on – I called John Torode a burger chef!' Then ten minutes later – 'Oh my God, I was frogmarched to the car!' And then, 'Was I tasered? Dawn, last night when I got in, did I say anything about being tasered?'

When it comes to *Masterchef*, I don't think I'll be invited along to a legends show.

15
'WORK'

As a kid, we'd supplement our main holiday with the odd day out. Dad had a Ford Cortina mk3 estate and we'd pile in and head off down to Brighton, occasionally Margate. My dad tended to regret these trips because for him it was just several hours of me nagging him for 5ps for the amusement arcade. For me, though, they formed a definite attachment to the idea of the day out. These days, I'm lucky enough to live not too far from the Surrey Hills and South Downs, great places for a stroll with a view and a bite to eat in a classic old English pub. I've been lucky enough to travel all over the world but, for a classic day out, there's nothing to match Britain on a glorious summer's day. The light and colours are just magnificent.

Epsom racecourse is also on our doorstep and me and Dawn have been known to head down there every once in a while, although I've probably spent more time at Cheltenham, a place where rather too many times I've reached the end of the racing day thinking, 'I'm skint. I've got a headache. And I'm three hours from home.'

Sometimes I'd go to Cheltenham for all four days of its famous festival and do a bit of corporate work. One time I was there early, about 10.30, to do some radio interviews. It was quiet, just a handful of people around. I nipped off to the toilet only to find a Welsh bloke and his friend in there, both in ill-fitting suits and white socks, who'd obviously got the early morning train. Nothing inherently wrong with that situation, except for the fact that one of them was lying prone on the floor.

'Oh my God,' I said. 'Are you all right?'

Well, they were so smashed that, at half ten in the morning, one of them had experienced – and I'm trying to be sensitive – a very unpleasant trouser-related accident. This was with the first race still three hours away. I'm not sure what happened to those two blokes but I think the safest bet of the day was that they never got to hear the famous Cheltenham roar.* I've not heard it for a while either. It's a long way to go to sit in a big tent eating guinea fowl with dauphinoise potatoes. And it's always so bloody cold!

Few people realise I was once a jockey myself. And when I say 'once' I mean it. There's a video that people happen across occasionally online and I have to virtually swear on the Bible to make them believe it's true. It features myself and the Australian quick Jason Gillespie pelting down the

---

* I expect the only roar one of them heard was that of 'Get out!' when they ventured into a shop for a new pair of strides.

final furlong at Warwick racecourse hanging on desperately to two suitably bemused nags.

As a fun warm-up for the Ashes in 2009, myself and Jason were asked to compete in a number of stunts, and a race on horseback was one of them. I'm not sure about Jason but my experience with horses was very much lacking.* To be fair the horses were a bit clodhoppery – no one was going to mistake them for Arkle and Nijinsky – but even so they were going at a half-decent pelt. I really had to hang on, not helped by being in George Cross jockey silks which had me sliding around everywhere. All I could do was close my eyes, sling my arms round the horse's neck, and hope for the best. If we'd fallen off we'd have done ourselves some serious damage. Occasionally, I look back at some of the things I've done and can't believe they've happened. Being a jockey is one of them.

Being a shepherd is another. I did exactly that for the ITV series *Celebrities under Pressure*, required to command Gwyn the collie to deposit several uncooperative sheep into a pen. Not that Gwyn was taking any notice of me. He saw straight away that I was utterly hopeless and pretty much did the whole thing himself. To have a good crack at the challenge I actually stayed with a Welsh sheep-farming family for three days. I got to know them well and saw what long backbreaking hours they

* I hadn't had a sponsored pony from Middlesex. It would have meant a terrifically unpleasant journey through central London at rush hour.

277

worked. If I completed the challenge, I'd win some great prizes for them. For me they deserved everything they could get, and genuinely the pressure to deliver was as big as anything I've felt on a cricket field. I could have hugged Gwyn when he completed the task, but I don't think he was interested. I didn't get so much as a lick. He was glad I was off and he could get back on with doing his job without some oaf from the telly getting in the way.

All through my career, I would be matched with animals who, in all honesty, wanted very little to do with me. On tour, it always seemed to be me who was chosen to do the press photo-calls. In Australia, I boxed a kangaroo. Well, I pretended. It wasn't a case of 12 three-minute rounds. And anyway, it had a longer reach than me. In India, meanwhile I was paired up with a snake charmer. I didn't mind that – I wondered if I watched his hypnotism skills hard enough whether I might be able to replicate them on Sachin Tendulkar. I was also pictured sat on an elephant which again triggered my vertigo. Why didn't we ever tour places with Shetland ponies?

It very much felt that, where photo-ops were concerned, no cultural stereotype was left unturned. Although the one with me sat on a beach smoking a spliff in the Caribbean never transpired.

Working for many years on *The One Show* also meant all sorts of trips to weird and wonderful places I'd never otherwise have clapped eyes on – like the Harlequin

Shopping Centre, Watford. It was here I was chased round by a bloke preaching the message of the Lord. I tried to explain to him that people don't want to turn on *The One Show* to see a message reading 'THE END IS NIGH!'.

People who've had a few drinks can also be a bit disruptive. I've learnt a few tricks down the years. When, inevitably, they spot the camera and stagger across to ask what we're filming, I either say *Songs of Praise*, at which point they walk off, or *Crimewatch*, at which point they run off.

Then there was the ITV cookery/reality show *Hell's Kitchen*, where I appeared, not as a contestant (thankfully), but as a guest at the restaurant where the various celebrities being beasted by Gordon Ramsay would serve up their food. It started off OK – there was a little reception area with free Champagne and what have you. But once we were seated in the restaurant itself it was absolute chaos. We didn't eat for about three hours, by which time pretty much everyone there, having drunk all the table wine on an empty stomach, was totally sloshed. There were tables going over, glasses getting knocked about. Eventually, a few scraps of grub appeared, but to be honest by then most of us had gone past it. All told, it was a very entertaining night because not only was everything free but you could hear old Ramsay shouting and swearing, pans getting chucked about, people weeping in the kitchen.

I've also been on *Who Wants to Be a Millionaire?* partnered up on a charity edition with Joe Pasquale. We actually did all right, getting to £75K (the prizes went up in different amounts from the normal show), but it's amazing how the pressure does come over you when you're in that hot seat. Sat at home, I'm like everyone else – 'Come on! You must know that!' But then you do it yourself and you start second questioning your own knowledge. 'Am I sure of that? Do I really know?'

Frustratingly, we hit a brick wall with 'Which country produces the most avocados?' We both knew it was Mexico, and Mexico was indeed one of the answers, but in the moment we doubted ourselves and took the money. I've always regretted that, but because you're playing for charity, in my case the Teenage Cancer Trust, you tend to be extra careful. That sort of money means a massive amount to such an organisation.

My biggest fear on *Millionaire* was looking a complete idiot. I think at least I avoided that, which is more than can be said for when I appeared on *Catchphrase*. This is another show which you watch at home screaming at the telly, and then under the spotlight you simply haven't got a clue. The first segment of the picture revealed a phone. I could also see some orange juice. I pressed the buzzer – 'Phone juice!' And in that moment you know everyone at home will be going, 'Jesus Christ! You stupid ****!' Thing is, all of these gameshows are great fun to do – I am a bit of a quizzer – and I'm happy to look a bit daft if the other option is to stand there half-petrified and not say anything.

* * *

280

Occasionally, TV producers' penchant for shoving my face on screen has taken me further afield. Iceland being a case in point. I'm not desperately keen on cold places. The only time I've felt genuinely cold touring with England was the Indian city of Chandigarh, right in the foothills of the Himalayas. However, the temperature was offset by it also being the most beautiful spot I've ever played cricket. I had also been to Scandinavia on holiday before – a short break in Sweden – and spent the entire time freezing my nuts off. It was like Bridlington with bagels and very expensive lager. All the time I was there I was wishing I was somewhere hot with a pool. So when Iceland was mentioned, initially I wasn't too sure. However, the idea for the show, *24 Hours to Go Broke* – basically spend a load of money given you by the show in the space of one day – sounded fun, and so, as ever, I gave it a go.

My episode was with the comedian Susan Calman. Together we were dropped off on a volcanic beach near Reykjavik and invited to spend two million krona in a day. That sounds a lot until you realise one krona is worth about 0.005 pounds. You need a bloody big wallet in Iceland.

Immediately on arrival, I understood why Iceland is called Iceland – it's absolutely bloody freezing. I wasn't keen then when I was told we'd be spending some of the cash going out cod fishing. My first instinct had been to spend 24 hours, and all the money, in Reykjavik's most expensive hotel, spa and restaurant, but apparently this wouldn't have made great telly. Also, I've been out fishing on boats before and never caught a thing. I've seen those pictures hundreds of times, some bloke off the coast of Barbados, bloody great fish in his hands, but every time I've done it the only thing I've returned to shore with is first-degree seasickness and a lungful of diesel fumes. I fully expected this Icelandic voyage to be the same, but colder, and when we got out there, bobbing up and down on a trawler, my expectations were very much becoming reality.

The first thing I noticed about trawlers is that everything's very hard and, like so many boats I've been on, they haven't made the doorways big enough. If you're not banging your head you're catching your funny bone on some bit of rusty old metal.* Going out on a trawler is like being a human pinball, ricocheting around all over the place. Anyway, we stuck a couple of lines down and then – miracle of miracles – up came this massive cod. I was astonished, not least by its lips. Here we truly had the Mick Jagger of the fish world. The fishing bloke we were with said I should give it a kiss. Well, you only live once. I leaned in, puckered up, expecting a little peck, and it nearly sucked my head off. For a first date it really was a bit much. We went back to the harbour where this very posh lady on a swish yacht cooked it up. I think I might have let someone else have the lips. Someone once asked me if I felt sorry for that fish, one minute swimming

* I really do think the fishing industry could benefit from a conversation with a soft furnishings manufacturer.

around in the North Sea, the next caught for the entertainment of a limited audience on the TV channel Dave. But actually when I cast my eyes over the cod even it looked cold. I think it was glad to be out of that sea. 'Thank God someone's caught me. Where's the stove?'

Full of cod, we stiffened ourselves for our next destination – the Iceland Phallological Museum, which bills itself as 'the world's only genuine penis museum'.* Here they have, among various whale penises and animal scrotum lampshades,† metal moulds of the penises of the country's silver-medal-winning handball team at the Beijing Olympics. Whether this is a traditional way to celebrate sporting success in Iceland, I'm unsure. I'm just glad no one thought of it when me and the England boys finished runners-up in the World Cup. Although, having said that, it might liven up the Long Room at Lord's.

Actually, look carefully on the Lord's stadium tour and you will find a willy already in situ. Thing was, the team photo in cricket – one of those long ones you used to get at school – was always an occasion for someone to mess about, pulling a stupid face, making obscene hand signals behind someone's head, nudging someone in the back. In the end, the England chiefs actually started doing them on

* If you ever happen to find yourself in a fake penis museum do please report it to trading standards.

† If ever you're after a penis-shaped bottle opener or backscratcher then the shop at the Iceland Phallological Museum really is the place to go. There's also a bistro – albeit a little heavy on nuts.

the day of the Test because in those circumstances people would be less likely to misbehave. Occasionally, however, at county level, someone would go a little bit too far and quietly expose themselves to the camera. It would escape the notice of everybody until it appeared in the county yearbook, sent out by the thousand to members.* There is actually such a photo at Lord's, unfortunately placed on the way to the lunch room, which features a player pulling this trick. You only see it if you really look for it, which, while perhaps being a little unflattering to the player concerned, is perhaps why it's survived for so many years.

As you might have ascertained, in and out of sport I've been on TV a lot. In all honesty, though, I don't remember the first time I saw myself on the telly. I never particularly watched the cricket highlights, especially if for me there weren't any. If I got a few out I might have a look, but spending half an hour with Peter West at half past ten never really compared to a night on the town. Even now I never watch myself back on anything. I've never sat and watched an episode of A Question of Sport for instance because I'd probably spend the entire 30 minutes cringing at what I'd done.

Away from the TV cameras, occasionally people will invite me along to make an appearance at an event. This is precisely how I found myself locking toes with a stranger

* No pun intended.

in a pub beer garden in Derbyshire. This was for the World Toe Wrestling Championships, yet to be covered by Sky Sports.* I didn't get past the first round. My opponent took his sock off to reveal the biggest big toe I have ever seen. This bloke was essentially the Mike Tyson of the discipline. With my very average big toe, weakened by repeated blows from yorkers, I didn't have a chance.

Rather more relaxing was an invitation to be star guest at a bed show in Shropshire. I spent the entire day horizontal. They picked me up in a nice limousine, which meant I could put my feet up, and then because we were a little late arriving I was ushered straight on to a bed where I chatted to the punters and had a few photos taken. A few hours later I stepped off the bed, back into the limo and went home. I walked about 15 steps to the front room and had a nice sit-down. Exhausting!

Another time I was working as the face of lager behemoth Foster's (funnily enough, I was never asked to be the face of cranberry juice). I pitched up at one event in Trafalgar Square where they'd set up a very nice little pretend beach. The idea was I'd play a bit of beach cricket while inquisitive passers-by came over to see what was happening and be wowed by the amber nectar brand. Except something strange occurred that day. My dad happened to be in the area and came over to say hello. What he told me amazed me – 'Did you know,' he said, 'I played the trumpet here on D-Day for the army band?'

* Toes cannot by law be shown in high definition.

Right there was a bit of perspective. One of those points where you really do stop and think about your life now and what past generations gave for those who followed.

Often with an invite, there'll be an element of judging involved. I've been asked to judge things I know nothing about on a remarkably large number of occasions. British Sausage Week is a case in point. The search for Britain's best sausage entailed embarking on a ten-city trail around the country to visit the various contestants' sausage-based enterprises, ending in an overall judging session at a country pub. Where this went wrong was that the judging session was a 10 a.m. affair. Nothing inherently bad in that – the sausage is after all an integral part of the full English – except I'd foolishly rounded off the previous night with a couple of tequilas after a few glasses of wine, a mix that's rarely recommended. Certainly, I don't remember Jilly Goolden putting it forward as a good idea on *Food and Drink*.

If you've never woken up with a severe hangover and then remembered that within the hour you'll be sat in front of ten plates of sausages, and required to taste them all, then let me tell you now it's a very unpleasant sensation indeed. To make matters worse, none of these were your everyday sausage. There was one with jelly babies in it. Another, if I recall correctly, was an unusual blend of caramel and warthog. One of them had gold leaf in it. If they'd meant tobacco I'd have been all right, but this was actual gold leaf – in a sausage. You won't find that in a greasy spoon on the Old Kent Road.

It didn't help that the pub in question was very old-fashioned, with dark woods, and smelt as if it had been soaked in three hundred years of beer. I nearly heaved on entry. Me and my fellow judges descended some stairs to find the assembled photographers and reporters from the surprisingly large sausage-based media. We then sat at a table and the judging began. Over the course of an hour, sausage after sausage was laid before us and, dutifully, I forced a mouthful of them all down. By the end of this process, I'm not saying I was pale but I could have been mistaken for the pub's resident ghost. We had a short debate* and, with the winner ready to be announced, I made a beeline for the toilet. The victorious sausage-maker stepped up to receive their award, and as the applause died down and they said a few words, the room was filled with the noise of me retching down the corridor. I dread to think what the publicity photos looked like afterwards – 'And here's the winner with ex-England cricketer and sausage fanatic Phil Tufnell. Phil's the one on the right with the winning sausage trickling down his tie.'

Over the years I've been asked to judge all kinds of things I know nothing about, from cream cakes to swine. This tends to happen when you accept an invitation to a village fete or country show. I'm a big fan of such inherently

* My contribution was a lot of sweating and a small amount of burping.

English occasions. No one loves looking at strangely coloured hen eggs laid on a small bed of hay on a saucer, or vast sheep, more than me. On several occasions, I've been tempted by a 'ferret for a fiver' offer or 'buy one bantam get one free'. I can wander round a country show for hours. If I hadn't been a cricketer there's a very good chance I'd now be leaning on a gate chewing a piece of straw and chatting with a passer-by about cattle. In the end the only snorting bull I encountered was Merv Hughes.

Usually, I'll just be stepping into the beer tent when I'm approached by an organiser who informs me that I'm responsible for judging the finest stick of rhubarb or most impressive radish. I use the word 'responsibility' deliberately, because, believe me, a lot hangs on these decisions. What might to the outside world seem like quite trivial matters are of intense importance to those taking part. A lot of time and effort goes into producing a top-end radish. To be awarded 'best in show' is reward for hour upon hour of love and attention. Honestly, there are radishes in this country treated better than minor royalty. So revered are they that when it comes to feeding and watering they essentially have staff. Get this kind of decision wrong and you are guaranteed to cause deep upset. Reaction varies from barely concealed disdain to your car being sabotaged with a large King Edward up the exhaust pipe. I do actually like my salad vegetables so hopefully there aren't too many growers out there holding this particular grudge. I haven't received hate mail on the subject for a number of years.

WORK

Cakes are the same. Especially in a post-*Great British Bake-Off* world where cake-making is taken only slightly less seriously than meetings of the UN Security Council. Thus, again, I'm very keen not to make the wrong decision. With this responsibility hanging over your head, what tends to happen is you become unexpectedly poetic. 'Lovely flan – it's like a magic carpet ride to the Amalfi coast.' At which point the organiser will point out that it's actually a Mr Kipling blackberry and apple tart they brought along for their lunch.

If it's not cakes and veg, it's hats. More than once I've been called upon to judge ladies' headwear at the races, and again, in the average race-going crowd, it would be hard to find anyone less qualified to do so. My knowledge of titfers basically stops at sunhats and caps. To hide my ignorance I have developed a number of key phrases, such as 'incredible structure', 'good use of fruit' and 'remarkable featherwork'. Flammability is also taken into account.

On occasion I've actually been roped in to choose the best horse in the parade ring. Now I like horses as much as the next bloke, but beyond the knowledge that they should have four legs and a head, and having a slight weakness for a plaited mane, I'm not best positioned to cast judgement. That's why I go for the one with the luckiest face. That's hard to define, but to me it's just got a look about it, a twinkle in its eye. Often these horses are a bit scruffier than the others, but they look like they might know a few tricks. If they were a cricketer, they'd definitely know the back way into the hotel at 3 a.m. Inevitably, they trail in

289

alone two furlongs behind the rest. The jockey is later found in a hedge.

The type of judging I've found terrifically hard down the years is when asked to look at the young spin bowlers at a cricket club. I hate the thought of pleasing one person and disappointing everyone else. Not just that but the possibility of missing a great talent hangs over me. I can just imagine ten years down the line when they're being interviewed after winning man of the match in a key Ashes battle – they'll look straight down the camera – 'And that's for Phil Tufnell who said I'd amount to absolutely nothing.' This is why very few types of judging can be taken flippantly. I don't care how long it takes, I'll cogitate and deliberate until I can honestly say there's no more than a 75 per cent chance I've made the wrong choice.

The problem with a lot of these events is I'm not told of my duties on arrival. I'll have enjoyed a long lunch and the offer of accompanying fine wines and only then will someone whisper in my ear, 'Oh, Phil, forgot to say, can you do a half-hour Q&A?' Or, if it's the races, 'Sorry, Phil, the TV people were wondering if you'd mind giving us your tip for the 3.30. The camera crew's just here.' And so next thing you know you're stood there with a glass of red wine and a lobster claw on your lapel going, 'Well, Refrigerator Boy's been looking good this year, and I believe good to soft running suits him perfectly. Refrigerator Boy – that's where my money will be going.' I'll return to my table only to be told 15 minutes later that Refrigerator Boy refused at the first and was last seen heading in the direction of Chessington World of Adventures.

Formula One at Silverstone was a bit more like it. Dawn and I got down there early, walked into hospitality, and were presented with a Champagne breakfast already being enjoyed by the superstars of showbiz. I spent a lovely few hours in there before someone popped in and announced the race was about to begin. We took our seats on the start line, watched a couple of laps and went back to hospitality for two hours until the same bloke reappeared to say it was the last two laps. Out we nipped to see the chequered flag being waved and that was it. Having fronted up to that particular bit of corporate idleness, I don't think I'll ever be able to talk about people going to the cricket and not seeing a ball being bowled ever again.

Oh, and before someone accuses me of turning up to the opening of an envelope, I do turn stuff down. Back in the Nineties, when Tony Blair became prime minister and there was all the talk of 'Cool Britannia', I was invited to one of the parties at 10 Downing Street. I didn't go. I had a feeling it might be one of those things that ends up being not quite as cool as you think, just a lot of standing around drinking warm white wine and trying not to drop ash on the carpet. I can do that at home if I want to.

* * *

Of course, aside from my work on TMS and TV cricket coverage for the BBC, my other main gig in Blighty was *A Question of Sport*. When my stint as team captain came to an end after 14 years I was naturally disappointed. On the other hand nothing lasts forever and TV is always developing and changing.

Initially it looked like that was it for me, fellow team captain Matt Dawson and host Sue Barker, and that was the hardest thing about it. We hadn't just recorded hundreds of episodes, we'd also become the greatest of friends – something which viewers had picked up on. There was a dynamic between the three of us that worked, and it came from spending a lot of time together not just in the studio but socialising as well. More often than not we'd go for dinner at the end of a day's filming, and that was how we really got to understand each other's characters. That showed on screen by how much we could make each other laugh – and by how we could so easily wing it when necessary.

Rather than go our separate ways, we began thinking how we could carry on. Doing a live theatre tour was one option. We all loved the idea. The audience had always been a big part of the TV show and making the move to a stage format really felt like it could work. That's exactly what happened – before we knew it we were off round the country, joined by a selection of sporting guests for each performance.

While me and Matt are more like rusting relics, Sue definitely qualifies as a national treasure, no better exhibited than by the public reaction to her retiring from the BBC's Wimbledon coverage in 2022. I agree, she is definitely a crown jewel, but you'd never know it. Sue is so down to earth. It's not like me and Matt are sharing a broom cupboard at a B&B while she's living it up at the best hotel in town. You don't walk into Sue's room to find her on a chaise longue being fed grapes. Although she might have a slightly better shortbread selection by the kettle.

Of course, when you're touring the theatres of this nation, some date right back to the 1800s and so not all dressing rooms are up to date. Occasionally you'll find an Edwardian sock down the back of a sofa or realise the phone charger socket is gas. I've walked into theatre dressing rooms and time-travelled back to 1974 from the carpet alone. But at the same time I've formed a great attraction to our theatres, especially the beautifully ornate ones designed by the late 19th- and early 20th-century architect Frank Matcham that just ooze closeness and warmth. More than once I've had to stop myself getting up and doing a music-hall turn. Audiences who come to any show I'm involved in should be mighty glad I can't play the spoons.

Getting up on stage would I'm sure for a lot of people be quite nerve-racking, but I think that little bit of natural showmanship I had as a cricketer has stood me in good stead. That side of my personality has always been in me, although I'm not quite sure why because I've never really liked or embraced being centre stage. It's not like I'm grabbing the karaoke mic down the pub or throwing open restaurant doors and bellowing 'Hello!' à la Brian Blessed.

Of course, when you get into TV you do encounter those who will launch into a song and dance routine at the drop of a hat – doing a two-step shuffle into the lift, that kind of stuff – and actually I've always liked those kinds of people because they tend to take you to unexpected places and open your eyes to a side of life you'd never otherwise see. But when I went on *Strictly Come Dancing* I had no intention of taking up the rumba fill-time and expanding into a West End show.

Perhaps more than natural showmanship, what I have is the willpower to make myself step outside my comfort zone. This is definitely where a cricketing career comes in. Often as a player I'd face a long drive ahead of a game. As the hours passed, sometimes I'd become more and more fixed in a mindset of just not fancying it. Questioning my ability. Wondering if I was doing the right thing. Live work can be the same. On both occasions you come to realise that what's making you feel like that isn't actually not wanting to get out there and do it – it's just a bit of natural trepidation. By the time you're at the theatre and in the wings – just like when you're about to come on to bowl – that trepidation has changed to a nervous excite-ment. Then you hear the words, 'Ladies and gentlemen, please welcome …' and you're off. Once you're out there you can't imagine what you ever worried about. Me and Daws have been good at supporting each other on that front. We want every show to be as good as the last and more often than not we'll meet beforehand to have a chat, relax one another and get in the right frame of mind.

I've also toured again and again with Aggers, and those shows, a mixture of playing memories and *TMS* anecdotes, with a Q&A thrown in for good measure, are some of the nicest bits of work I do. Aggers is quite theatrical in his own way and very good at putting an audience at ease – which then puts me at ease! – and a really lovely couple of hours passes by in a blur. Of course, I get the best of those occasions because Aggers is the one who goes out and introduces the evening and then wraps everything up at the end. By the time he finishes I'm in the car on the way home! We always laugh about that. Other times, if we're staying over, I'll make sure I've got a drink waiting for him in the bar. Well, we need a little time to appraise the show! Can I just say, neither of us could ever be mistaken for rock stars. Our backstage rider is little more than a sandwich and a glass of Vimto. Well, maybe a glass of wine if we're feeling unusually raucous.

One obvious thing missing from my stage CV is panto. I've been asked a couple of times but to me it's always seemed quite a hard gig. Two shows a day for six weeks, with only Christmas Day to stick your feet up – you need to be an Olympic athlete to do that. Never say never – there's a big part of me that can see myself as Widow Twankey – and I'll bet it's good fun, but it would have to be somewhere round the corner. The Glasgow Empire's one hell of a hike.

Having said that, one thing I've always loved about theatre shows is they've taken me to parts of the country I'd never otherwise have seen. There are 17 first-class counties in England and so, as a cricketer, you can end up in the same place again and again. But there are 48 counties overall, plus the many and varied areas of Scotland, Wales and Northern Ireland. Like I say I'm actually quite a nosey bloke and will more than happily wander off in any given direction and see where I end up.

If that's chest-deep in the River Clyde as a pantomime dame so be it.

16

THE DAWN OF TOURISM

Me and Dawn like nothing more than to get away somewhere special. We're lucky to live in a beautiful part of England, but we're no different to everyone else – we love a change of scene. Even if half the time we can't be bothered to do anything when we arrive!

Take Rome, for example. We'd been there a week and still hadn't visited the Colosseum even though it was pretty much right outside the hotel. Instead, we'd been busy drinking wine, eating pasta and generally having a lovely time. As the last day dawned, we thought it would be remiss if we didn't at least try to have a little look round. I suppose that is the idea of a city break after all. Otherwise, you might as well just go to Waitrose and have a week at home.

I was keen to avoid any hanging around in queues, especially since it was boiling hot, and so went down to reception and asked if there was such a thing as a hotel car. The bloke on the desk confirmed they had exactly that, an air-conditioned Mercedes. Before we knew it, we were in the back of this luxury vehicle with the reception-ist at the wheel.

'Right,' I said, 'now please can you take us to all the places that people usually want to see, the Trevi Fountain and what not? But don't let us out and drive off. If you could, we'd like you to stop right by each attraction while we all quickly jump out and you take a picture of us.'

Well, we did Rome in an hour and a half.* At the Colosseum, we nipped out, stuck a Roman re-enactor's hat on Dawn's head, and were back in the motor before the traffic warden could even sharpen his pencil. We abso-lutely smashed it.

The only time we stopped was to have a little look round the Vatican City. But again we tried to keep the time down, this time by avoiding the translated tour. It was perhaps an efficiency measure too far. Everyone else was stood gazing earnestly at these statues, taking in all the information on their headphones, while we didn't know who the heck anyone was. We were just licking ice creams while walking past blokes with missing append-ages. We then got hustled through the Sistine Chapel with only a few seconds to look up at Michelangelo's famed ceiling. I'll be totally honest with you, I wasn't particularly impressed. If it was a toss-up between Michelangelo and Sid's Painters and Decorators to do my kitchen up, I know who I'd choose. I said as much as I came out, although refrained from making an entry in the comments book.

* Maybe it was built in a day after all.

298

We took the same whizz-around approach in Venice, only this time by gondola. Early on in the trip I'd seen a sign saying, 'Queue for the Doge's Palace, three and a half hours.' The Doge's Palace is one of the city's main landmarks. A masterpiece of Gothic architecture it ranks alongside anything in the whole of Britain.* Venice is known for such incredible architectural feats. The downside is that vast cruise ships daily disgorge thousands of tourists into the city and so the queues to get inside any of them are legendary. I didn't fancy that and so instead of going in anywhere we just floated past outside.†

I know people will consider this kind of tourism lazy but, thing is, I've headed off to visit famous landmarks in the past only to end up wondering if it was really worth the fuss. Take the Taj Mahal. It was very lovely and everything (quality domes), and I had a nice wander around, admired the plasterwork, but was then faced with a four-hour coach journey back to the hotel. Same with Uluru, also known as Ayers Rock. Yes, it's an unusual sight, rising up out of the landscape. But was it worth a never-ending bus trip across mile after mile of featureless scrub? I sometimes

---

* Even the Harlequin Shopping Centre, Watford.

† Just to say, this wasn't one of those blokes with the stick, like him off the Cornetto ads, this was a motorised gondola. Even so, he was the coolest boat driver I've ever seen – aviator shades, pair of pristine white trousers, jumper thrown over his shoulders. I think he'd studied the boxset of *Howards' Way*.

think we get swept up in a vacation mindset that we have to see something or else we'll regret it at some later point. But think about it. If someone came up to you in the street and said, 'There's a big rock four hours up the A1 – do you fancy it?', chances are you'd say no. On holiday we're struck with FOMO (fear of missing out). Rest of the time, we're quite happy to go home and watch *Emmerdale*.

Even when me and Dawn went to Paris, we didn't go up the Eiffel Tower. We were heading that way, only to happen across a very nice little restaurant where you could see the structure from the window. We were more than happy to sit there admiring the bolt-work while eating bread and olives.

I know this sounds a bit flippant – clearly we've been fortunate in having travelled widely – but I actually think staying clear of the really big tourist attractions can save a lot of holiday stress. Take what happened when we went to the Egyptian coastal resort of Sharm El Sheikh. We'd got it in our heads that we really should take the opportunity to see the Pyramids while over there. However, as the holiday went on, we were having a great time just chilling by the pool and the thought of several hours on a bus to Cairo became less and less appealing. Luckily for us, we got chatting to a couple who'd already made the Pyramids trip.

'What were they like?' I enquired.

'OK,' they replied. 'If you like that kind of thing.'

Well, this very unenthusiastic answer was exactly what me and Dawn were hoping to hear. When the couple also told us they'd travelled the last couple of miles on a very disgruntled camel, we both looked at each other, each thinking exactly the same thing – no way we were going to bother. We'd both seen the Pyramids on the telly – big things, pyramid-shaped. Were they going to be any different in real life? Another day by the pool it was.

Before anyone accuses me of being unenlightened when it comes to the ancients, I have been to Stonehenge.* I wasn't part of a hippy convoy, I was sent there for *The One Show*, fortunate enough to be allowed into the actual circle of stones – an incredible feeling to be in the midst of something so sacred. It was very early in the morning, really quiet, misty and incredibly atmospheric. So taken was I by the moment that I actually stood for a couple of minutes giving one of the stones a hug. I'm not saying I experienced a spiritual awakening – I didn't become a practising Druid – but it did give me a feeling of being connected to something very special. And before anyone asks, no I didn't chisel 'Tuffers woz 'ere'.

To some degree I'm still playing catch-up with some parts of the world, Europe especially. The fact I played cricket every summer for two decades meant I never went to the classic sunspots of Greece, Portugal and Italy. There didn't seem much point in booking two weeks in Corfu in the middle of winter. Even so, I do prefer Europe to America, a place with which I've had a mixed relationship. I find it all a bit full-on. There's just way too much noise,

---

* I've also spent a lot of time around MCC members.

although I'll admit when I went to Las Vegas for my fifti-eth – five days of absolute carnage – it was me making the most of it.

I knew I was in for an unorthodox little break the minute we left the airport and saw two beggars with a sign – 'SPARE CHANGE PLEASE – FOR COCAINE AND WHORES'. So much for, 'Excuse me, guv, any chance of ten pence for a cup of tea?' At least they were honest I suppose.

About 30 of us embarked on this trip. How many made it back I'm not entirely sure. We barely slept the whole time, properly getting stuck into the whole experience. I mean, I've done the slots on Brighton Pier but this was next level.

The birthday celebration itself was in a very posh nightclub at the top of the Mandalay Bay Hotel, hangout for the real Vegas top brass. It was all very Cirque du Soleil-ish. Women in vast winged costumes wandering around on stilts, everyone with huge diamond rings and massive expensive watches.* And, for one night only, a retired Middlesex leg-spinner. People were stood around sipping Champagne and Courvoisier. I enquired after a brown ale but the waiter looked through me like I was invisible.

At one point me and my mate thought we'd go for a fag. The only problem was we had to get through this vast sea of VIPs to reach the balcony. My pal had a plan. 'Just

* Not to be confused with Southend.

watch this,' he said. Instead of inching apologetically through the crowd, he just went for it, high-fiving strangers, whooping and doing the odd 'Yee-hah!'. At one point he bearhugged a quarterback from the Cincinnati Bengals. I'd never seen anything like it. It was like the parting of the Red Sea. Everyone moved out of our way as we powered through. Of course, after we'd had a fag the pressure was on for the return trip. The gap we'd made had totally disappeared. It would take something special to get back through this lot.

'Introduce me!' said my pal. I stood by the balcony door. 'Ladies and gentlemen,' I announced, 'all the way from Surrey ...' I'd barely got the words out before my mate got down on his belly and started caterpillaring across the room.

Vegas was huge fun from start to finish, but, like a say, a one-off blowout, a departure from the peace and quiet I usually prefer. If I do find myself in a casino then I'm happy to have a drink and stay for an hour. I don't want to still be there three days later.

New York is a good example of an iconic American city I couldn't quite come to terms with. Well, for someone renowned for loving a kip, 'the city that never sleeps' was always going to be a challenge. Strangely enough, I had actually played in a game against West Indies in the Big Apple as part of an attempt to broaden the game's appeal in North America. It didn't work. A couple of thousand people turned up but cricket has always fought a losing battle in a continent so dominated by baseball. I wasn't particularly bothered that New York was unlikely to be a permanent addition to the international schedule – I find the noise and sheer energy of the place to be exhausting. Take the old traditional diners, great little places which serve the most amazing food – it's just the staff can be a little terse. 'Come on, talk to me! Waddaya want?' And I'm thinking, 'Chill out, mate! I've only come in for an omelette!'

Me and Dawn did a Christmas trip there. Did the old ice-skating, had a look round Bloomingdale's department store. Every time we jumped in a cab, it'd be, 'OK, whereja wonna go? Whatja wanna do?'

'Well, have a nice relaxing ride in your cab would be a start,' I'd think. 'But I don't think it's going to happen!' It's weird. You find yourself raising your game a bit, like you have to be quite full-on back. 'Heh, man! Take me to Brooklyn! I wanna jump off the bridge and swim to Noo Joisy.'

I think maybe I'm better suited to somewhere a bit quieter, like New England; somewhere with silence and trees rather than 24-hour police sirens and honking.

You get back from New York and you're totally exhausted. You need a holiday just to get over someone constantly demanding if you want a top-up on your coffee. Having said that, I've also been to places there where they do free top-ups on Bloody Marys. I can stay somewhere like that all day!

You might think that having travelled pretty widely, my home would be full of global nick-nacks. Actually not. As a cricketer I went through a short stage of buying representations of Indian gods, although none of them could ever bring about the meeting with Britt Ekland I so desired. Generally, though, aside from a tan and a sun-bleached mop, you'd never know I'd been away. Even now I'm not much of a shopper for myself. Dawn, on the other hand, likes a sarong. She has a collection which will at some point form the basis of the National Sarong Experience. I've yet to go down that route.

If anyone can trace the Tufnells back to Scotland, though, I'm willing to invest in the family tartan and a kilt.

17

YOU ONLY LIVE ONCE

It's easy when writing a book like this to stick on the old rose-tinted glasses and start banging on about how everything was better 'in my day'. I'm lucky – memories of Demis Roussos, green custard and cars with chokes prevent me from doing that.

I am, however, constantly told there's not enough characters in cricket anymore. I think the truth is more that we've just got a different type of character. The explosiveness of modern cricket means that big personalities can express themselves through the sport. On the international and T20 scene they play in front of huge crowds across the globe. Yes, they have to look after themselves and live a stricter, more athletic lifestyle, but the sport itself delivers huge dramatic highs.

Playing for England in the Nineties was different. Yes, there were great times on the pitch – well, a few! – but being an international cricketer was incredibly unpredictable. You quite literally didn't know whether your next innings, your next over, would be your last. That meant playing for England came with a slightly different perspective. If you were so minded, you enjoyed the experience in its entirety. My attitude was – and remains – you only live once, enjoy it. Some might say I overdid it once or twice. I would say I was only being true to myself – something which Mum and Dad had always encouraged in me. I remain hugely grateful for that.

Look at it this way, being good at cricket opened up horizons that would otherwise have been totally denied to me. I was no more going to be able to travel around Australia and the Caribbean – put up in top hotels, and meeting incredible people at every turn – than I was going to sledge to the North Pole. The fact that Mum and Dad had ingrained a love of the different in me – be it culture, food or characters – also meant that whenever I was picked to tour with England I was going to take in as many facets of a country as humanly possible, not just the inside of hotel rooms and sports stadiums. Cricket gave me a very privileged and rare opportunity to see a world that might otherwise pretty much have begun and ended in London and the south-east. The fact I have seen so much of this planet – good and bad – is actually a source of personal pride. For a bloke like me, it should never have been like that. I was selected for all those trips because I was the best at what I did.

I was then lucky enough to continue to see the world through *TMS* and being invited on to weird and wonderful TV shows. Had that alternative career not been there, I'm not sure what I'd have done. I was aware that quite a few Middlesex cricketers had gone on to make a good living in the City, and that, for those who'd worn the blazer with pride, certain mysterious contacts known to frequent Lord's seemed ready and willing to smooth the path to these streets paved with gold. Others, like our spinner Phil Edmonds, had made inroads in that area while still in their whites. But I never saw myself in that kind of world. I'd seen those TV images of blokes in weird outfits shouting at each other across the trading floor and it seemed a little too near to one or two dressing-room dust-ups I'd seen for my liking. Similarly, I could never see myself working in an office. I've been in one or two and they never seem to have a physio's bed to get your head down for half an hour.

What I did have in abundance was the travel bug – caught young and remaining active. I've been incredibly fortunate to travel so widely in and out of cricket, but even now there remain places I'd like to go. The Maldives is one of them. I've heard so much about how beautiful the islands are, how terrific the light is, and would really like to take Dawn there one day. Bali is another for similar reasons – that feeling of just being surrounded by the most mesmerising blue ocean.

I've also always had a little bit of a tingle for South America – Cuba for its history, Peru for the culture and Argentina for the steaks. I'd also love to go to Brazil for the rainforest and the beaches. Having said that, I was slightly put off when Aggers returned from covering the dressage at the Rio Olympics and reported that a random bullet had come hurtling through the press tent from which the journalists filed their copy. Call me odd, but I always like to honour the 'return' part of a plane ticket.

Dawn, meanwhile, is keen to go to explore Canada, and, having only nipped in and out for a quick cricket match (part of that aforementioned ill-fated North American tour) at the home of the Toronto Blue Jays baseball team, I'm also keen to see what the country as a whole has to offer. Famously, in Vancouver, you can ski in the morning and be on the beach by lunchtime. I might have a go at that – perhaps without the morning part.

And so, the big question – where's the favourite place I've been? Somebody once said the Caribbean is my natural home, and it's hard to disagree. Most of the places cricketers travel to are in big cities, whereas a tour of the West Indies takes you round a succession of beautiful party islands.

In fact, I've just had an idea – 'Cat in the Caribbean'. It's definitely got a ring to it. TV execs, I'm available for filming!

ACKNOWLEDGEMENTS

I would like to thank all those in and out of cricket who have helped me enjoy seeing so much of the world. I have been to some amazing places but none of it would have meant anything without so many terrific companions along the way. You have provided me with endless incredible memories, many of which, I'm glad to say, are still fresh enough to make me laugh all over again today.

I'd also like to thank Adam Humphrey and all those at HarperCollins for seeing the potential in my many and varied touring anecdotes, and also John Woodhouse for the many lively chats and transferring my words to paper. Thanks too, as ever, to my manager Mike Martin.

There is one person in particular to whom I'd like to say a massive thank you – my lovely wife Dawn. You truly are the best companion in life a bloke could ever want.